King of the Bowery

1. The apotheosis of Timothy D. Sullivan. Big Tim as depicted on the menu of a banquet given in his honor at the Hoffman House, 1901. Courtesy of the Rare Books Division, the New York Public Library, Astor, Lenox, and Tilden Foundation.

King of the Bowery

Big Tim Sullivan, Tammany Hall,
and New York City from
the Gilded Age to the Progressive Era

Richard F. Welch

excelsior editions

AN IMPRINT OF STATE UNIVERSITY OF NEW YORK PRESS

Published by
STATE UNIVERSITY OF NEW YORK PRESS, ALBANY

© 2008 by Rosemont Publishing and Printing Corp.

Printed in the United States of America

Originally published in 2008 by Fairleigh Dickinson University Press.
First Excelsior Editions paperback printing, 2010.

Excelsior Editions is an imprint of State University of New York Press, Albany.

For information, contact
STATE UNIVERSITY OF NEW YORK PRESS, ALBANY, NY
www.sunypress.edu

Production, Laurie Searl
Marketing, Fran Keneston

Library of Congress Cataloging-in-Publication Data

Welch, Richard F.
    King of the Bowery : Big Tim Sullivan, Tammany Hall, and New York City from the Gilded Age to the Progressive Era / Richard F. Welch.
        p. cm.
    Originally published: Madison [N.J.] : Fairleigh Dickinson University Press, c2008.
    Includes bibliographical references and index.
    ISBN 978–1–4384–3182–6 (pbk. : alk. paper)
1. Sullivan, Timothy Daniel, 1862–1913. 2. Legislators—United States—Biography. 3. United States. Congress. House—Biography. 4. Politicians—New York (State)—New York—Biography. 5. Tammany Hall—History. 6. New York (N.Y.)—Politics and government—19th century. 7. New York (N.Y.)—Politics and government—20th century. 8. Political corruption—New York (State)—New York—History. 9. New York (N.Y.)—Biography. I. Title.
    E664.S95W45 2009
    974.7′044092--dc22
    [B]

                                                              2009029113

10 9 8 7 6 5 4 3 2 1

For Bill and Mike—For Everything

Contents

Illustrations

Acknowledgments

MANY INDIVIDUALS AND INSTITUTIONS PROVIDED CRUCIAL EXPER-
tise and support in the creation of this book. The author would
like to thank Corie Trancho-Robie and the staff at Columbia University's Oral History Research Office for permission to quote
from Columbia's extensive oral history collections. Likewise, a
tip of the hat to the librarians at Hofstra University, C.W. Post
College, Long Island University, and Stony Brook University
who provided expert assistance in accessing their microfilm
collections.

Professor Wilbur R. Miller of Stony Brook University and
Deborah Gershenowitz of the New York University Press read the
manuscript, and volunteered thoughtful observations and helpful
suggestions. The book has benefited greatly from their input. A
special nod of appreciation is due Kevin Baker who enthusiastically shared his extensive knowledge of New York history and
long experience in writing and publishing as I struggled to get the
project off the ground. Similarly a note of gratitude is owed Harry
Keyishian and the staff and readers at Farleigh-Dickinson University Press who recognized the drama and significance of Big
Tim Sullivan's career and opted to take on the project. Lastly,
thanks to Christine Retz, Managing Editor at Associated University Presses, for cheerfully guiding authors through the mine-
fields of book preparation and academic publishing.

Introduction

THE FIGURE OF TIMOTHY DANIEL "BIG TIM" SULLIVAN LOOMED over New York from the 1880s to 1913 in ways few others could match. Revered, respected, and loved in the congested neighborhoods of the Lower East Side of Manhattan, he was feared and loathed in those precincts dominated by the "respectable classes." Sullivan wielded more political power than any other contemporary, and though a member of the Tammany Hall Democratic machine, he ran his own fiefdom in the Bowery as a personal satrap. Although he declined the role of Tammany boss for himself, no one could assume that position without his consent. While the Lower East Side always remained his power base, Sullivan continuously broadened his political reach until it extended across the length and breadth of New York City. The open-handed social and economic support he provided his constituents was legendary long before he died, and his legitimate investments helped nurture live theater and film. On the other hand, his involvement with vice, especially gambling, and his friendships with underworld figures, tainted his personal and political reputation.

Paradoxically, Big Tim Sullivan became not only the last great practitioner of nineteenth-century urban politics, but an early supporter of progressive legislation in New York State, confounding his enemies and again delighting his followers. For the working classes and poor, the new immigrants and their children, Big Tim was leader, advisor, fixer, banker, employment officer, social worker and, when the need arose, funeral director. The day before his own funeral a steady stream of New Yorkers filed past his bier tendering their last respects. The following day the streets of the Bowery were jammed with 20,000 mourners straining for a glimpse of the cortege as it rolled through lower Manhattan and across the Williamsburg Bridge to Calvary Cemetery.

Big Tim's fame was so great, his energies so strong and his accomplishments—in the eyes of many New Yorkers—so obvious, that it seemed as if his place in the pantheon of New York politicians was both fixed and exalted. For a brief time it was. But the onset of a world war, the self-destruction of Tammany Hall under Mayor Jimmy Walker, and the catastrophe of the Great Depression quickly relegated Tim Sullivan's life and career to that of a dimly recalled memory. His era—its passions, pastimes, failings, and achievements—were reduced to a few dry sentences in textbooks, and Tim's legend faded away until, like the Cheshire Cat, all that remained was a smile—a vague recollection of a powerful, slightly roguish politico from a vanished world. Perhaps a few others remembered the Sullivan in New York's famous Sullivan Law which made it illegal to carry a concealed weapon without a permit. Otherwise, even in most studies of the politics of the time, Tim Sullivan slid down a memory hole.

But examining nineteenth- and early twentieth-century urban politics without Big Tim Sullivan is like discussing the 1960s without the Kennedys. He stood at its center, he made it go, he gave it its juice, and if he was hobbled by the limitations of his traditions and outlook, he proved a feisty harbinger of the measures and methods which triumphed in the 1930s. Sullivan was a master of mass politics in an age when personal contact was everything. The loyalty he engendered in the multi-ethnic population below Fourteenth Street was based on his bighearted solicitude for his constituents. He gave them jobs, provided housing, and organized the largest and most celebrated social outings in New York. Moreover, he became an early and aggressive proponent of Progressive reform in labor and women's issues.

Tim Sullivan's story—a classic rags to riches, poverty to power journey—illuminates a key transitional period when American politics was becoming truly modern, adopting many of the forms, methods, and issues which would characterize the twentieth century. It also provides a glimpse of New York in the process of becoming the great metropolis, still trying to master the secrets of efficient and effective government. Sullivan worked with and sometimes butted heads with many who would become celebrated political players and government leaders—Robert Wagner, Sr., Al Smith, Frances Perkins, William Randolph Hearst, and the two Roosevelts. In his day he was better known and more important than any of them, excepting Theodore Roosevelt. But Big

Tim would not live to see many of these acquaintances, allies, and opponents achieve their hours of glory. Nothing was more surprising about Big Tim Sullivan's life than how suddenly and gruesomely it ended.

But that was the last act. Between the mid-1880s and 1913 Big Tim Sullivan was a powerful, constant, and irradiating presence in politics and popular culture. To borrow a line from a song which would have been familiar to him, he did indeed "trip the light fantastic."

King of the Bowery

2. Tammany Hall. From *Munsey's Magazine,* 1901.

1

The City and the Machine

The network of party clubhouses and the hierarchy of party committees with a citywide leader or "boss" at the apex constituted a "shadow government," a supplementary structure of power that performed some functions more vital than those of the nominal, legal government.
—William V. Shannon, *The American Irish*

Tammany is corruption with consent . . .
—Lincoln Steffens

THROUGHOUT THE NINETEENTH CENTURY THE FORCES OF INDUS- trialization, expanding global enterprise, and dizzying demographic increases and mutations made New York City the nation's most dynamic and influential metropolis. The inexorable rise of the city's financial, commercial, and manufacturing sectors created a large and aspiring middle class that drove the city's economic machine. Ranked above them was a smaller but economically and socially dominant upper class secure in the wealth and position that their ownership of the great business combinations had won for them. The rich advertised their status in a number of ways, none more visible than the opulent homes they built for themselves along the then upper reaches of Fifth Avenue in the forties. Through natural growth and incessant immigration from the American hinterlands and Europe, the city's population pressed against the outer boundaries of established neighborhoods and spread ever northward, swirling around Central Park and engulfing old villages such as Harlem and Spuyten Duyvil. By the 1880s some voices were called for outright annexation of the southern sections of Westchester called the Bronx, as well as Kings County, Staten Island, and those parts of Queens County that lay in the city's ambit despite lying across the East River.

The wealthy dominated high society and owned the high-end businesses and firms with their continental and global connections. The optimistic and striving middle class contributed the countless small and middling businesses that gave the city much of its energy while providing the personnel that staffed the white-collar professions. But it was the lower class that provided the muscle and the sweat that drove the great metropolitan machine. The major stronghold of the working classes and poor—often one and the same—was the Lower East Side, the area below Fourteen Street, or "south of the line" as the locals phrased it. Here stood the swarming households, pre-Civil War structures, and older tenements and row houses, as well as the myriad of small businesses, recreational, and entertainment places that catered to, and were often owned by, the largely immigrant population that dwelt there.

Two large thoroughfares stretched south to north through lower Manhattan, running directly through the area. The first was Broadway, one of the oldest streets in the city. More than a major artery, Broadway was a commercial street of considerable importance, and the address of many theaters, dance halls, barrooms, and popular museums. Slightly to the east, but noticeably different in character, ran the Bowery, which took its name from Pieter Stuyvesant's old *bouwerie*—Dutch for "farm." Many years had passed since the Bowery could claim anything bucolic, but the avenue, which ran from Canal Street to Fourteenth Street, was home to a wide variety of commerce and recreational enterprises. The area surrounding the avenue, especially to the east, which also bore the name Bowery, had been densely populated since before the Civil War. Between 1880 and World War One, it had the ambiguous distinction of being the most congested residential area in the city. The type of entertainment that was found on Broadway also lined the Bowery. But almost from its very beginnings, Bowery amusements were considered more raffish, rowdy, bawdy—or outright disreputable and dangerous. The Bowery was home to more whorehouses, dives, and flophouses than Broadway—whose legitimate theater was migrating toward midtown as the twentieth century approached—and fielded greater numbers of gang members, gamblers, and pimps. Not to mention politicians.

None of this necessarily hurt the proprietors of the Bowery's multifaceted enterprises. In addition to the locals who enjoyed the ruder, proletarian fare, Bowery amusements attracted visitors from uptown and out-of-town, including significant numbers from allegedly respectable classes, who sought the livelier entertainment available in the dance halls and theaters, or perhaps some of the readily available illicit action dispensed at after-hours gin mills, gambling dens, and brothels. The Bowery's expanding notoriety was proclaimed in a popular tune first aired in the comedy *A Trip to Chinatown* in 1892. The chorus, widely known well into the twentieth century, went

> The Bowery, the Bowery!
> They say such things and they do strange things
> On the Bowery, the Bowery!
> I'll never go there anymore.

In 1878, an elevated line was opened along the Bowery, casting a shadow over the street during the day and threatening to plunge it into darkness after dusk. However, in 1882, electricity was extended along a mile of the thoroughfare, and it was soon ablaze with streetlights and electric signs advertising a wide variety of amusements. Edison banished the gloom, and the Bowery may have been at its peak between 1880 and 1900, when it was described as "the liveliest mile on the face of the earth."[1]

The Bowery was home to some of the city's most infamous dives, such as McGurk's Suicide Hall, so-called after a number of prostitutes ended their careers and lives in its halls. Owney Geoghegan, part-time boxer and friend of Tammany politicians, opened his doors at 105 Bowery in the 1870s, and it quickly earned the reputation as one of the toughest "resorts" in town. Raw whiskey went for ten cents a drink, and a "free and easy" amateur boxing bout was held nightly. Complaining customers might be invited to settle their dispute in the same manner. Unwary visitors had to dodge the pickpockets, and off-duty professional beggars could be seen relaxing, their public infirmities vanished as if Geoghegan's was an auxiliary of Lourdes. Less disreputable was Steve Brodie's saloon, a hangout for professional athletes and those who came to gawk at them. The main barroom featured a painting of Brodie's claim to fame, a jump from the Brooklyn Bridge whose authenticity was questionable, but whose celebrity became a career. The tougher saloons and dives could be dangerous, and anyone who flashed big bills might find himself taken one way or another, but locals, or experienced "slummers" who avoided attracting attention and paid in small change, could usually enjoy the ambience unmolested.[2]

But the Bowery was more than dives and flophouses where overnight accommodations were sometimes a chalk outline on the floor. "Outside men" acting like carnival barkers enticed passersby into the various "dime museums" where they could gaze at freaks such as albinos and "dog-faced" boys, as well as more conventional acts like sword-swallowers and fire-eaters. The Bowery was home to many theaters, whose performances might be in English, German, or, a little later, Yiddish. Some presented upscale fare such as Shakespeare or Oscar Wilde, but the variety theaters, fast evolving into vaudeville, were more popular. Variety theater offered a panoply of entertainment—comedy, juggling, minstrelsy, singing, short dramatic pieces, amateur nights—for a modest entrance fee. Twenty cents would admit a patron to the National Theater, where the bill often ran over four hours.

Alcohol was served at most theaters, which no doubt encouraged the tradition of razzing and heckling the performers, who were perfectly at liberty to hand it back. To prevent things from getting out of control, Henry Miner, the politically connected owner of the Bowery Theater, stationed security guards—bouncers—on each level of his theater. The guard on the orchestra level stood with back to the stage searching the audience for potential problems. As the curtain opened and a show began, the balcony bouncer shouted "Hats off, youse . . . Hat's off, all o' youse."[3] Enthusiastic, even boisterous behavior was acceptable at the Bowery and most East Side theaters. Prohibited acts included tobacco spitting, throwing paper, or annoying women. Violators were summarily ejected.[4]

"Gilded Age" New York had a pronounced Irish accent, and much of downtown sported a Celtic character between 1840 and 1900. In the 1880s, a full 40 percent of the city's inhabitants were of Irish extraction—either immigrants or first American generation.[5] Only the Germans, more likely to keep to themselves and less politically active, rivaled the Irish in numbers. Arriving in large numbers only after 1840, the dispossessed Famine Irish had been pitied, despised, and feared. The first non-Protestant group to appear in great numbers, their appearance triggered the anti-Catholic bigotry that had characterized British popular culture since the sixteenth century. Nor did the old-stock—Anglo-Saxon—citizens of New York forget that their ancestors had conquered and colonized Ireland, beating down several attempts at rebellion between 1641 and 1848. The poverty of most of the Famine refugees, their unfamiliar customs—in many cases unfamiliar language—their concentration in the cheap, dilapidated housing the native born had fled, and the increasing presence of crime and prostitution in their neighborhoods further inflamed anti-Irish feelings. In the decade before the Civil War gangs of Irish and native-born Americans were battling in the streets of the Five Points and other downtown neighborhoods.

Yet the Irish persevered. Some—a few—had come to America with money, skill, or professional acumen. Others parlayed work, talent, luck, or connections into a middle-class lifestyle. By 1875 the Irish could boast two major accomplishments in America—mastery, if not virtual creation, of the American Catholic Church and control of the Democratic Party in most northern cities, especially New York. Irish dominance of New York's Democratic Party was exercised through their control of Tammany Hall. Tammany, the leading Democratic organization in the city, was founded as a political-fraternal order in 1789. Originally nativist, it became an important part of Thomas Jefferson's Democratic-Republicans, which evolved into the Democratic Party in the 1830s. The organization's name was taken from a mythical Indian chief, Tammany, which led to the society's adoption of a number of pseudo-Indian terms. The Tammany leader was the grand sachem, district leaders sachems, rank-and-file members were braves, and the headquarters was dubbed "the Wigwam."

Seeing the possibilities of the huge numbers fleeing Europe in the 1840s, Tammany welcomed the newcomers—especially the Irish—and baptized them as Democrats. Before the Civil War, Irish loyalty helped Tammany establish itself in the slums of the Fourth and Sixth wards—the so-called "Whiskey Wards." In 1861, William Marcy Tweed assumed the leadership of the Hall, initiating a ten-year reign of municipal looting and bequeathing the organization its soon-to-be famous tiger symbol.[6]

Celebrating Tammany's grip on city politics, in 1867 Tweed erected a new Wigwam on Fourteenth Street. By that time, the Irish were not only "braves" but ward leaders, municipal officials, and Tweed's most trusted lieutenants. Tweed himself would be the last old-stock American to run the Hall. After Tweed's fall, triggered by a disgruntled organization functionary who revealed the extent of Tammany's looting of city funds—about $200 million between 1861 and 1871—the organization came under the control of an all-Irish hierarchy.[7] Until 1932, small breaks excepted, Irish-led Tammany would dominate New York City politics and make it the gold standard of political machines everywhere.

John Kelly, later "Honest John," was the first of a line of powerful Irish grand sachems. Kelly assumed control of the organization at its nadir, drifting and discredited after Tweed tumbled from power in 1872. In the words of later chroniclers of Tammany's fortunes, Kelly "found Tammany a horde and left it an army."[8] Born in 1822, Kelly was the ambitious son of Irish immigrants who had established a successful grate and soapstone business by the time he was twenty-one. Like many young men in the city, he joined one of the several volunteer fire companies that competed, and sometimes brawled, for the privilege of extinguishing the many blazes that plagued the then largely wooden metropolis. In addition to their basic duties, the volunteer fire companies in the antebellum period functioned as social and political organizations, and membership was a prerequisite for any young man with political ambitions.

Kelly, who had an appetite for self-improvement, acted in amateur theatricals, read Shakespeare, taught himself French, and finished his secondary education at night. He was also devoutly religious and had originally intended to study for the priesthood. The young Irisher was drawn into politics by the rise of the nativist Know-Nothing Party, which grew in strength in the late 1840s and 1850s. Anti-immigrant, especially anti-Irish immigrant, the political leaders of the American Party, as the Know-Nothings were officially named, demanded restrictions on immigration while their underlings fomented anti-Catholic rioting and battled Irish gangs in the streets. Ironically, Kelly began his career with one of Tammany's smaller Democratic rivals, opposing both the Hall and the Know-Nothings. Nativist gangs, supporting Know-Nothing candidates, raided Kelly's electoral district and were probably responsible for his defeat in his first attempts at a seat on the New York City Board of Aldermen. On his third try, Kelly lined up support from Irish gangs and fire companies— often interchangeable—and in a pitched battle at the polls, the

Irish defeated the nativists, breaking Know-Nothing power in the Sixth Ward and handing Kelly his first political victory.[9]

Kelly entered the House of Representatives in 1854. The only Catholic out of 241 representatives, the new legislator was frequently engaged in verbal warfare with Know-Nothing or other anti-Catholic representatives.[10] But in 1858 he returned to local politics, winning the election as New York City sheriff on the Tammany ticket. The position was unpaid, the salary to derive from the collection of fees. The system, which was ancient, allowed certain officials, such as sheriffs, to levy an amount for their services above what the city demanded. The differential was pocketed by the officeholder. Kelly was diligent, efficient, and successful, earning $800,000 fulfilling his duties and earning the sobriquet "Honest John."[11] Though some later claimed he drastically overcharged for his services, others countered that he was restrained compared to other officeholders. At any rate, the nickname stuck.

Kelly broke with Tammany as revelations of Tweed's chicanery emerged, and he allied himself with reform Democrat, later governor, Samuel J. Tilden. At about the same time, his personal life unraveled as he watched his wife and three children die in the space of five years between 1866 and 1871. Grief stricken, Kelly again spoke of joining the religious life, but Tilden and Democratic lawyer Charles O'Conor convinced him that his true vocation was that of a political leader, and he agreed to take charge of the faltering Tammany organization. Assuming the office of New York County leader and chairman of the Committee on Organization, "Honest John" purged Tweed's supporters from the Hall. The new leader tightened Tammany's chain of command, according to some observers by using the Catholic Church as his model, and made himself more of a boss than Tweed had ever been. During Kelly's tenure as leader, the Tammany Society and Tammany Hall became separate, though related, organizations. The Hall became a purely political operation, while the Society functioned largely as a social and fraternal entity.

After 1871, the assembly district replaced the old wards as the basic unit in the Tammany hierarchy—although it remained common to refer to neighborhoods by their former ward designation into the twentieth century. New York's thirty-five assembly districts were subdivided into election districts, each with it own captain who was appointed by the district leader. The district leader commonly held a state or municipal office in addition to his position in the party. But the district leaders' real power was with the organization. Leaders could make or break aldermen, assemblymen, state senators, or even congressmen. Theoretically, the district leaders were elected, but in practice they were usually appointed by the Hall's leader—the ultimate "boss." Such appointments were usually, though not invariably, bestowed on men who had already built up a significant following in their districts. The district leaders sat on the New York County Executive Committee, which elected the leader of the Manhattan County Democracy—Tammany's boss. Kelly also created the General Committee, which numbered thousands of members elected from the assembly districts. Basically window dressing, the General Committee was Tammany's version of the Supreme Soviet, as it had no real power.

Functioning as the party's eyes and ears, and sometimes enforcers at the neighborhood level, the election district leaders— the captains—made it their business to know everyone in the area, their needs, wants, and how they voted. The captains reported back to the congressional district leaders, who were in turn accountable to the boss. Ultimate power resided with the Hall's leader, whose authority depended on his success in winning elections and distributing spoils to his lieutenants and the party faithful. This system, which Kelly constructed from the wreckage of Tweed's operation, became the model for urban political machines throughout the United States. Kelly's reorganization soon proved its worth, and the Tiger's first Irish Catholic leader oversaw the election of New York's first Irish Catholic mayor, William Grace.

To finance electoral contests, Kelly introduced a campaign funding system that also became standard with virtually all American political machines. Candidates for office were required to contribute a fixed sum to the fund, while party officeholders were assessed a percentage of their salaries. As election day neared, the district leaders, Kelly's bishops to his pope if the Catholic model is accepted, received a share of the war chest as Kelly thought best. After the election, if Tammany was victorious, district leaders, after consulting with their captains— the parish priests—would submit a list of deserving job seekers for Kelly's approval. Kelly would run them by his executive committee, his curia, and if there were no objections, the appointments were confirmed. Each assembly district was entitled to a quota of the municipal jobs, which the assembly leaders passed on to their captains, who doled them out. Officially, of course, the appointments were made by the mayor, who received the list of worthies from the Tammany leader and who had the honor of conferring the offices.[12]

By the time Honest John was firmly ensconced in the Wigwam, the contractual nature of Tammany's operations were well entrenched. Tammany power depended on the support of the lower and working classes, especially the immigrants and their American offspring. Kelly's success in shaping an effective organization was matched by a diligent campaign to create a reliable electorate. By the time of his death, Honest John had overseen the naturalization of 80 percent of New York's German and Irish immigrants.[13] These were soon registered as voters with a natural tendency to vote Democratic—a tradition they passed on to their children. While not automatic, the Irish and German electorate gave Tammany a "manageable" vote, one they could count on, barring unforeseen or unusual problems, and one that allowed the Hall to consolidate its hold over the city during the 1890s.

Tammany provided jobs, legal support, social events, and food, fuel, and shelter if necessary. The emerging machine was itself a profession, offering young men opportunities for advancement and power. The Hall also defended and supported the immigrants' religion and culture against the sneers and slurs of old-stock nativists, and protected such popular immigrant pastimes as Sunday drinking from reform-minded politicians who wished to enforce Sunday blue laws. The Hall's political leaders also held patriotic and seasonal celebrations and festivals that provided the working poor with cheap amusements to break up an often dreary existence. For all these services, Tammany leaders wanted three things: votes, spoils, and power.

The money—often in huge amounts—flowing into Tammany's coffers depended heavily on corruption and graft. Graft came in two forms. The first, most controversial and a potential source of a backlash, was "dirty" or "police" graft. "Dirty" graft followed from Tammany's control of the police. When in power, the Hall controlled appointments to the police force, and often promotions and specific assignments as well. Gamblers of various stripes and levels, running from back alley practitioners to owners of upscale gaming rooms, madams, pimps, prostitutes of all classes, and purveyors of illegal alcohol, all paid tribute to Tammany. The payoffs were ordinarily collected by the police, who received a cut depending on rank. Additionally, those who engaged in a legitimate trade were also expected to feed the Tammany kitty if they did not want the local copper looking too hard at a license or inquiring about the hours or days of business operations. Payments to the police meant contributing to Tammany on one level or another. Failure to do so meant raids, arrest, loss of city contracts or licenses, and maybe beatings. Many Tammany politicos maintained contacts with the underworld, and their gangster allies might be dispatched to do a job too controversial for the police to undertake.

The second form of graft used political power or connections to gain lucrative contracts from the city. Alternatively, a Tammany man might use insider knowledge to purchase property he knew the city intended to acquire and resell it to the municipal government at a steep markup. The colorful Tammany district leader, George Washington Plunkitt, whose candid, humorous descriptions of Tammany's philosophy and practices, *Plunkitt of Tammany Hall,* remain in print, dubbed such activities "honest" graft. Some Tammanyites specialized in one form or another. Not a few were involved in both.

Reformers of all stripes railed against Tammany's corruption. Republicans—no novices at chicanery though their power lay outside the city—reform clubs, city leagues, and Good Government clubs (sneered at by Tammanyites as "Goo-Goos) repeatedly endeavored to break Tammany's hold on city government. Occasionally the scandals involving "dirty" graft were sensational and outrageous enough to allow the reformers to oust the Democrats from power. But the Tiger proved hard to kill, and like his smaller cousins had nine lives. Defeat led to reorganization and recalibration, and the Hall kept coming back, reclaiming its status as the most potent and enduring force in New York politics until 1932, when the nature of the game changed, and its methods became obsolete.

The reformers, often college-educated, generally old-stock Protestants, were viewed skeptically by the largely Catholic and later Jewish workers who made Tammany's rule possible. The reformers who tried to entice the immigrant and first-generation

Americans away from the machine, often lacked direct knowledge of the poorer neighborhoods and their inhabitants and were not infrequently insensitive, if not contemptuous, of the culture and mores that held sway "south of the line." The air of political and moral superiority often displayed by the Goo-Goos grated on the sensibilities of the downtowners and rendered reform gains ephemeral. Above all, the Reformers misunderstood the essential ingredient in Tammany's hold on its supporters—whatever its sins, the Hall served their interests. In 1900, reporter Harley Davis attempted to educate his readers of this fact in an article published in *Munsey's Magazine.*

> Tammany Hall does more for the daily personal comfort, happiness and well-being of the average tenement dweller than all the charitable and philanthropic institutions in New York. . . . It is not true that Tammany is uplifting the people of the metropolis. It is not true that it is making them better men and women. But it is true that in relieving distress, in providing for daily wants, in furthering ambitions, in helping men out of their troubles, and in assisting them to get on in the world, Tammany does wonderful work. . . .[14]

It took a lot to shake the loyalty of people to an organization that provided such practical support.

Despite his dedication and organizational skill, Kelly's effectiveness as a political boss was undercut by a deep contrarian streak. An early ally of Tilden, he later broke with New York's governor, though he grudgingly supported his losing run for the presidency in 1876. Three years later he bolted the state Democratic convention when it renominated Governor Lucius Robinson, whom Kelly despised for reneging on a pledge to pardon Tweed. Already suspect in many Democratic circles, Kelly's tepid support for the party's 1880 presidential candidate, Winfield Scott Hancock—which may have cost Hancock New York and the White House—led to his ostracism from state and national party functions. Despite his isolated position, none of the other "Democracies"—rival Democratic clubs—could turn him out of his power base in New York, and Kelly worked his way back into the party's good graces through his early support of Grover Cleveland's political career. But once safely in possession of the governor's chair, Cleveland declined to give Tammany the patronage it expected, infuriating Kelly, who then tried to block Cleveland's nomination as Democratic presidential candidate in 1884. Increasingly beset by health problems, and depressed at Cleveland's victory that year, Kelly relied more and more on his chief aide, Richard Croker, in running Tammany's operations.

Born in Cork in 1841, Richard Croker and his family arrived in New York three years later. The Crokers' first American address was the Irish shantytown on the western fringes of what became Central Park. Young Croker's connection with Tammany came early when the Hall got him a job as a veterinarian's assistant on the horse-drawn Hudson Railroad, which allowed him to move to better quarters on East Twenty-eighth Street. Croker left school at thirteen to work as a locomotive machinist, but most of his time was spent with the Fourth Avenue Tunnel Gang. Though a Protestant, Croker was no Orangeman, and, at least in his case, Celtic background trumped sectarian divisions, and he was running the gang by nineteen.

Aspiring political leaders—like their criminal counterparts—were expected to demonstrate physical prowess as well as organizational acumen. Tweed had proven his mettle as a battling fireman. Kelly was a fireman, amateur boxer, and opponent, both physically and verbally, of the nativists. Croker's forte was boxing, and he announced his arrival as an up-and-comer by knocking out his instructor. He added to his reputation by taking on and defeating several professional pugilists.[15] In addition to their criminal activities—robbery, shakedowns, burglary—New York gangs functioned as farm teams for political clubs, and the young immigrant soon attracted the attention of Tammany leaders.

Jimmy "the Famous" O'Brien, Tammany alderman and district leader, befriended Croker and persuaded him to operate the Fourth Avenue Tunnel Gang in Tammany's interests. In addition to applying necessary street muscle, Croker and his crew became adept repeaters—men who voted several times on election day. O'Brien brought Croker into the inner circles of Tammany power, introducing him to Tweed and launching his political career. When O'Brien moved up to become sheriff, Croker moved into his alderman's seat. A shrewd judge of people and situations, Croker stayed with O'Brien and Honest John Kelly as Tweed began to topple, and remained with Kelly after "the Famous" defected from the Hall and attempted to set up a rival Democratic organization.

The falling-out between former friends led to an election day melee in 1873 when O'Brien, running for Congress against Tammany's candidate, Abram S. Hewitt, crossed into the Lower East Side with a gang of West Side repeaters. Croker and his Tammany posse were patrolling the area and confronted the group. O'Brien, smarting from what he viewed as Croker's disloyalty, called him "a damned loafer." [16] Croker rejoined that he was no such thing, and O'Brien shouted, "You damned cur. I picked you out of the gutter and now you're supporting a rich man like Hewitt against me for Congress."[17] Verbal exchanges quickly degenerated into a brawl, during which someone pulled a gun, leaving one of O'Brien's men dead in the street. Croker was charged with the murder, most likely committed by his friend, Joe Hickey.[18] He stood trial, but the jury deadlocked and the case was never heard again.

Despite the odor emitting from the trial, Croker retained Kelly's loyalty. As Honest John's health declined, he became increasingly dependent on the younger man, who had shown toughness, loyalty, and an ability to keep his mouth shut under pressure. After Kelly's death in 1886, Tammany's district leaders were unsure of what course the Hall should take—should Tammany adopt committee rule or keep a boss at the helm? The day after Kelly's funeral, as the leaders convened at the Wigwam to debate the issue, Croker arrived on the scene. He strode past the district leaders, walked into Kelly's office, and sat down in the chair behind his desk. There would be no committee running Tammany.[19]

Croker had his work cut out for him. Kelly's intransigence and grudges had left Tammany weakened both in and out of Democratic circles. But Croker proved he had the right combination of talents to resuscitate the Tiger. In addition to an iron will and perceptive intellect, Croker was more flexible than Honest John. He was ready to compromise when necessary and worked to avoid schisms and self-defeating maneuvers. The new boss set about to reestablish Tammany's power in the city, combating Republicans and Henry George's popular Independent Labor Party. His first task, however, was to reassert Tammany's unchallenged control of New York's Democrats by defeating the rival County Democracy, which had gained prominence during Kelly's last contentious year.

The County Democracy was the most successful—however briefly—of the anti-Tammany Democratic organizations that appeared after the Civil War. The rival Democracy drew its support from recently arrived German and Irish immigrants, and wielded considerable power over construction and employment patronage in several municipal departments. Moreover, it fielded effective district leaders, many of whom took advantage of the competition between the two Democratic organizations to enhance their local power.[20] Among the County Democracy's weaknesses was internal dissension, an Achilles' heel that Croker exploited after it allied with Tammany in the face of the mutual threat posed by Henry George's surging Independent Labor Party in 1886.

George's third party movement drew on widespread labor unrest, fed by the dislocations and often misery of workers in the industrializing city. Popular among both Irish and German workers, especially those of a socialist bent, George's campaign heralded the arrival of labor issues as a potent force in municipal politics. George's popularity and potential victory frightened Democrats, Republicans, and businessmen, who feared his pro-union, pro-labor agenda. The Catholic Church, whose leaders smelled socialism in George's policies, also denounced him, providing additional support to the Independent Labor Party's enemies. Nevertheless, Tammany ballot stuffing and ballot theft were necessary to prevent George's capture of city hall.[21]

Croker took the initiative in forming a joint front against George by co-opting the County Democracy's leader, Abram S. Hewitt, as his candidate for mayor. Hewitt ran on both lines and won, providing Croker access to some crucial city patronage.[22] Already playing the role of a junior partner, the rival Democracy began to unravel due to internal disputes and weaker organization, with most of its district leaders joining Tammany or forced from office.

The Tammany boss's alliance with the old-stock mayor lasted just long enough for Croker to rebuild his organization. Hewitt, pressured by Protestant reformers and bitter over perceived slights to his overtures for higher office, advanced Croker's program to regain Tammany's dominance through self-defeating actions. He forced peddlers off the streets, enforced Sunday closing laws for saloons, called the Knights of Labor "highwaymen," and derided the Grand Army of the Republic, the largest Union army veteran's organization, as nothing but office seekers. Unsatisfied, the mayor alienated the city's largest voting bloc by refusing to review the St. Patrick's Day parade and went on to assert that the percentage of Irish in city jails and almshouses was double their percentage of the city's population.[23] In the next mayoral race, Croker nominated his close friend Hugh Grant. Grant and most of the Tammany ticket won in a blowout, defeating Hewitt, who had only the hollowed-out County Democracy line, along with the Republicans.

Croker and Tammany were back in the saddle, free to dispense municipal jobs and contracts to friends and supporters while they entered lucrative alliances with businessmen. Croker was unapologetic about his spoils-system approach to city government. "Now since there must be [city] officials, and since these officials must be paid, and well paid, in order to insure able and constant service, why should they not be selected from the membership of the society that organizes the victories of the dominant party? In my opinion, to ask this question is to answer it."[24]

Croker's personal wealth increased in parallel measure with Tammany's grip over city government. The boss became an inactive partner in Meyer & Croker, the most prosperous real estate auction house in New York. During Grant's term as mayor, the Tammany leader held the post of city chamberlain, which paid $25,000, along with ample opportunities for financial enhancements. The money raked in from his take of kickbacks, bribery, and protection was likely much higher yet. After 1890, Croker moved into an $80,000 brownstone in the East Seventies, which he refurbished for another $100,000. He then purchased a $500,000 stock farm near Utica to indulge in his passion for horses. The Tammany boss also owned a Palm Beach estate, "the Wigwam," and took to traveling to Democratic National Conventions in a private Pullman car.[25]

Between them, Kelly and Croker had not only revived Tammany Hall, they had made it the central fact of life in New York politics. Tammany provided the ladder a sharp, young man might climb if he had a mind and the drive to make his name and fortune in the empire city. Many a lad from the dirty, impoverished byways below Fourteenth Street would do so. None would do it as flamboyantly and as successfully as Timothy Daniel Sullivan.

2
Upward Mobility

We could tear down half our prisons and shut up three quarters of our almshouses.
　　—Reverend Charles Parkhurst on the benefits of removing
the Irish and rum from America

BEFITTING A MAN WHO CLOSELY GUARDED HIS PERSONAL LIFE,
the exact date of Timothy Daniel Sullivan's birth is uncertain.
Some sources claim February 6, 1863, while several cite July 23,
1863.[1] The best evidence is that he was born July 23, 1862.[2] He
entered the world in the squalor of New York's Hudson River
tenements, an appropriate first address for a man who came to be
idolized by thousands of poor and working-class people. His par-
ents, Daniel Sullivan and Catherine Connelly, were fugitives
from the serflike conditions that prevailed among the poor in
British-controlled Ireland. Daniel Sullivan died about 1867, and
his widow remarried Lawrence Mulligan, who moved the family
to the Five Points, then the epicenter of Irish New York. The
Mulligans had three children, two girls and a boy, to add to Tim
and his brother, Patrick. But Mulligan proved a nasty drunk who
beat his wife and children, and the marriage disintegrated.[3] His
stepfather's negative example turned young Tim into a lifelong
teetotaler, though he saw no problem in providing drink to those
who wanted it. While he erased Mulligan from his autobiography, his reverence for his mother, who took in laundry to make
ends meet, and a sister who began working in a sweatshop at
fourteen, instilled an appreciation of women that later manifested itself in an unexpected feminist streak.[4]

Survival in the Five Points was a full-time occupation, and Tim
learned the importance of money early on. His first nickname,
"Dry Dollar," supposedly originated when he was a young boy and
discovered a revenue stamp on an empty barrel of beer. Mistak-
ing it for a greenback, he carefully peeled it off, dried it, and ran

home to tell his mother he had found a "dry dollar."[5] He soon found out what the real thing was, a necessary lesson as the Sullivan-Mulligan clan hovered on the edge of destitution. Tim later recalled that the three boys slept in a "three-quarters bed not big enough for two, and the girls in a shakedown on the floor."[6] What little the family owned in material possessions was often stretched beyond effective usefulness. When he was a boy of ten going to the Elm Street School, Tim's teacher, a Miss Murphy, asked him to remain after school. The lad feared he had been set up to take the fall for another student's antics, but found out that the teacher had noticed that he was wearing a broken-down pair of shoes. Realizing the family had little money, Miss Murphy sent the boy to Timothy Brennan, brother of a Tammany politician, who handed him a voucher for new footwear.[7] Tim never forgot the kindness, and its memory would inspire conspicuous acts of charity in later life.

In any event, Tim was not destined to remain long at school. His working life began when he was eight and lugged bundles of newspapers to men who would go out and peddle them.[8] By the time he was ten he was leaving school at 2:00 PM to start his day with the *Commercial Advertiser* where he worked as a "fly boy" on the presses. Despite his long hours at the newspaper, the future political leader did well enough at school that he was one of seven boys selected to attend the "free academy" on Twenty-third Street. But, as he later put it, "free as it was it was not free enough for me to go there. I had to go downtown and commence the struggle of life for four children younger than me."[9]

The future Tammany leader showed himself a quick study, and his natural intelligence, ambition, and winning personality shortly made him leader of the local newsboys. He staked poorer children so they could purchase papers to sell, and later, when he was the city's most successful politician, Sullivan never forgot the boys who worked the streets hawking the news.[10] According to Bowery historian Alvin Harlow, "Early in life he was instinctively assuming leadership and drawing others to him like a magnet by kindness . . ."[11] Personable, openhanded, ambitious, and sharp, Tim's apprenticeship as "newsie" and "fly boy" grew into a profitable career as supplier of newspapers all across the city. By eighteen he was handling five different newspapers, forging contacts with newsdealers throughout the city, and adding new papers as they appeared.[12] In addition to income, Tim's newspaper

activities gave him an education in the expanding metropolis—
its peoples, classes, neighborhoods, institutions, failings, and opportunities. For a young man from the Five Points, the lessons
learned in the news trade were more valuable than what he
would have received at the "free academy."

The real rulers of the Five Points, Bowery, and the Lower East
Side in general were the Tammany Hall politicians. Tim received
his first lessons in their importance and potential from Miss
Kelly, who knew where to go if a needy lad lacked shoes and the
money to buy them. Tim's enterprises brought him into frequent
contact with Tammany men of different stripes. A smart kid from
the Five Points would see how the game was played and appreciate the possibilities—and the responsibilities—of the system.
And a shrewd Tammany politico would quickly recognize the
potential of an aspiring, clever kid. Sullivan's leadership of the
downtown "newsies" caught the attention of Tom "Fatty" Walsh,
the Hall's Sixth Ward boss. Walsh took Tim under his wing and
gave him his first political assignments, using him as a mes-
senger and source of street news.

Besides the parish church, the social hub of the Irish neighborhoods was the local saloon, which often doubled as a de facto
political club. At twenty-one, Tim bought his first saloon on
Leonard Street.[13] By 1889, Tim had at least two others, including
one on Center Street directly across from the Tombs Police Court.
Whether Tim purchased his first drinking establishment with
his own money or found a backer is unclear. In either case, the
saloon business was so good that he left—probably sold—his
newspaper enterprise soon after. Dry Dollar's first saloon became
the headquarters for the most notorious downtown gang of the
time—the "Whyos." Nineteenth-century gangs were often controlled or linked to political leaders, providing muscle on election
day and occasionally supplying new blood. Tim secured the loyalty and informal leadership over the Whyos by successfully
fulfilling the test of physical prowess requisite for political advancement in the downtown neighborhoods. Sullivan made his
name when he came across a local man—a boxer—beating a
woman in front of the Tombs, New York's municipal jail. Sullivan
intervened, and when words could not dissuade the thug, he went
after the woman beater with his fists, taking out the boxer and
winning his reputation as a man of principle and action. The
story might have been apocryphal, though it was widely repeated

and fits the known parameters of Tim's character. As a "creation myth" the dual forces of chivalry and physical courage were a strong brew.[14]

Sullivan's waxing popularity in the Sixth Ward, and his following among the young men of the area, especially the Whyos, convinced Fatty Walsh to nominate him for the state assembly in 1886. With the support of the Whyos, who probably intimidated opponents and served as repeaters, the novice candidate won his first race. He was destined never to lose a bid for an elective office he coveted. Ironically, in his debut campaign, Tim ran on the line of Tammany's Democratic rival, the County Democracy. Tim made his presence felt in Albany. He was keen, effective, and, though never given to oratory, could exchange barbs with the best in the assembly. But from the very beginning, his connections with the underworld elements in his district left him vulnerable to attack. In his personal and public life, Sullivan placed loyalty to friends in first place among his guiding principles. If he adopted someone's case, he stuck with it, and when some members of the Whyos ran afoul of the law, the young legislator exerted his influence to help them.

His instinctive loyalty to friends and supporters was used against him in a dispute with New York Police Department inspector, Thomas F. Byrnes, who alleged that Tim was an "associate of criminals and thieves," charges that would surface repeatedly throughout his career.[15] Sullivan had incurred Byrnes's wrath by opposing a bill that would have given the police the right to apprehend anyone who had ever been previously arrested. Byrnes retaliated by raiding two of Tim's saloons. The novice representative rebutted Byrnes's charges on the floor of the assembly when, not for the last time, he recounted his humble origins and hardworking mother, and denied Byrnes's allegations by asserting that he had risen by virtue of his own sweat and diligence. "I am not looking for sympathy," he began,

> But I think I owe it to this house to show you that you have not been sitting with a man who has been a chum of thieves. My father died when I was four years old, leaving me the youngest of four children. My mother struggled along as best she could, but when I was seven years old I had to go downtown and sell newspapers to keep the family together. A year later I began as a flyboy in a pressroom, and I worked in a press room till the very morning of my election, and I think you will agree that I had no time to associate with thieves.[16]

3. Timothy D. Sullivan at the start of his career. *Tammany Times,* **1893.**

According to the *New York Herald* "the speech was given in the tone and manner of a genuine fourth warder, and . . . its tone was so manly that Tim gained much sympathy."[17] The speech was also partly disingenuous. Tim's descriptions of his childhood and early upbringing were accurate enough, but by the time he entered the assembly, he was involved in far more than newspaper pressrooms, which he had left behind when his saloons took off.

Tim's gift for the well-turned phrase was largely responsible for killing a bill desired by one of the larger corporations in the city. A fellow assemblyman had taken the floor eloquently explaining why, having previously opposed the legislation, he now favored it. His earlier hostility, the speaker proceeded, was caused by the influence of a special-interest lobby, which was offering securities to those who would vote for it. "This year, Mr. Speaker," he went on, "I thank God that this bill is in new hands and no one charges that stocks and bonds are being distributed to effect its passage." "No Mr. Speaker," Tim interjected loudly, "this year it's cash."[18] Not that Sullivan had any aversion to accepting honoraria in exchange for his favors in considering legislation. Referring to a bill whose payoff potential was uncertain, Tim advised, "Well, let's give it a toss," meaning it was worth a try.[19]

Taking note of Tim's vote-getting abilities and skill in dealing with Byrnes, Tammany invited him to come over from the County Democracy. Quite likely, the young assemblyman saw that Tammany's rival was fading fast and readily recognized the advantages that Tammany offered. For openers, the Tiger could field about ninety-thousand precinct workers who labored under the direction of the district leaders.[20] Tim understood the district leaders themselves typically held a state and municipal post, and he likely envisioned such a dual role for himself. In addition to organization backing and advancement, Tammany ordinarily controlled the largest source of patronage in the city. The smaller Democratic clubs offered none of these inducements, and never endured as well. Sizing up the pluses and minuses, Tim threw in his lot with Croker.

The freshly converted Tammany man soon proved his value. In the presidential elections of 1892, he delivered his electoral district for the Democratic candidate, Grover Cleveland, by a margin of 388 to 4. "[Benjamin] Harrison got one more vote than I expected," Tim confessed to Croker, "but I'll find that fellow."[21] The remark amused Croker, who was equally impressed by the young man's energy. The boss decided such talents deserved a larger stage on which they could be displayed. The only question was where. The Sixth District slot was filled. Alderman Patrick "Paddy" Divver was the leader in the Second. Sullivan would probably have beaten him in a primary, but Divver was Croker's man and would stay put. Nor would Croker accede to moving

John F. Ahern out of the state senate to make room for the rising politician. So Croker hit on the idea of moving Tim out of the Sixth and into the Third which adjoined it.[22] Here he could be district leader and still be free to run for the state senate. Sullivan agreed and took command of the Third Assembly District— the heart of the Bowery. Tim already had a beachhead there in the form of a saloon, and, along with his circle of retainers and lieutenants, he moved westward into his new domain.

3

Running the Game

Being Irish, [Big and Little Tim] took to politics naturally, and being Irish they succeeded in New York politics very well.
—New York Times

THE THIRD ASSEMBLY DISTRICT THAT TIM SULLIVAN TOOK OVER was not then a Tammany stronghold, and Croker hoped the young, ambitious Irishman could shape its polyglot, teeming neighborhoods into a reliable voting bloc. The area had been heavily Irish and German until the 1880s, when increasing numbers of Italians and Eastern European Jews began transforming the area. In 1890, four years after Tim began his tenure as Bowery district leader, a United States government report observed that Italians were seen in formerly Irish neighborhoods and Jews in those recently German. "Wherever these newer peoples came the older began to move out," the report noted.[1] While more than a few Irish and Germans remained as Tim took the helm in the Third, the earlier immigrant groups and their first-generation children were already more evenly distributed across the city and were pressing uptown, the Germans primarily on the East Side and the Irish on the West. Some of the ethnic change was a result of decreasing immigration from Ireland and Germany. Some was the natural process of dispersion that accompanied social mobility and acculturalization to American mores. To the older or more assimilated Irish and Germans, the Lower East Side was beginning to look foreign, and they pulled away from the newer groups as the Yankees had recoiled from them earlier in the century.

The influx of the newer immigrants made the Lower East Side the most pluralistic in New York. German, Irish, Irish-English, Italian dialects, Hungarian, and virtually any language spoken in Slavic Europe could be heard, and often read, in the downtown neighborhoods. With three hundred thousand people living within its general area, the Bowery was also New York's most

congested district. The housing stock into which the residents
were crammed were dominated by multistoried tenements whose
apartments were often home to more than one family or such
extended grouping that the buildings contained more people than
could healthily or comfortably live there. Most of the Bowery's
residents were working people, heavily immigrant, who performed many of the tasks that drove New York's economy. But the
Bowery was notorious, with some justification, as the home of a
large number of thugs, gangsters, pimps, whores, and bums. This
was unsurprising since, in addition to the rowdy plebeian amusements that titillated and frightened reformers, the Bowery wards
contained a large concentration of establishments offering vice or
low-life diversions. In 1891 reporter Julian Ralph estimated that
one-fifth of the city's pawnshops and one-sixth of its saloons were
found along Park Row and the Bowery between city hall and
Cooper Union. Police Department records revealed that 27 percent of New York's arrests were made in the Bowery district. Half
of the city's pawnshops and more than half of its saloons were
located south of Fourteenth Street—the Lower East Side.[2]

If Sullivan felt any trepidation about his new job, he hid it well.
Rather, he assumed the helm of his new bailiwick as if it were his
by birth. Profoundly Irish by birth, heritage, and experience, the
new district leader held little in the way of ethno-religious prejudices and took people as he found them. Brought up in abject

4. The Bowery, c. 1905. Postcard. Author's Collection.

poverty himself, his worldview was refracted through a prism of class-consciousness that owed nothing to theory or ideology and everything to experience and practicality. As one chronicler put it, "[Sullivan] took [the immigrants] as fast as they came, [and] flung them into his melting pot. They went Silvestros and Gordzinskis and they came out Sullivans. He naturalized them, registered and voted them for Tammany Hall. They wondered and adored him. . . ."[3]

The "Big Feller," as Tim was becoming known in his new domain, did more than just vote them. If he found non-Irishers with the talents he valued, he showed no hesitation in placing them in command of the electoral districts. Soon a number of his captains were Germans, Jews, or Italians whose rapport with their brethren kept the Bowery Democratic and instilled a sense of loyalty to Sullivan that transcended ethnic and religious divisions. Within two years, Tim's hold on the allegiance of the Bowery was so strong that he had effectively created "a machine within a machine." As one historian later concluded, "below 14th Street Big Tim Sullivan was Tammany Hall."[4]

Like a medieval fiefdom, Sullivan's organization ran on personal fealty, and its hierarchy was primarily made up of members of his extended family. Known locally as the "Wise Men" or the "Sullivan Clan," this coterie/cadre included Tim's brother Patrick, "Paddy," and his half brother, Larry Mulligan. Three of Tim's cousins—all brothers—also took their seats in Tim's inner sanctum: Florence "Florrie" Sullivan, who managed some of Tim's saloons and helped run the polls on election day, Christopher D. "Christy" Sullivan, and Dennis "Flat-Nose Dinny" Sullivan. The Sullivan clan was augmented by Tim's personal bodyguard, "Photo Dave" Altman, Thomas F. Reilly, called "Sarsaparilla" or "Soda Water," and, somewhat later, "Colonel" Michael Padden, sometimes called the "Secretary of War in the Sullivan Cabinet."[5]

Colorful nicknames were common in the Bowery, and it was taken as an honor to be addressed by Tim with one's moniker. Seen by many in the Bowery as Big Tim's mascot, Photo Dave's name derived from his role as the official photographer of the Sullivan Association. Until 1902, it was Altman's job to officially put Sullivan's name forward in nomination for whatever position he was running for at the time.[6] Reilly got his nickname from his practice of drinking sarsaparilla during champagne toasts. He was also known as Tim's valet. According to Bowery tradition,

Big Tim once traveled to Washington to call on Grover Cleveland at the White House. He purchased a formal suit for the occasion, and under the impression that protocol called for his retaining a valet, he pressed Reilly into the service. When the two checked into the Shoreham Hotel in Washington, Tim registered them as (state) "Senator Timothy D. Sullivan and valet" to the amusement of the staff.

But first among equals in the "Wise Men" was yet another cousin, Timothy Patrick Sullivan. Timothy Patrick was born in Pearl Street June 22, 1876, but went to Boston as a young child, which gave rise to his first nickname, "Boston Tim." He returned to New York about age ten with the ambition of becoming a lawyer. But he soon became devoted to his older cousin and namesake. As the Big Feller climbed up the political ladder, the Little Feller, as Timothy P. came to be called, followed and learned. He started as a "Tombs Runner" carrying messages or bail money from the political clubs to those incarcerated in the city jail.[7] When Big Tim went to Albany, Little Tim came along as a page and later became his cousin's secretary. According to some, he functioned as Big Tim's "satchel man." In 1896 he won his own assembly seat representing Tammany-Sullivan interests in the assembly as the Big Feller did in the senate. Their time in Albany, where they both boarded at Keeler's Hotel, a Tammany favorite, cemented the bond between the two men who became as close as brothers.

During his early days in Albany, Big Tim was never much for speeches—his lengthy forays usually reserved for impassioned defense of his name and reputation—and originally Timothy P. followed suit. But in 1901, his last year in Albany, he assumed the leadership of the Tammany forces in the assembly, where he revealed a gift for political repartee that provided much amusement for his colleagues. Few wished to miss his performances, and his fellow assemblymen seldom left the chamber when Timothy P. rose to speak.[8] It was noted that while Little Tim was well educated, he readily played "to his constituency when all sorts of Bowery barbarisms are inserted into his speeches."[9] Nor was the younger Tim's wit reserved solely for public settings. While at Albany the two Tims traveled back and forth from their hotel to the Capitol in an ancient black hack that showed many years of wear. A Republican legislator, seeing them alight from the hard-used carriage, good-naturedly suggested they should get a "re-

5. Timothy P. "Little Tim" Sullivan, c. 1905. *Munsey's Magazine,* December 1913.

spectable looking outfit" that would "preserve the dignity of your office." "It may be different with you," Timothy P. rejoined by way of explanation, "but all we get here is our salary."[10] Whether literally true or not, the rejoinder stiffed the Republican and amused the Democrats.

When Big Tim left Albany for the United States Congress, Little Tim—he was actually of average height and so-called to distinguish himself from his larger cousin—took his place as district leader while simultaneously serving as majority leader of New York's Board of Aldermen. He was highly successful in advancing Sullivan and Tammany interests on the board, and was considered as "a lightning manipulator of men" a skill that was attributed to "his long time association with his cousin."[11] Other observers noted that Timothy P. had "absorbed all the finesse and cunning of the old [Tammany] leaders without their blundering disregard for the consequence."[12] While the Big Feller was fond of all his family, it was Timothy P. who held first place in his affections and whose counsel he sought. Little Tim lacked Big Tim's personal charm and charisma, but his more restrained air hid a probing, calculating intellect that missed nothing. A reporter for the *New York Tribune,* describing Little Tim, stated that "[h]is eye is smaller than his cousin's, but if anything is more active."[13] Until Timothy P.'s death in 1909, the two Sullivans reigned as the dominant force in New York City politics, and the Big Feller was personally grieved and politically weakened by the Little Feller's untimely passing.

Big Tim's power, which soon extended beyond the Lower East Side, sprang from his shrewd intelligence and engaging personality. Over six feet tall and weighing two hundred pounds, his popular nickname, the Big Feller, was well earned. He had dark hair and a handsome Irish face. Even as he grew older, stouter, and began to lose his hair, he remained an impressive man. According to a contemporary observer, "his smile could adequately be described only by the word beautiful. He radiated kindness."[14]

Some sources maintain that Tim was adverse, even uncomfortable, with public oratory. This was not the case. While not one of those who seized every opportunity to harangue the public as some of his colleagues did, Dry Dollar counterattacked ferociously when his character was assailed, especially if he was accused of involvement with prostitution. He could promote himself and slam his opponents with the best of them at election time, and he was quick, energetic, and effective in fighting for legislation he desired, especially in his last session in the Albany senate. In debating opponents and rebutting their arguments, he showed a keen eye for his foe's weakness, which he exploited with wit and irony.

Whenever necessary, Sullivan rang the chimes of neighborhood solidarity, delivered in flawless, and authentic, Lower East

Side argot, stirring his followers and confounding his opponents. After he had established himself, his endorsement of allies for local posts tended to be straightforward. When he spoke in support of Battery Dan Finn for the Board of Aldermen, he declared "Boys, I'm a Democrat (Cheers.) I've been a Democrat all my life (loud cheers.) I have voted the Democratic ticket straight all my life (uproarious cheers.) I never scratched a ticket since I cast my first vote when I was seventeen and I never will (pandemonium.)."[15] As Alvin Harlow somewhat hyperbolically observed, "The critic may think that Tim wandered from the subject in this oration, but not so. If he had merely recited the multiplication tables in Finn's behalf, it would have been valid material. Anybody that Tim was for was good enough for the voters, and Finn was elected."[16] Interestingly, in his brief statement of support, the Big Feller admitted that he had cast an illegal ballot, the voting age being twenty-one.

Big Tim understood that running the Bowery was a profession, and all the benefits that accrued from his position were dependent on his running the district for the perceived benefit of its inhabitants. Following the traditional stance of virtually all American politicians, at least since Andrew Jackson, Sullivan publicly denied possession of any greater talent for leadership than could be found in any of his constituents. "All this talk about psychological power and personal magnetism over man is fine business for pretty writing," he remarked in 1909, "but when you get down to brass tacks it's the work that does the business . . ." Expounding on his theory of political leadership, he added

I'll take any man from the Bowery or the prairies and set him down anywhere, and if he'll follow my instructions he'll be a leader of men sooner or later, according to how much he has in the go-in. Most men are lazy and do only what they have to do for their immediate comfort; lots of men are born with the unfortunate ability not to think for themselves, and other men, for no known reason in the world, have to have someone to look for a leader for them

Every community has to have some man who can take the trouble to look out for their public interest while they are earning a living, and it don't make any difference whether he's tall, short, fat, lean, humpbacked or with only half his teeth, if he's willing to work harder than anybody else, he's the fellow.

That'll hold the job. They're not always grateful, and when they catch a man fourflushing, no matter how good his excuse—Skidoo!

> Back to the old home for his. And so, after all, there ain't much to it to
> be a leader. It's just plenty of work, keep your temper or throw it
> away, be on the level and don't put on any airs, because God and the
> people hate a chesty man.[17]

Of course, everyone knew that a politician like Sullivan was a
rarity in any age. In his heart, Sullivan knew it too.

Powerful as he became, Tim was by nature and calculation
munificent. He was approachable by all, provided myriad of social and legal services, and dispensed his favors without regard
to religion or ethnicity. Early in his career in the Third Assembly
District. he sent cops to raid the clubhouse of an Irish gang that
had harassed a group of Orthodox Jews. Tim then rented the
former clubhouse for the Jews to use as a synagogue.[18] The lesson was not lost on all involved, and Sullivan's standing among
the neighborhood Jews was secured. Later, he introduced a bill in
the New York State legislature making Columbus Day a state
holiday, winning a strong following in the Italian community as
well.

The business of politics was a full contact sport in turn-of-the-
century New York, and nowhere was this truer than in the congested districts of the Lower East Side. Tim was popular, but like
other Tammany leaders—and their opponents—his first duty
was to win elections. As the Big Feller's hold on the Lower East
Side grew, New York's reformers denounced his use of street intimidation to control or expand the vote, as the situation required. His methods were well established when he decided to
move up and run for a state senate seat in 1893. Lodging house-
men, often nonregistered transients—and sometimes nonciti-
zens—were organized and voted. A Republican poll watcher
named Henry Cunningham later testified before a state investigating committee that in the 1893 elections, after he ordered a
man arrested for illegal voting, Big Tim grabbed him by the collar
and pulled him into the street. "If I wasn't running for senator I
would do so and so," Cunningham quoted Tim with the expletives
deleted. As it was, the Big Feller restrained himself and left it to
Florrie to hand Cunningham "a severe beating."[19]

During the 1901 municipal elections when Republican candidate for district attorney, William Travers Jerome, threatened to
dispatch outside poll watchers to the Bowery, Sullivan responded
at a public gathering at Miner's Bowery Theater with a threat of

his own. "If Jerome brings down a lot of football playing, hair matressed college athletes to run the polls by force, I will say now that there won't be enough ambulances in New York to carry them away."[20] Tim's use of strong-arm tactics on election day was usually done in the service of his allies in Democratic primaries or on behalf of Tammany's state and municipal candidates. By 1892 he himself was so popular that even the *New York Times,* then a Republican organ and bitter critic, later admitted, "there is no doubt that he was the real choice of the majority of voters in his district when he ran for the State Senate or National Congress . . ."[21]

The supporters of good government—contemptuously referred to by Tammany men as Goo-Goos—took Big Tim's words seriously. To the "silk hats and silk socks with nothing in between," as Sullivan described them, his supporters even looked intimidating. In the words of the *New York Herald,* they were "bullet headed, short haired, small eyed, smooth shaven, and crafty looking with heavy vicious features, which speak of dissipation and brutality, ready to fight at a moments notice."[22]

Some of Dry Dollar's followers had more in common with bullets than the shape of their heads. Sullivan employed the century-old practice of employing gangs for muscle when necessary. The two most actively used while he ruled the Bowery were Monk Eastman's Jewish gang and Paul "Kelly" Vaccarelli's Italian crew. In addition to intimidating opposition voters, Eastman could turn out four to five hundred repeaters, while Vaccarelli reportedly could supply one thousand.[23] Tim preferred "guys with whiskers" as repeaters. The repeater made his initial vote in his bushy state. Then, according to Sullivan, "you take 'em to a barber and scrape off the chin-fringe. Then you vote 'em again with side lilacs and mustache. If that ain't enough, and the box can stand a few more ballots, clean off the mustache and vote 'em plain face. That makes every one of 'em good for four votes."[24] If any of his repeaters or hard cases fell afoul of the law during an election, the Big Feller would bail them out and provide them with legal counsel if necessary.

Big Tim's burgeoning political power was paralleled by deep involvements with sections of New York's underworld. The connection between crime and politics was an old one in New York and most major cities, and Sullivan was following a well-trodden path in this regard. Nevertheless, while many Tammany men had interests in the vices that flourished in the "Gilded Age," Big Tim presided over an unusually extensive system of graft, kickbacks, and shakedowns. According to newspaper accounts, "There is not a saloon in the [Bowery] which does not work in his interest, and he personally selects the men who shall work in the various saloons. In every poolroom, gambling and disorderly resort the employees are named by Sullivan and must be taken by the proprietor. These men, alone in number, give Sullivan a big following."[25]

Some charged that under Big Tim's rule, the Bowery had become "more wide open than ever before. . . . He made politics and crime more comprehensively synonymous than even such a master as Tweed had been able to do."[26] Most of Dry Dollar's dealings were with practitioners of "victimless crimes"—gamblers, illegal saloon/dive keepers, and after-hours or Sunday bars. His support for those who purveyed alcohol without regard to legal limitations reflected the attitude of most of his constituents in the immigrant communities that defined his district. The forces of reform—primarily old-stock Protestants—generally wanted to curb alcohol sales on Sundays and closely regulate the places where it was sold. The Irish, Germans, and Italians resented this intrusion into the social life they conducted in their saloons, beer gardens, and neighborhood wineries. They were also well aware that many of the measures designed to curb alcohol sales were hatched in private clubs that were immune from the strictures of early closing and Sunday blue laws. It was Tammany policy to protect the ethnic watering holes, and Tim, who owned several saloons himself, was a company man in this regard. Though neither he nor Little Tim drank themselves, they took care to make sure plenty of alcohol was available at their neighborhood celebrations and rallies for those who did not share their avoidance of "the creature." More problematic was the extent of Sullivan's involvement in prostitution, a "victimless crime" that aroused ire among reformers and alarm among many in the downtown neighborhoods as well.

The blatant presence of gambling, prostitution, and the variegated dives did not go unchallenged. In February 1892, the Reverend Charles Parkhurst, a Protestant clergyman soon to assume leadership of the Society for the Prevention of Crime, took to the pulpit to condemn the politically protected vice that he claimed was rife in the City. Tammany officials demanded that he back up his allegations with fact, and the abashed minister was forced to concede that he had no direct knowledge of the nature and extent of criminality in the city. Unexpectedly, however, Parkhurst determined to rectify that deficiency and began his own personal investigation into the prevalence of gambling, illegal alcohol joints, and prostitution. Affecting a disguise and engaging the services of several knowledgeable and experienced guides, the reverend got a practical education in low-life New York. Armed now with firsthand information, Parkhurst began attacking Tammany control of New York, especially the Lower East Side—Big Tim's domain. Parkhurst's revelations sparked the creation of a "Committee of Seventy" who, supported by the Council of Good Government clubs and much of the city's social and economic elite, set out to break Tammany's hold on New York.

The aggressive and energetic reform movement of which Parkhurst was a part owed a great deal to the Protestant evangelical revival, which was a force in municipal politics ca. 1880–1900. Those caught up in its enthusiasm believed it was both a possibility and a duty "to establish the kingdom of God on earth; to create a thoroughly [Protestant] Christian state and social order."[27] The reform evangelical impulse led to a multifaceted reform movement aimed especially at social problems, deploying the considerable resources of wealthy Protestants to achieve its goal. Among its more militant manifestations were the Society for the Prevention of Vice and the Society for the Prevention of Crime. Both assumed quasi-legal status, and both held themselves above the law, an assumption that led them into nonviolent vigilantism.[28] The old-stock reformers endeavored to address the needs of the poor, often immigrant, neighborhoods through charitable and labor organizations that often included, implicitly or explicitly, a Protestant missionary adjunct. Though they attempted to understand the Catholic and Jewish immigrants, the reformers' backgrounds and religious zeal impeded their goals.

The largely Protestant reformers denounced Tammany Hall as a fountain of vice, a stance that sold well in many middle- and upper-class neighborhoods, but did them less good in poorer areas. Unless Tammany overreached—or stooped too low—the Irish and Germans, as well as later groups, tended to view the Hall as their source of protection and employment. The reformers and their clubs, organizations, and societies were accurately perceived as inherently anti-Catholic, an attitude that alienated the Catholic neighborhoods and set the Catholic Church, with its own charitable and social institutions, against them. As one historian put it, "the same impulse that led many wealthy Protestants to seek an alliance with non-Protestant immigrants also made it impossible to sustain the alliance."[29] But with the odor of political corruption rising, the reformers might achieve temporary victories before their internal inconsistencies and a revived Tammany could oust them.

Parkhurst's denunciations, and the gathering of reform opposition, stirred the state Republicans into action. With the Republicans in control of Albany, New York GOP boss, Thomas Platt, directed state senator Clarence Lexow to initiate an investigation of corruption in New York City's government.[30] Platt's own operations on a statewide level were far from the standards of civil virtue (Parkhurst once condemned him in a sermon), and he was simply taking his opportunity as he saw it. Some suspected that the inquiries of the Lexow Committee were a Republican gambit to coerce some city patronage out of Croker.[31] Whatever the motivation, the Lexow Committee, which began hearings in March 1894, amassed a mound of evidence—six thousand pages in all—that detailed the connection between Tammany and the police and police protection of vice. Among other things, the Lexow Committee discovered that Tammany district leaders controlled the board of police, which in turn authorized all appointments, promotions, and transfers within the Police Department. Despite ample testimony regarding payoffs, kickbacks, and sundry other forms of corruption, neither Big Tim nor any other Tammany leader was indicted as a result of the damaging material presented.

The Panic (Depression) of 1893 had put the public in a sour mood, and Parkhurst's nocturnal rambles combined with the Lexow Committee's report to throw Tammany on the defensive. In 1895, the Republicans nominated William L. Strong, a millionaire dry goods merchant turned banker, for city hall. Croker initially convinced Nathan Straus to take the Democratic line, but Straus bowed out after nine days of social ostracism. Tammany then persuaded former mayor Hugh Grant to lead the ticket. Grant himself had been tarred in the Lexow hearings, and the Republicans captured city hall, adding Albany and Congress to their conquests the following year. Before the ballots were counted in the municipal elections, Croker told reporter Lincoln Steffens that Strong would be elected. When Steffens and his fellow newsmen seemed stunned by the declaration, Croker continued, "You knew all along it was a reform wave, didn't you?" he explained. "Our people could not stand the rotten police corruption. They'll be back in the next election; they can't stand reform either."[32]

Croker spent most of Strong's term in England where he amused himself with horses and hounds. Back in New York, the district leaders, Sullivan chief among them, had to deal with the Republican mayoralty, which attempted, only partly successfully, to cut them off from all patronage. Among the luminaries in the Strong administration was its president of the police commission, a young blue blood named Theodore Roosevelt.[33] By background, temperament, and politics, the police commissioner and the Big Feller were natural antagonists. Sullivan, Roosevelt recalled in his autobiography, "represented the morals of another era; that is, his principles and actions were very much those of a Norman noble in the years immediately succeeding the Battle of Hastings. (This will seem like flattery only to those who are not acquainted with the real histories and antecedents of the Norman nobles in question.) His application of eleventh century theories to our nineteenth century municipal democratic conditions brought him into sharp contact with me. . . ."[34]

Nevertheless, some were convinced Sullivan was able to use some of his legendary charm to wheedle some patronage from Roosevelt. Roosevelt adamantly insisted that his appointments were made exclusively on the basis of merit. In just such an instance, Roosevelt put aside his opinions of the Big Feller to promote yet another of his numerous cousins, Jerry D. Sullivan, a patrolman whom he deemed both effective and honest. Considering the nature of his relationship with Tammany in general and Tim in particular, Roosevelt's action was a pleasant surprise to both Sullivans. "I do not know whether Jerry or Jerry's cousin (Senator Sullivan) was more astonished," Roosevelt remembered.[35] "The Senator called on me to express what I am sure was a very genuine feeling of appreciation. . . . The Senator, though politically opposed to me, always kept a feeling of friendship for me after this incident."[36] The expression of gratitude was very much part of Tim's nature. He remembered those who helped him or his family, and evidence suggests he always had a touch of

6. Richard Croker. *Munsey's Magazine,* **1901.**

sympathy for Roosevelt despite political warfare. Roosevelt's account hints that he might have slightly mellowed his attitude toward the Big Feller.

Though never totally shut out of patronage, and able to provide places for followers from corporate supporters, the loss of city hall always pinched, and the Tammany men girded themselves for the next contests. Croker finally returned from England in September 1897. His reception was less than warm, and John Sheehan, whom he had left as titular boss, informed him that the district leaders were planning to dump him in favor of Sullivan, the most powerful of them all.[37] On October 5, 1897, Croker arrived at an executive committee meeting at the Wigwam. He pushed past the district leaders who were supposedly preparing to oust him and entered his office. Shortly after, he sent word that they should join him. Once the leaders were in their seats, Croker challenged them. "I've heard some of you have complaints to make. What are those complaints? None? Well! I just want to say that I'm tired of hearing that certain leaders are dissatisfied. Tim Sullivan, are you dissatisfied? No? Very well, then there is no dissatisfaction. Now I want you men to go back to your districts and get to work. We have a show to carry New York this time, and if you go about it right, we'll do it. But I don't want to hear any more grumbling."[38]

Bluffing with a weak hand, Croker reasserted his leadership over Tammany. If the account is accurate—and lengthy, verbatim accounts of Tammany councils are suspect—Sullivan backed down in the face of Croker's bluster. On the other hand, all evidence indicates Big Tim never wanted the job. He certainly could have brushed aside Sheehan, essentially Croker's cipher, while Croker dallied in England. Moreover, throughout his career he consistently demonstrated he was content to rule his own bailiwick while exerting his influence over the entire Tammany organization from behind the scenes. In any case, Croker's subsequent actions showed that the restored boss remained fearful of the Big Feller's clout, and if he pushed him once, he never did it again. Indeed, the reverse proved the case.

Whatever the acrimony resulting from Croker's return, Sullivan and the other Tammany leaders needed each other if the Democrats were to retake the city in the 1897 elections. The stakes were even greater with the creation of the city of Greater New York, which was scheduled to come into being on January 1, 1898. The expanded city now included Manhattan, the centerpiece, plus the new outer boroughs of the Bronx, Queens, Kings (Brooklyn), and Staten Island. Republican boss Thomas Platt had supported the consolidation, thinking Republican prospects would be enhanced by the incorporation of the outlaying areas that——outside of Brooklyn—were not under Democratic control. In contrast, Tammany believed that it would continue to hold Manhattan and then extend its dominance over the other Democratic borough organizations that, expecting Brooklyn, were weak and not well organized. For his mayoral candidate, Croker secured the nomination of Robert A. Van Wyck, a descendent of an old Dutch family. A venerable Knickerbocker name was about the only thing Van Wyck had. A little-known chief judge of the city court, lacking both wealth and a political following, Van Wyck was chosen precisely because he would be Croker's puppet—a role he accepted enthusiastically.[39]

Tammany faced a split opposition. The Fusion reformers nominated former Brooklyn mayor and serving president of Columbia University, Seth Low. Henry George ran again on a Labor Party ticket, though his moment had passed. The expected Republican endorsement of Low did not come. Platt, perhaps having made a deal with Croker, ran his own candidate.[40]

Low was hurt by the efforts of the Strong administration to enforce Sunday closing laws in the ethnic neighborhoods. These attempts reinforced the suspicion with which the largely Anglo-Saxon reformers were viewed on the Lower East Side and in the Irish and German neighborhoods to the north and west and across the East River. For its part, Tammany presented itself as the voice of low- and middle-income groups, provider of opportunities for the poor, and the opponent of religious prejudice—including Sunday closing laws. They also began emphasizing their supposed superiority in representing the interests of the city's increasingly diverse population.[41] The result was a huge blowout for the Hall, and the Democratic wards erupted in glee. Downtown Democrats danced in front of the Wigwam on Union Square, waving upraised brooms—traditional symbol of a sweep—and taunting their defeated adversaries with the chant, "Well, well, well, reform has gone to hell."

Shortly after, Sullivan organized an elaborate victory parade from the Bowery to the Murray Hill Hotel where Croker had taken up residence. The Big Feller rode at the head of the procession on a charger, the other district leaders following on their own mounts. A collection of downtown political and social organizations tailed after them, hoisting the broom of victory and shouting contempt for reformers, Republicans, and Fusionists. Tim's own club, the Timothy D. Sullivan Association, led the way, followed by the Elmwood Athletic Club, the Palm Pleasure Association, the Chop Suey Club, and the Bowling Green Wheelmen. After them came two floats. The first bore the largest tiger obtainable surrounded by Bowery braves "in appropriate war paint."[42] Two children dressed as Uncle Sam and Columbia rolled by on the second float. However, for unstated reasons, probably because he did not want to acknowledge a manifestation of Sullivan's political power, Croker declined to address the jubilant revelers, an act that further poisoned his relations with the Big Feller.

Throughout the December following the elections, Croker and Van Wyck vacationed together at the Lakewood Hotel in New Jersey where their agenda was less recreation than spoils—forty thousand municipal jobs, innumerable contracts, and key governmental positions. Indeed, the expansion of the city's boundaries had resulted in a parallel increase in the number of positions the Democratic machine controlled or influenced. By the time the celebrations heralding the birth of the city of Greater New York were held on New Year's Day, the work was complete, the patronage and power apportioned. Tammany was back.

The roller coaster of mayoral politics, the excoriations of Parkhurst, and the charges of the Lexow Committee had little effect on the Big Feller's political or financial position. Indeed, despite the drumbeat of criticism, both continued to expand throughout the 1890s. In the middle of the decade, Big Tim formed a syndicate with Frank Farrell and Police Commissioner (and later owner of the New York Highlanders, renamed the Yankees) "Big Bill" Deverey that provided protection—for a price—to gamblers and gambling houses. Between them the trio represented the police, state senate, and state gambling commission. Control of the police was crucial. According to the *New York Tribune,* "Sullivan and the gambling combine use Deverey and the police as a collection agency to secure revenue from the gambling houses and other illegal resorts."[43]

After conducting its own investigation, the *New York Times* published a list of the triumvirate's supposed assets. According to the paper, 400 poolrooms, which were banned by law, paid $300 per month apiece for protection, or $1,440,000 annually, to Sullivan-Deverey-Farrell. Five hundred crap games contributed $150 to $175 a game, averaging about $75,000 a month. Two hundred small gambling houses kicked back $150 a month or $30,000 per month. Twenty upscale sporting establishments forked over $1,000 a month or $240,000 a year. Fifty envelop games provided $50 per month or $2,500 monthly for all, and policy operators were down for $125,000 a year. Altogether, the *Times* reckoned that the syndicate divvied up $3,075,000 between them.[44] Moreover, the Sullivan-Deverey-Farrell combine controlled boxing in and around the city—Brooklyn excepted. Only a handful of venues were licensed for the sport and the partners owned them all, a monopoly that netted them another $50,000 annually.[45] Tom O'Rourke, one of Big Tim's lieutenants, explained the situation to a group of boxers. "If you don't fight in our clubs, you don't fight anywhere else in the state."[46]

Another source of Tim's income flowed from the state senate in Albany. The Big Feller was widely considered a member of the Empire State's "Black Horse Cavalry"—a bipartisan group of legislators who collected annual fees to block certain bills. Pawnbrokers, for instance, who did not wish the interest rates lowered made regular payments to the group.[47] Each year, the "Cavalry" killed fifty to seventy-five "strike bills" that benefited parties whose identities were cloaked, but whose money spoke. The process was so well organized that a single law firm, acting for those who contracted the mounted troop's services, paid off all the cavalrymen after each legislative session. In cash, of course.[48]

Undisputed "King of the Bowery," Tim was almost "King of the City," certainly the king of its illicit amusements. He likely viewed his arrangements and exactations as a fair return for providing the populace with the kind of entertainment it wanted, but was denied by a hypocritical old-stock establishment. Others, unconvinced of the harmless nature of the diversions he provided, repeatedly tried to label him with the sobriquet "King of the Underworld." In a way, Tim and his supporters, as well as his critics, were all right. The Big Feller's interests ranged across the city into every borough, and in a surprising variety of enterprises. Excoriated by many, even more lauded him as the personification of the city's brash exuberance and the embodiment of poor-boy immigrant success—the American Dream come true. From the mid-1890s until his death, Sullivan's hold on the public imagination was greater than any other politicians in New York, and the devotion he inspired among his constituents and followers became the envy of his fellows and the despair of his enemies.

4

Taking His Opportunities as He Saw Them

The newspapers and a lot of people are always insinuating
things about me. . . . They oughtn't to go around always insinuating, insinuating, and insinuating without proving nothing
at all.

—Big Tim Sullivan

By the time the municipal elections rolled around in 1901,
Big Tim, Dick Croker, and Tammany Hall as an organization
were all on the defensive. When reform "went to hell" in 1898, the
Tiger once again closed its paws over municipal power, distributing city contracts, jobs, and funds to those who fed and stroked it,
while casting a benign eye on the vice—petty and grand—that
spread across New York's neighborhoods.

The overt, almost casual, presence of graft—"honest" and
otherwise—soon provoked a backlash. In 1899, another state
commission, this time led by assemblyman Robert Mazet, convened to hear evidence of corruption in New York City. The most
damaging testimony exposed the existence of an "ice trust." The
American Ice Company, owned by Charles W. Morse, had been
granted a virtual monopoly over the sales of the commodity,
which was a necessity in the pre-refrigeration era. Croker, Van
Wyck, and Docks commissioner Charles F. Murphy were substantial beneficiaries of the company, thanks to the large number
of shares they received from Morse despite having shown no evidence of paying for them.[1] The monopoly's practices were especially hard on the poor who needed the ice to keep their children's
milk from going bad. Morse had discontinued the earlier practice
of selling chunks of ice for a nickel, and demanded that buyers
pay sixty cents for one-hundred-pound ice blocks.

Besides exposing the Tammany connection with the "ice trust,"
the Mazet Commission charged that Sullivan headed a city "vice
commission." The Big Feller loudly retorted that the committee

59

had never subpoenaed him nor asked him to appear before its hearings even though he was in Albany while it was in session.[2] Croker, however, was called to testify and, as usual, was remarkably candid and unapologetic about Tammany's interests. If newspaper readers were shocked by his bravado, his admission that "I am working for my pockets all the time" wasn't much of a revelation for those who had been paying attention.[3]

By the fall of 1901, the anti-Tammany forces, smelling victory, had reconstituted a Fusion movement. The core of the revitalized reformers was the Citizens' Union, first organized in 1896, and led by the president of the Charity Organization Society, Robert Fulton Cutting. The "Cits," as Tammany men dubbed them disparagingly, drew support from old-stock, German, and Jewish charity trustees as well as the usual wealthy members of the Protestant moral reform clubs.[4] The likelihood of a reform victory increased dramatically when Republican boss Thomas Platt endorsed Seth Low, president of Columbia University, who already had the Citizen's Union backing, creating a genuine reform Fusion movement. The Fusionists' prospects were heightened by dissension in Tammany. Croker's visits away from New York to his English estate rankled many, while the failure of his chosen candidate to defeat Theodore Roosevelt for governor, and his unpopular support for William Jennings Bryan in 1900, left him vulnerable to attack. If it was true that the Big Feller had backed down when Croker returned form England in 1897, he now showed no hesitation in opposing Croker's policies while pursuing his own interests—not necessarily for the better—within the Democratic organization.

Although the Fusionists denounced Tammany control of the police, the "ice trust," and various forms of "honest" graft, they concentrated their fire on Tammany's protection of vice. Protestant Episcopal bishop Henry Codman Potter condemned Tammany for permitting—if not abetting—the open operation of brothels and other forms of prostitution. Supported by Protestant and Jewish reformers, the bishop was the primary mover in the creation of the Committee of Fifteen, the latest in a line of such bodies organized by the wealthy and prominent to tackle political and social corruption. Among its members was William Travers Jerome, a former investigator of the Lexow Committee, judge of the court of special sessions, and Fusion nominee for district attorney, who became personally involved in exposing

Tammany's criminal connections. Jerome, a maverick with a Democratic background, encouraged the Committee of Fifteen to hire their own detectives to amass information about gambling dens and brothels. Their findings were passed along to Jerome, who soon discovered the police would not raid the places or did so only after sending warning to the intended targets. With a nose for publicity, Jerome began leading the raiding parties himself. Armed with an ax and John Doe warrants, the judge, accompanied by a few bailiffs and volunteers from the Committee of Fifteen, smashed his way into the betting clubs upon which he would declare court in session and proceed to dispense justice.[5] Jerome's nocturnal forays made good copy, and reporters and photographers were soon accompanying his posse on the missions. The resulting newspaper stories further exposed the extent of "police graft" and jacked up the pressure on Tammany.

In April, Jerome's Committee of Fifteen raiders crashed a number of poolrooms that were protected by Sullivan's organization. Police officials, Tammany allies, denounced the raids as politics, maintaining there was no evidence that the raided establishments were actually poolrooms.[6] Some newspapers carried accounts claiming that no poolrooms connected with Big Tim's gambling syndicate—excepting two examples too notorious to shield—were among those busted. Supposedly, Sullivan, Farrell, James Mahony, and Bob Davis raised a $60,000 war chest that went to someone who could "nullify" Jerome.[7]

Even if the Big Feller had some success in blunting Jerome's campaign, the heat was on. On April 18, a banquet was held in Tim's honor at the Hoffman House. Though the exact reason for the celebration was unannounced, it was no doubt connected with the upcoming election. Forty-eight Tammany luminaries, city officials, judges, and business partners assembled for a multicourse dinner. The highlight of the evening was the presentation of a six-foot-high silver and onyx loving cup to the Bowery's master.[8] Each of the diners was given a small bust of Tim, in matching silver and onyx, as a memento of the occasion. Though reporters were kept away from the proceedings, some of the participants were heard to make disparaging remarks about the Committee of Fifteen and their activities, an indication that not all of Tim's investments were being spared.[9] Significantly, Croker was not invited to the gathering. The meeting was a Sullivan organization affair, and the presence of powerful and well-connected attendees testified to the independence of the "machine within a machine."

Jerome continued to lace into Croker and Sullivan at every opportunity, declaring that his candidacy was "a movement against vice and the protection of crime."[10] Responding onstage at a rally at Miner's Bowery Theater, Big Tim damned Jerome as "a liar, a four carat lawyer, and"—worst of all—"a collegiate."[11] At another appearance, Sullivan condemned Jerome for indulging in two vices he himself eschewed. "Jerome lives on high balls and cigarettes," he pronounced contemptuously.[12] Jerome, who was no prig, turned the comment to his own advantage, repeating his opposition to Sunday drinking laws. The statutes were unpopular in Tammany strongholds, and his stance attracted votes from those dismayed by Tammany corruption, but fearful that a reform admonition would curtail their social activities.

Concerned over widespread prostitution, many members of the clergy also stepped up to the plate to take a swing at the Demo-

7. *Harper's Magazine*'s take on the 1901 election. The bedraggled Democratic mayoral candidate Edward Shepard enters Tammany Hall riding the Tammany tiger which is led by Police Commissioner William Deverey. The "burning blot" is the term Shepard had used to describe Tammany Hall in 1897. A dissipated Richard Croker presides, while Big Tim Sullivan, dagger in hand, warily observes the spectacle.

crats. Bishop Potter issued an open letter condemning the police and politicians for promoting gambling and prostitution. Croker, seeing the array of forces massing against him, tried to deflect the criticisms by creating his own investigating unit, the Committee of Five, under the reputable Lewis Nixon. Croker supposedly urged the district leaders to drop the "dirty" graft, but some, led by Sullivan, balked. Indeed, even as Tammany seemed headed for a defeat, Big Tim continued to expand his own alliances, creating what the newspapers called an anti-Croker "combine."[13] He also showed little inclination to reduce his high-profile connection with gambling, poolrooms, and policy shops. After the state legislature effectively removed Sullivan's ally, William Deverey, from power by abolishing the office of chief of police, Tim found his gambling dens raided. Convinced that Nixon was cooperating with Jerome, he wired Croker, who was again visiting his English estate, "Wantage," and told him that unless Deverey was reappointed, the gamblers in the Deverey-Sullivan-Farrell network—supposedly ten thousand in all—would no longer contribute to Tammany's coffers.[14] Croker was fully aware that the crass and blustering Deverey was an albatross around the Tiger's neck, but he also knew he lacked the power to stand up to Dry Dollar. He sent word to Van Wyck to restore Deverey to power over the police by giving him a new title.[15] Things returned to the status quo ante and, as the *New York Tribune* put it, "Sullivan's word is law at Police Headquarters and even Croker can not controvert it."[16]

Nixon intended to present the Committee of Five report to Tammany's Executive Committee in the expectation that it would be approved and released. The three-page typed report boasted of Tammany's efforts to shut down gambling and vice interests. It was also reputed to contain information of potential interest to the district attorney.[17] But before the Executive Committee could convene, Big Tim made a surprise visit to the Wigwam, an event that attracted notice, as he was known to skip meetings devoted to routine business. Sullivan spent his time conferring with the district leaders, the police commissioner, and the other movers and shakers in the Tammany universe. Shortly after Tim touched base with the sachems, word spread that the Committee of Five report would not be presented that night.[18] Tim's intervention seems to have been decisive in the decision to supress the report. Whether it actually contained damaging information or Tim simply quashed it to prevent un-

8. William Travers Jerome, Sullivan nemesis who reluctantly conceded the Big Feller had redeeming qualities. *Munsey Magazine,* **1901.**

necessary complications is uncertain. In any event, it was never released.

Sullivan's deliberate pursuit of his own interests in the face of imminent defeat for his party seems self-defeating at first. A Fusion victory would deprive Tammany of both the mayor's and district attorney's office. The organization's control of the police, a prime requirement for the protection of Tim's illicit operations, would be jeopardized. Electoral defeat would also cut Tammany off from the patronage it used to reward supporters and foster loyalty. The Big Feller's actions might have been motivated by a deepening dislike of Croker, and it had become common knowledge that he addressed the supposed boss in a way that "no other Tammany leader dares and he has flatly refused to obey Croker."[19] His attitude may also have stemmed from confidence—his belief that whatever happened to Tammany elsewhere in the city, the "King of the Bowery" was impregnable in his Lower East Side bastion. Having successfully survived, even prospered, during one reform administration, Sullivan was probably convinced that his organization could tough it out, and his gambling interests would survive even if they were forced to keep a lower profile.

The most explosive vice issue was not gambling, but prostitution. The reformers lacerated Tammany, especially Sullivan, for providing protection for, or participating in, the sex trade. William Travers Jerome, who was proving an energetic and effective campaigner, began appearing at rallies waving a leather belt studded with brass checks that Lower East Side madams gave their customers to prove they had paid. "If these conditions existed in other communities," he shouted, "there would be a Vigilance Committee organized and somebody would get lynched."[20]

Without doubt, brothels flourished in New York throughout the nineteenth century, with the greatest number concentrated in the Bowery and Tenderloin, the latter of which stretched roughly from Twenty-third to Fifty-ninth Streets west of Sixth Avenue. Part of the costs of running such operations were payoffs to police and the politicians who generally controlled them. Additionally, whores plied their trade in gambling rooms, saloons, and theaters, left unmolested by the law if they had purchased their "license." In the words of historian Timothy J. Guilfoyle, "although prostitution was never legal, New York's police and political machine developed an elaborate system of maintenance and control over the most prominent institutions of prostitution. In effect, public sexuality was shaped and protected by a system of de facto regulation during New York's Century of Prostitution" (ca. 1820–1920).[21]

Among the more sordid aspects of the business was the coercion or enticement of many poor girls and women into the trade by pimps and whoremasters, a practice that produced dismay and outrage in many of the immigrant and working-class neighborhoods. It was largely due to the prostitution issue that Fred Stein began publishing a Yiddish-language weekly supporting the Fusion ticket, which evolved into the *Jewish World*. Such backing helped Jerome triumph in seven of ten heavily Jewish districts, which were usually solid for Tammany.[22]

Big Tim's actual connection with prostitution is unclear. At least in the abstract, he held a somewhat idealized view of women, which is traceable to his devotion to the memory of his mother. "No one who knows me," he protested, "will believe that I would take a penny from any woman, much less the poor creatures who are to be pitied more than any other human beings on earth. I'd be afraid to take a cent from a poor woman of the streets for fear my old mother would see it. I'd rather break into a bank and rob a safe. That would be a more manly and decent way of getting money."[23] Unfortunately, Sullivan had also publicly stated "I never got any money from any thief, gambler, or dive-keeper. That's so, so help me God," a statement that was patently false in regards to the latter two professions.[24] The fact that Dry Dollar raked in enormous amounts from his gambling interests—deny them though he might on occasion—plus his entertainment profits, suggests he didn't need any tainted money from whores, pimps, and madams. That does not mean he did not receive any.[25]

Whatever Tim's exact connection with prostitution, and it was a charge that always provoked a heated rebuttal from him, he had to have been well acquainted with the sex trade, which was rife in the city. Though there is no direct evidence that Big Tim was personally invested in prostitution, some of his captains and allies certainly were, and some of that money would have flowed back into his coffers.[26] Moreover, Sullivan was vice president of the Max Hochstim Association, putatively a Jewish fraternal and businessmen's club that provided its members with services such as death benefits and burial plots. It was, however, the parent—or front—of the Independent Benevolent Association (IBA), an alliance of real estate agents, concert saloon owners, and brothel managers that dominated prostitution on the Lower East Side.[27] Martin Engel, downtown district leader and Sullivan ally, was second in importance only to Hochstim in the IBA. Controlling much of the prostitution along Allen Street, he took his responsibilities to his employees and their clients seriously, arranging regular medical inspections for his women and girls to prevent or treat venereal diseases.[28] Minimally, Sullivan's close relationship with Engel belied his public utterances that he knew nothing about the downtown sex trade and those who ran it. Unsurprisingly, Hochstim's operations were believed to operate under the Big Feller's protection. Yet, it may have been the case, as the *New York Times* later conceded, that Tim "could be distinguished from his intimates, and yet be their leader."[29] Nevertheless, it seems incontrovertible that commercial sex on the Lower East Side benefited from the Big Feller's passive consent if nothing else.

The Big Feller's supposed connection with prostitution arose during the Democratic primaries of 1901. Paddy Divver, Tammany leader in the Second District, faced a challenge from "Big Tom" Foley, later Al Smith's mentor, who was backed by Sullivan. Divver, whose district was virtually engulfed by Tim's territory, made much of his refusal to allow what he termed Sullivan's "red light cadets"—procurers—to operate in the Second.[30] Though Croker initially saw Divver's candidacy as a favorable opportunity to polish the Hall's tarnished image, Big Tim threatened to bolt the party if Divver received help from the titular boss. Croker publicly backed off, though he supported Divver as much as he could behind the scenes. On primary day, Paul Kelly's crew moved in to the polling places and blackjacked Divver's supporters while the police looked on.[31] Newspapers summed up the contest stating that "Sullivan and Foley literally drove Divver out of the district."[32]

Divver blamed his defeat on Croker's shrinking authority. Tim concurred and publicly expressed his contempt for the beleagered Tammany leader. In September, just before the Democrats' municipal convention, a *New York Tribune* reporter asked for Sullivan's thoughts on the upcoming contest. "Tammany Hall will win in a walk, no matter who heads the ticket," Tim predicted, knowing it wasn't true. "[A]nd I want to say," he continued with what the newsman described as a sly smile, "that Croker don't boss us; he only advises. Croker could stay in Europe and the district leaders would fix up the state. Croker ain't the whole thing as I remarked before."[33]

Although Sullivan and Tammany were not helped by Divver's raising the prostitution issue, Big Tim's support of Foley had little to do with sex trafficking. Nor was the use of muscle itself unusual, in intraparty squabbles. Political alliances and power were the key issues, and Sullivan promoted Foley's candidacy as another opportunity to extend the reach of his "machine within a machine." Croker's support of Divver, in contrast, was taken as meddling in Big Tim's sphere of influence. Whatever the Big Feller's political calculations, the dispute reinforced the connection between Sullivan and illicit sex in the mind of the public.

The negative publicity, the impending Fusion triumph, and possibly his growing interest in trying national government, led the Big Feller to hand over his role as district leader to his most trusted lieutenant, Little Tim. His ally, Martin Engel, whose involvement with organized prostitution was manifest, also gave up his seat. Little Tim and Florrie led public assaults on brothels, smashing up the premises, and beating the pimps. It was to no avail. The outcry over vice and corruption swept the Fusion candidate, Seth Low, into the mayor's chair, though the Sullivans held much of the Lower East Side for the Tiger. With the Big Feller stepping aside, Little Tim, who had left Albany to take over as majority leader of the New York City Board of Aldermen, officially ran the Sullivan organization downtown. Of course, everyone knew Big Tim was engaged behind the scenes and working with the Little Feller to keep the clan machinery running smoothly. Whatever Little Tim's considerable talents as a political tactician, it was Big Tim who held the love and loyalty of the Bowery.

After the returns came in on election night 1901, Sullivan summoned the rank and file to the association's clubhouse at 207 Bowery. "Boys it looks like a hard winter ahead and light picking for you for a couple of years," he told the assembled members. "My distinguished friend, the Human Turnip [Low] is going to be mayor of New York."[34] Facetiously, the Big Feller advised his followers to join the Republicans in order to get city jobs and even offered to pay their dues for them if they needed it. But Tim knew that the city's flirtation with reform was always short-lived. "Be Republican and do the best you can till the next election; then come around to me and we'll throw the hooks into them fellers downtown."[35]

Big Tim also called on Croker the night of the election. "Well, boss," he announced striding into the Executive Committee Room at the Wigwam, "you see *my* district came through OK."[36] Croker could not have missed the implications of the statement and the emphasis on the possessive pronoun. For some time, Sullivan had been bragging that it was easy for him to get votes for himself and his team, but hard to secure them for Croker.[37] Now Tim and his "Wise Men" had survived the Fusion wave while Croker's ticket had lost. Content that his fiefdom had weathered the worst the Goo-Goos could bring against him, Sullivan was probably not unhappy that the Democratic failure citywide spelled the end of Croker's rule as Tammany leader.

Despite Tim's public indifference, if not disdain, for Croker, the *New York World* ran a story claiming that Tim offered his "allegiance" to Croker on election night. According to the *World,* after it was clear Tammany had lost city hall, Croker, Sullivan, John F. Carroll, and Maurice Untermeyer left the Wigwam for a dinner at Ennis Restaurant. As the meal began, Tim supposedly pledged his continued support of Croker as Tammany's leader.[38] The story is feasible since the Big Feller never coveted the job himself and had just proved that he could survive nicely even as the Hall itself went down. Never a mean man, Sullivan was likely making a gesture of sympathy and consolation to a beaten man whom Tim knew could not continue. He was not surprised when Croker replied that he had made his last political fight. The abdicating boss then asked Tim whom he wanted as the Hall's leader, and Sullivan replied that Carroll "would be pleasing to him." Croker assented, and all agreed that the transfer of power would be made official at a meeting of Tammany's executive committee the following week.

Business concluded, the Tammany leaders began to leave the restaurant. As they filed out, they were recognized by a man who made an unflattering remark to Croker. Though the dig was directed at the departing boss, it was Tim who responded to the heckler. According to the *New York World,* "Senator Sullivan punched him in the face knocking him down. Several patrolmen were present but Senator Sullivan's assault passed unnoticed."[39] The politicos then walked out into the night without further interference. One thing did change between the conference at Ennis and the meeting of the Tammany Executive Committee. For some reason Carroll did not become Croker's successor. The calculations that led to the change are unknown.

The 1901 debacle finished Croker, who soon left New York for England and Ireland where he devoted himself to horses and pseudobaronial living. The boss's chair at Tammany was Tim's for the asking—or more accurately, taking—but he let it pass. Sullivan never sought control of Tammany for himself. Rather, he preferred to operate independently, strengthening his system of alliances and influence so that whoever sat in the boss's chair did so at his sufferance. At the same time he avoided the burden of responsibility for the entire organization. From his perspective it was the best of all possible worlds. The Big Feller watched, probably amused, as Croker's successor, Lewis Nixon not John F. Carroll, tried to run the democracy. According to some researchers, Croker left Nixon in charge to prevent Tim from taking over.[40] It is hard to see how Nixon could have withstood any serious challenge from the Sullivan clan or their allies. Nixon was installed as titular boss precisely because he had no support among the district leaders. Croker apparently intended him to serve as a figurehead, keeping his seat warm until the smoke from the election had cleared and he could return from England as he had done in 1897. If that was his plan, the old boss was doomed to disappointment. Nixon, one of Tammany's more reputable figures, stepped down in May 1902, declaring, "I could not retain the leadership of Tammany Hall and at the same time retain my self respect."[41]

Nixon was replaced by a triumvirate, which in turn did not last. In September, Charles Francis Murphy, an ambitious district leader who grew up in the Gas House District adjoining the Bowery, pushed his fellows out and assumed sole leadership of Tammany Hall. It was all right with Tim. If it weren't, Murphy would never have gotten the job. As the *New York Tribune* observed, "More than any other [Sullivan] put Murphy in the leader's chair."[42] As long as the Big Feller lived, Murphy, for all his considerable talents, was dependent on the Bowery leader's support.

Murphy was another product of the Irish diaspora that reached New York. His father was either a John M. or Dennis Murphy, a tenant farmer from County Kildare who emigrated to America in the Famine year of 1848. The future Tammany leader's mother was Mary Prendergast or Pendergass. Charles Francis Murphy was born June 20, 1858, the second of the couple's nine children. Like Sullivan and most Irish immigrant children, Murphy's for-

mal education ended early, in his case at age fourteen. Young
Charles held a succession of manual laboring jobs, a worker in a
wire factor, caulker in a shipyard, and driver on the horse-drawn
"Blue Line" in 1878.[43] Murphy joined the Gas House Gang, but
seemed more interested in their athletic than criminal potential.
He organized two baseball teams, the "Senators" and the "Syl-
vans," and played catcher himself. When the teams toured New
York State in 1877, Murphy's play was good enough that he received offers from professional clubs, but he saw his future in a
different field.

In 1880, Murphy opened a saloon—the first of four—at Nineteenth Street and Second Avenue. The top floor was reserved for
the Sylvan Social Club, an organization for boys from fifteen to
twenty. While not exclusively abstemious, Murphy himself drank
little, a small glass of beer on social occasions.[44] Unlike Sullivan,
he was puritanical—or since he was Irish, Jansenistic—and permitted neither women nor profanity in his drinking establishments. Despite the latter prohibition, his fourth saloon, at Twentieth Street and Second Avenue, became the headquarters of the
Anawanda Club, the local Democratic organization.

At about this time Murphy passed the mandatory test of physical courage or ability requisite for a successful career as a Tammany politician. Breaking tradition from Kelly, Croker, and Sullivan, whose early reputations included proven ability with their
fists, Murphy made his name as an athlete. While he was still
just an electoral district leader, Barney Biglin, Republican boss of
the Twentieth District, immediately north of Murphy's bailiwick,
challenged the Democrats to a rowing race on the East River
from 100th to 129th Street. Murphy's Sylvan Club took up the
challenge. On the day of the race, however, the Sylvan's stroke
fell ill. Murphy took the place of the stricken rower and led the
team to victory.[45] The triumph over the Republicans marked
Murphy as a rising star, and he was borne from the boat on the
shoulders of a group of young men from the neighborhood.

Like Sullivan, Murphy's first foray into politics was against
Tammany. In 1883, Honest John Kelly blocked Edward Hagan's
bid to secure renomination as assemblyman from the Eighteenth
District. Hagan turned to the ambitious saloonkeeper for advice.
After pondering the question, Murphy told Hagan to run as an
independent. Hagan did so and won, defeating the Hall's candidate.[46] Again like Sullivan, Murphy understood that maverick

Democrats lacked the organizational and financial resources to continue successfully, and he never bucked the Democracy again. Instead, he set out to run it. Hagan, who also returned to the fold, became district leader in 1887, and appointed Charlie Murphy as his lieutenant.

Five years later, as he lay dying, Hagan reportedly told his confidants to "see that nobody gets the district but Charlie."[47] But when Hagan finally expired, rumors surfaced that one of the dead leader's relatives had ambitions in the district. Murphy realized that only Croker could guarantee his appointment, and he quickly sought a meeting with the boss. Croker was initially put off by Murphy's persistence. "Why didn't he wait until the man is cold?" he snorted irritably.[48] But he soon realized the potential of the hungry young athlete-saloonkeeper and handed over leadership of the district to the "young fellow who beat the starting gun."[49]

Murphy could get the vote out as well as Sullivan, and the Eighteenth District often piled up the largest majorities for Tammany, a somewhat easier task in a less heterogeneous area. Unlike the Bowery leaders, he never built up a personal organization. His fealty was pledged to Tammany and whoever was its leader. After he took over Hagan's district, Murphy made himself accessible to all his captains, subordinates, and those who had a problem or request. He preferred to conduct district business every night beneath the old gas lamps that stood in front of the Anawanda Club. As an organization stalwart, Murphy stood by Croker as the boss began to lose his grip in the election of 1901.

Prim, proper, with a hard, calculating mind masked behind the face and demeanor of a seminary student, Murphy was as opposed to the Tammany connection with "police graft" as he was determined to pursue "honest graft." His leadership in the Eighteenth was noted for "his determined effort to keep his district morally clean."[50] Whatever the charges hurled by the Goo-Goos, none would accuse Murphy of involvement with prostitution.

Murphy's tight-lipped style was early in evidence and sprang from his character. He created his own version of the "Wise Men," close advisors he consulted when making difficult decisions or pondering policy. When VanWyck became mayor in 1898, he appointed Murphy to the Dock Commission. The appointment was the only city post he ever held, and he carried the title "Commissioner" for the rest of his life. While serving on the commission, he made the acquaintance of J. Sergeant Cram, a Harvard graduate who introduced Murphy to genteel society and gave him some social and cultural polish. As George B. McClellan Jr. waggishly put it, Cram "taught Murphy to eat peas with a fork."[51] Cram became Murphy's closest confidant, and many believed that Cram provided the brains and Murphy the nerve in their odd-couple partnership. Together they turned the Dock Commission into a moneymaking business corporation. Murphy, who was worth perhaps $400,000 when he took the job, left office a millionaire.[52]

Murphy's remarkable rise in income as dock commissioner—and afterward—was probably related to his stake in the New York Contracting and Trucking Company, which he founded in 1901 with his brother, John L., Alderman James E. Gaffney, and political leader Richard J. Couch. Murphy later denied that he kept any interest in the company, and no evidence exists that he did. Nevertheless, a silent partnership provides the most likely explanation for his growing fortune. The company leased two piers from the city for $4,800 a year and then released them at a steep markup. Within two years, New York Contracting and Trucking secured city-related contracts amounting to $15,000,000.[53] Additional business came from firms that received grants from the city. Altogether, the years of Charlie Murphy's leadership in the Hall were good ones for New York Contracting and Trucking.

Taciturn by nature, Murphy believed it was wise politics for a Tammany boss to keep a low profile and avoid becoming a target for reformers, such as Croker had been. On assuming leadership, Murphy stated, "I won't do much talking. The vote speaks for itself. I will be at Tammany Hall every day, and spend the hours between three and five o'clock in the afternoon at work. There is plenty of work to be done and the less talking the better."[54] The immediate task was polishing the Democracy's tarnished name.

Shortly after taking the boss's chair, Murphy and the Sullivans initiated a public campaign to groom the Tiger's pelt by attacking the most notorious whorehouses. With Big Tim's approval, Murphy sent Florrie Sullivan to oust Martin Engel, whose brother was heavily involved with the largely Jewish red-light district on Allen Street, from the Eighth Assembly District clubhouse. Joined by other members of the Sullivan organization, Florrie began throwing pimps out of the brothels that had been protected by Engel.[55] Though the Big Feller did not publicly participate in the neighborhood cleansing, the campaign clearly had his blessing. The closing of the whorehouses removed the most egregious display of commercialized vice, but it sent their workers into the streets, dance halls, and gambling houses, which might not have been much of an improvement, especially for the women.

Murphy also took steps to expel some of the more odious characters from the Democracy. The most conspicuous of these was Big Bill Deverey, ex–police commissioner, notorious dirty grafter, and former ally of Big Tim. Ostracizing Deverey would publicly demonstrate Tammany's commitment to purging vice, at least the most offensive kind, from its repertoire. Indeed, both Tammany and the reformers began to use the term "Devereyism" as shorthand for "dirty graft"—especially "white slavery." Although Sullivan had also been charged with conniving with prostitution and other forms of corruption, his repeated and vociferous denials led many—especially Democrats—to believe him. At any rate, even if Murphy was uneasy about Big Tim's connections, there was little he could do about it. Deverey, however, was a different story. The new boss may have also been gaining a little payback in his campaign against the former police commissioners. When Murphy forced out his two partners and assumed sole control of the Hall, Deverey publicly predicted disaster for the Democrats. "If three lobsters can't run the organization," he asked "how can one do it—and the one with the least brains?"[56] Deverey soon discovered who had the brains and who had only mouth and attitude. In 1902, he became leader of the Ninth Assembly District in a blatantly corrupt election—reportedly he simply handed out money on street corners. Murphy, after checking with Tammany lawyer, Max Steuer, altered the traditional rules of membership on the Executive Committee and blocked Deverey's attempt to take his seat.[57]

Murphy struck again at the Democratic nominating convention in October when the party faithful selected nominees for federal and state elections the following month. First, he prevented Deverey from being seated at the convention and followed that by blocking Deverey's candidate for the Eighth Judicial District. Though Deverey maintained "I am a Democrat—a Tammany Hall Democrat—and I have always been one," he was clearly humiliated by the Tammany boss he had belittled as the "sport" of the previous triumvirate.[58]

The ex–police commissioner did not take defeat gracefully. Although Deverey was a former ally of the Sullivans, Big Tim and the "Wise Men" stood with Murphy. Frozen out of the organization, Deverey bucked Tammany in the 1903 municipal elections and ran as an independent against Murphy's mayoral candidate, George B. McClellan Jr. Greatly overestimating both his popularity and political skills, Deverey proclaimed "the downtrod will arise in their might and make the Murphys and Big and Little Sullivans look like calico dogs stuffed with saloon sweep-ins."[59] Neither the Sullivans nor Murphy were impressed and were content to let Deverey rage in isolation.

Deverey was only part of the political calculus of 1902. Tammany also had to select its candidates for the state supreme court. Newspapers reported that the nominations were virtually for sale as they had been in Croker's day. Supposedly, no nominations were considered for those who failed to contribute $30,000 to Tammany's campaign fund.[60] Though the amount may have been exaggerated, cash was probably exchanged for a judicial line.[61] On October 8, Big Tim spent most of his day at the Wigwam, going over judicial selections with Murphy and pressing for the nomination of Edward E. McCall, a political ally. Murphy accepted McCall, though he refused to countenance anyone who had been nominated during Croker's reign, a policy with which the Big Feller had no quarrel. Once determined, the Sullivan-Murphy judicial slate sailed through the nominating convention.[62]

The most important nominations were for Congress. Exactly when Big Tim decided to take a fling in Washington is uncertain. He may have been toying with it before Tammany's defeat in the 1901 elections, having grown somewhat tired of Albany. Certainly after the Republicans took power in the city and Albany, Washington may have seemed a good place for some rest and recreation before returning to the fray. "The graft is played out," he reportedly, if hyperbolically, concluded.[63] According to Alvin Harlow, a friend of Tim's suggested a stint in Congress during a conversation downtown. "Me in Congress," the Big Feller exclaimed incredulously. "To the itzy house with youse! Do you want me to put on the bum, like Tim Campbell and Sulzer? Nit!" When Tim's friend persisted with the proposal, Tim inquired,

"What's the graft over there?" The response was satisfactory, and Dry Dollar began mulling it over, voicing some concern about distance from New York. When informed Washington was only five hours by train, he was pleasantly surprised. "Only five hours? That ain't such a long time. Them guys that flag the Washington graft get famous and get to be the main squeeze at the White House when their gang is in, don't they? They're the whole cheese in national conventions. That ain't such a bad lay. I'll think it over. If it ain't a piker's game, I might take a stack and sit in."[64] To a reporter who asked if it was true he planned to run for the House of Representatives, Tim replied, "Who knows? It might be a grand game with the limit off. They pulled the blinders so tight at Albany that it got to be heavy goin' and I pulled out. Maybe on a bigger track in faster company it would be worth entering. I may take a hand."[65] The lengthy, slangy direct quotes may have been complete or partial fabrications—newspapermen were happy to invent good copy if reliably sourced news was unavailable—but they probably convey the germ of Tim's interest in Congress.

Tim's wish was Tammany's command. On October 3, the Democrats chose Sullivan, William Randolph Hearst, and George B. McClellan Jr. as their candidates for the Eighth, Eleventh, and Twelfth congressional districts, respectively. Little Tim placed his cousin's name before the convention and was quickly seconded by Battery Dan Finn. The election was a foregone conclusion, a fact that did not go down well with those who saw him as a malign exemplar of Tammany power. "Tammany has sunk to a lower and dirtier depth than it ever reached before," the *New York Times* wailed.

> The nomination of Timothy D. Sullivan in the Eight District is so disgraceful and revolting that a petition to wipe the district off the map and leave it unrepresented would receive thousands of signatures in the city. If Sullivan is not the most disreputable predatory politician in Tammany he is at least not more than one or two places distant. . . . All his life he has been the type and embodiment of everything that is corrupt and vile in the organization. The Tammany policy of levying blackmail upon gamblers and the proprietors of evil resorts in payment for police protection finds in Sullivan its best known representative. Anywhere outside a Tammany barroom it would be supposed that Sullivan could be elected to Congress only in a district inhabited by the very scum of the earth. What is the dis-

trict? . . . That part of it that lies upon Manhattan Island [it also included Staten Island] . . . includes the financial center of the United States of America, and it is to be represented in Congress, if its legal voters so determine, by a person who is simply not fit to be at large in a civilized community.[66]

Downtown where Tim grew up, the *Time*'s excoriations were fighting words. He gave his reply a week and half later at Battery Dan's clubhouse on Hudson Street. Tim was never much for oratory. The only lengthy speeches he ever delivered were counterattacks against those who accused him of corruption and his performance at Battery Dan's fit that tradition. He told the crowd that the night's address was the only one he expected to give during the campaign and he would not speak of tariffs or trusts—major national issues—since his listeners were familiar with what their operations had done to the poor of the Lower East Side. "De papers, several of them, within the past week, has paid some very severe attention to your candidate," Tim began, getting into his topic. "I intend to speak to that now, and I am not apologizing, and I ain't afraid of any newspaper."[67] The Big Feller then recited the story of his poverty-stricken upbringing, struggling mother, and entry into the world of work at eight. Tim made a virtue out of his truncated schooling, playing the class card against his enemies. "My opponent will hold me up to ridicule on my mannerisms," he explained, "But they are the mannerisms of the people. And they are the mannerisms of your children and your children's children."[68]

After demonstrating his credentials as an authentic—and proud—downtown New Yorker, Big Tim took on the explosive charges of his alleged protection of vice that had been raised loudly the previous year and that the *Times* had hurled against him in their editorial. Though the grammar was strained in places, the message couldn't be clearer.

Now, I am not a reformer. I am not an agitator or an investigator. I don't know whether any police got blackmail money or not. But I can say now without fear of contradiction—and this will be the last time in the campaign that I shall make any explanation in relation to this infamous business—that I don't know any crime on the calendar that I would not be [less] guilty of than in any way being a collector of blackmail from unfortunate women or any other body that would be forced to give it up.[69]

Tim next dealt with the question some papers had raised regarding the source of his wealth. Newspapers reported he was worth $400,000 (he clearly had much more), but received only $1,500 as a state legislator. The Big Feller declared that the day after the issue was raised he met with five reporters at Tammany Hall and showed them receipts from his investments totaling the income he was believed to have. Probably he could have produced receipts for any number in question. At any rate, Tim complained that the papers would not run his explanation. Having disposed of all the negative charges, the congressman-in-waiting pledged to devote his time in Washington to the service of his constituents. "Your interests are my duties. I was born here and raised among you, and I think I am better, if I do say so myself, to represent you than Daniel Webster, if he was to come back to earth."[70]

After the applause died down several prominent Democrats rose to attack the tariff and the coal mine operators whose dispute with the miner's union had only recently been settled through the intervention of Theodore Roosevelt. Congressman William Sulzer warmly recommended Big Tim, averring that he had always loved him and that Tim never let down anyone who put his trust in him. Commenting on Tim's statement that he was no orator, Sulzer advised his audience, "What you want is a man who can initiate legislation and get it through—get something for the district. If [Tim] can do what I have seen him do in Albany, there will be no constituents in his district who will not be able to get what he wants. And Tim can do it. Tim's a worker."[71]

Though Tim had vowed his Battery Dan performance would be his only speech of the election, he gave a punchy talk at an election eve rally at the London Theater. The hall was "packed from pit to dome" with Sullivan supporters and various party functionaries. When some of the better-heeled men settled in the front rows of the box seats, Tim's plebeian followers shouted for them to "Go way back and sit down, de ladies is what we wanter see, bless 'em. We like the goils and we want to see the fair wives of de conspicuous leaders."[72] Chastened, if not frightened, the men did as they were bidden and wives and girlfriends took the front row, from which they could receive the admiring glances of the hoi polloi.

Little Tim, who presided over the exuberant rally, gaveled the high-spirited, partisan crowd into something approaching silence, and congratulated them on their confidence in his cousin's ensuing victory. Then the speakers took the floor. State senator Henry Grady, whom some believed seldom made a speech entirely sober, extolled Tim's candidacy as the choice of the "plain people."[73] He took a few swipes at the corporate giants of the day, asserting that Carnegie, Rockefeller, and Armour were unexceptional men who "had the favors of the Government which made their wealth possible."[74] After exhorting the throngs not to split their vote, he turned the floor over to Congressman George B. McClellan Jr., son of the famous, if controversial, Civil War general. McClellan declared that the settlement of the recent coal strike, which was widely credited to the president's personal intervention, was, in fact, the result of "the rising anger of 80,000,000 people."[75]

William Sulzer, who had so heartily endorsed Tim at Battery Dan's, succeeded McClellan on the floor. Sulzer launched into a short speech in which he praised the Big Feller and attacked Roosevelt, comparing the president's supposedly timorous treatment of the trusts with his strict enforcement of the law against the poor and working people while he was New York City police commissioner. According to the congressman, the president was "afraid of the trusts and their power. If he were as strenuous as he was when police commissioner, he would not fear them. He has the power and he could crush them as he did the police man and the ice man on Sunday, or the poor fellow who sold a glass of beer on the Sabbath."[76]

When Sulzer finished bloviating, Little Tim returned and introduced his cousin as "Congressman Sullivan." The audience erupted into cheers, which newsmen believed might have gone on all night had not Tim quieted the crowd. He then produced a copy of the *Brooklyn Eagle,* which he claimed he had never seen before. The paper contained an article by Republican Party official Timothy Woodruff, later state Republican Party chairman, which charged that Big Tim and Deverey had arranged for one hundred thousand illegal voters to cast ballots for them on election day. Tim felt no need to remind the crowd that he hadn't been an ally of Deverey's for over a year, but pointedly ridiculed Woodruff as "Lilliputian Tim." He challenged Woodruff by pledging $1,000 to the Republican campaign if the *Eagle*'s writer would give up the name of the informant who supposedly revealed the plan to use repeaters and floaters. Satisfied that he had stiffed "Lilliputian

Tim," Sullivan then repeated his belief that he would be as good a representative as Daniel Webster, who was apparently his ideal as a congressman. "I meant what I said," he assured the crowd. "I don't look through the colored glasses of some overcultured, educated gentlemen, but as my constituents look, and, therefore, I think I will make a better representative than the educated gentlemen with the colored glasses."[77]

"Have you ever heard of any criticism of my votes at Albany, my labor votes?" Tim asked the assembly.

"No," the crowd shouted back.

"I haven't sat a day in the state senate that I did not think how lucky I was that I was not on the front platform nor the rear platform of a motor [street] car. When you get your ballot Tuesday, don't go looking for my name and don't do no quitting. Look for the star [Democratic symbol] and put your x under that star."[78]

The election went off with a bang—literally. A cache of fireworks stored at Madison Square intended to celebrate Hearst's election went off prematurely, killing seven people and injuring several more.[79] The Republicans did well in New York, keeping control of the legislature and taking the governor's chair. Charlie Murphy was satisfied, however. His gubernatorial candidate, former commissioner of public works Bird S. Coler, drew the highest number of votes ever cast for a Democratic candidate for governor, a result that augured well for the municipal elections the following year. Although the Republicans held Congress, all of Manhattan's representatives were Democrats. These included Big Tim Sullivan, whose supporters marked an X next to the star 24,835 times as opposed to the 9,996 who did the same by the Republican eagle.[80] The Big Feller was on his way to Washington.

5

Extracurricular Activities

He would not drink a drop of liquor; he wouldn't smoke a
cigar; he wouldn't utter an oath—he was absolutely ideal
from that standpoint, but he would sit up five nights in succession around the poker table playing for high stakes and
hardly get up. They'd eat sandwiches.

—J. T. Hettrick on Big Tim

CONSTITUENT SERVICE

AMONG THE BENEFITS THAT TAMMANY BESTOWED ON ITS SUP-
porters—proven and potential—were the social and economic
services that governments of the time did not provide and that
churches and private charities could not match. The Tammany
men not only understood the needs and expectations of their
neighbors and constituents, they knew how to arrange such
favors in accordance with the customs of the immigrant and
working-class neighborhoods that they ran and represented. The
common Tammany practice of sneering at college graduates—at
least those in the ranks of their opponents—was not simply
a matter of class envy or antagonism. It stemmed from their belief, not altogether unjustified, that college-educated reformers,
Fusionists—largely old-stock Protestants—viewed the Catholic
and Jewish populations of the Lower East Side and Hell's Kitchen
with condescension. From the perspective of the Democratic politicos, for all their book learning, reformers were generally ignorant of the sensibilities, potential, talent, and culture of those
whom they professed to save from the Hall's corruptive coils.

In 1908, referring to college-educated Goo-Goos who were fond
of slipping a little Latin into their speeches, Little Tim rhetori-
cally asked if "that ever [paid] a widow's rent? Does the college
graduate who talks politics in evening dress at Carnegie Hall
know what it is to bring a spoon to a christening? Did he ever

81

think of bailing out a poor fruit peddler who has been run-in by some too-officious policeman? Does he know how many votes a ton of coal will bring in?"[1] The Little Feller then went on to spell out the philosophy and methods which made Tammany—and the Sullivan clan—so successful. "Organization to be effective in representation as well as action must mean organization all year round . . .," which was a roundabout way of saying politics is a profession and Tammany never sleeps.[2] Little Tim went on to describe the effective politician, starting with the neighborhood leaders, the captains, and working up. The local politician, he explained, "knows everybody's troubles and is expected to remedy them as far as he is able. If he can't he goes to his district leader. . . . These men are the great bulwark of Tammany Hall. Without them we would be helpless. They must be in court when a citizen is in trouble, ready with bail if the case demands it. They must feed the starving, clothe the naked, bury the paupers, and be good friends with everybody."[3]

Timothy P. left a few things out regarding the Tammany playbook, such as intimidation and fraud when necessary, but as a description of the Hall's positive program, it was on target.

In addition to running interference with the police or obtaining bail, Big Tim and his Wise Men provided a wide array of constituent services. They arranged building permits and secured railroad passes and extensions on commercial loans. The two Tims never overlooked the small, thoughtful, and fondly remembered gestures, such as flowers for the sick or funerals.[4] Nor were the Sullivans daunted by emergencies. As coal became scarcer before the 1902 miners' strike was settled, Big Tim organized the distribution of a half-ton of coal to every needy family in his district.[5]

Big Tim himself was a well-known soft touch for personal loans. While some borrowers were insistent that he take their notes for the cash extended, he never made such a document a condition of lending, although he knew full well that he would probably never see much of the money he lent. Indeed, the Big Feller once smilingly inquired if an IOU pressed on him by a borrower were "one of those Kathleen Mauvoureen things?" The reference was to a line in a sentimental Irish American tune that included the refrain "it may be for years, it may be forever."[6] In any event, even when he did accept a formal note, his loans to friends bore no interest.[7]

It was his personal involvement and concern for the poor, troubled and simply down on their luck that won the affections and loyalty of so many in the Bowery for Big Tim and his organization. Some traced Sullivan's well-attested sympathy for those who had run afoul of the law to the memory of his mother. The Big Feller told his longtime friend and advisor, William B. Ellison, that her selfless example led him to the conclusion that he should be kind to boys who made "mistakes," because the good boys could take care of themselves. There is no evidence that he himself was ever in any serious trouble with the law as a boy, but growing up in the Five Points certainly made him familiar with those who were. From Tim's somewhat idiosyncratic view, men in trouble with the courts or police had made "mistakes," their prison sentences amounting to "cruelties." As early as 1893, Sullivan's solicitude for those who fell on the wrong side of the system was well known. In that year Governor Roswell D. Flower, who believed he owed Tim a favor, offered him anything his administration could provide in return, with one exception—a voice in pardons.[8]

Sullivan would come to the aid of a distressed constituent or friend even if it meant petitioning a political opponent and critic. A poor widow whose son badly beat another man while drunk went to Tim to ask his help. Tim was moved by the mother's plea and agreed to see what he could do, even though that meant dealing with District Attorney William Travers Jerome, who had castigated him during the 1901 election. Tim made a heartfelt case for leniency and told Jerome that he had warned the saloon keepers in the Bowery that anyone who sold the young man a drink would be put out of business.[9] Jerome was affected by Tim's intercession and promised to do what he could within the law. The incident also altered Jerome's attitude toward his political opponent. The district attorney never overlooked the Big Feller's faults, but he did come to appreciate his complexity—and his virtues.

While all the Tammany leaders provided support, services, and entertainment to their followers, none indulged in it on Dry Dollar's scale. Starting in the Depression year of 1894, the Big Feller began hosting massive Christmas dinners for the poor and not-so-poor of his district. As early as 8:00 AM, lines of hungry men—women are never mentioned in the coverage—formed outside the

9. Men standing in line for one of Big Tim's Christmas dinners. *Munsey's Magazine,* **December 1913.**

Sullivan Association headquarters at 207 Bowery waiting for the doors to open. Frequently, Big Tim would appear before the meals began, walking down the lines shaking hands and telling the crowd how happy he was to have them as his guests.[10] When the meal began at 11:00 AM, the diners ate standing in relays, as the Sullivans' captains oversaw the distribution of turkey, potato salad, and assorted fixings. Also on hand was "enough beer on tap to float [a] dreadnaught . . ."[11] Near the beginning of the meal, one of Tim's lieutenants, in later years William Dorf, secretary of the Sullivan Association, would slam his gavel on the table and announce, "Boys we're all here to partake of the hospitality of Senator Sullivan." The declaration was followed by cheers for Big Tim after which Dorf would continue "and the senator wishes you all a Merry Christmas and a happy and prosperous New Year."[12] As the relays of diners entered, ate, and departed, Sarsaparilla Reilly stood guard keeping an eagle eye out for "repeaters." To add to the festive nature of the day, Tim's guests were usually treated to performances by vaudeville singers and performers as they enjoyed their holiday meal.[13]

In 1903, the Big Feller began handing out vouchers for shoes and socks at his Christmas celebrations. The items themselves were usually distributed in February, the anniversary of Tim's receiving his badly needed shoes through the intervention of his teacher and the aid of the local Tammany politician.[14] A notable characteristic of the Bowery leader's largesse was his no-questions-asked policy. Whoever showed up for a Christmas meal got it. Indeed, reporting on Sullivan's 1910 Christmas dinner, the *New York Times* noted the presence of "unusually large numbers of young men . . . [who] appeared big and strong enough to do a day's work."[15] No matter. Tim welcomed them along with those more visibly in need.

Big Tim knew his philanthropy was good politics—no matter how much he may have extended and refined such practices, he didn't invent them. But there is no doubt that his openhanded generosity was an integral part of his personality and his concept of the social contract. "I believe in liberality," he once stated. "I am a thorough New Yorker and have no narrow prejudices. I never ask a hungry man about his past. I feed him, not because he is good, but because he needs food. Help your neighbor, but keep your nose out of his affairs. I never sued a man in my life. I am square with my friends, and all I ask is a square deal in return. If I don't get it I am still with my friends."[16]

For the denizens of the Lower East Side, the biggest event of the year was the long-anticipated "chowder" that Big Tim hosted around Labor Day at the end of each summer. The chowders were daylong extravaganzas, including breakfast and dinner, featuring boat rides to a nearby amusement park. Exactly when Tim first initiated the outing is uncertain, but it was well established by 1895.[17] In that year the Timothy D. Sullivan Association picnic and outing was held at Sulzer's Garden in Harlem River Park. No admission fee was charged, the association recouping some of its money by selling the beer concession for $2,000.[18] The crowd grew larger throughout the day, reaching two thousand by eight in the evening when Tim presided over the "grand march."

While Tim clearly enjoyed throwing the party, he also made sure that everyone knew who was responsible for the celebration. In addition to the prominent display of the Timothy D. Sullivan Association name, photographs of the Big Feller were sold during the day at ten cents apiece. By nightfall, with the event winding down, they were discounted to a nickel.[19] The printed program

for the event featured an encomium to Dry Dollar in such preten-
tious purple prose that the *New York Tribune* ridiculed it on page
one the following day. The program began by stating, accurately,
that few New York politicians achieved the celebrity of the Big
Feller. Then, after extolling Tim's combination of "indomitable
Celtic courage and nerve" with "those eminent qualities of broth-
erly love and charity," the anonymous hagiographer hit his
stride. Tim's political history, he declared, was "synonymous with
all that is laudable, beneficial and patriotic, his heart beats especially for the poor, the suffering and the downtrodden. . . . His
lofty aims and refined ideas would never tolerate discrimination
as to a citizen's race, color or religion. . . ."[20] When it came to
Tim's senate career, the program's author became unexpectedly
reticent, stating, "Suffice it to say that our feeble words in exten-
uation of [Tim's] beautiful life would be but 'painting the lily.'"
The *Tribune* writer, gagging on the "lily" reference, dryly remarked that "the crop of lilies has been a trifle short this year,
owing to the new style of gardening introduced into the municipal garden."[21] The program description concluded with a torrent
of flowery rhetoric culminating with the wish that after death
God would grant to "Our Tim" the opportunity to "renew his
former love and friendship with his legion of friends and admirers in the realm of heaven."[22]

In another setting, the gushy flattery of the program might have
proven embarrassing, but probably few read it at the chowder. If
Tim saw it, it's hard not to imagine him laughing—or dismissing
it with a vulgarity. At any rate, the scorn heaped on the panegyric
by the *Tribune* may have had the happy result of insuring no such
inanity appeared again. Many friends, followers, supplicants,
and sycophants praised the Big Feller during his career, but if
another such piece of cloying propaganda appeared in a Sullivan
Association publication, it is lost to history.

But the chowders themselves continued, becoming bigger—
often feasting 15,000—and more elaborate. The destination
changed to recreation/amusement parks on Long Island, usually
Donnelly's Grove at College Point, which allowed the introduction of the legendary boat ride. In the early twentieth century,
chowder tickets went for $5.00.[23] Many were bought by mer-
chants or those who felt obligated to the clan, and then given
away. On the morning of the chowder, partygoers lined up at
Tim's headquarters at the Metamora Club from which they left

10. **The Sullivan Association steps off on the way to the excursion boats at an annual Labor Day Chowder, c. 1905.** *Munsey's Magazine,* **December 1913.**

for the East River piers about 10:00 AM. The order of the procession might vary from year to year, but Sullivan Association leaders always held primacy of place. In 1903, Big and Little Tim, along with Florrie, marched at the head of the throng just behind the first of several bands. Another Sullivan, the celebrated boxer John L., stepped out with his clansmen, the entire party decked out in white automobile hats, American flags, and festooned with photographic buttons of Big Tim himself.[24] On other excursions, the day-trippers were equipped with "chowder caps" and green and gold Sullivan Association badges.[25] Major district leaders and allies of the Sullivans customarily joined the party, and Charlie Murphy himself was often a participant.

In later years, the number of partygoers often exceeded the capacity of the boats—ordinarily two—and latecomers were forced to take the railroad and trolley to College Point. The possibility of injury as Bowery celebrants rushed to get on the vessels presented a problem with crowd control as it was not unusual for more than seven thousand people to board the steamers.[26] To prevent the crowd from becoming unruly, a guard of mounted patrolmen was stationed on hand, and in some years their intervention proved necessary to keep order.[27]

Those who boarded the steamers were treated to breakfast, drink, and, of course, the opportunity to partake of games of chance. Reporting on the 1909 chowder, the *New York Times* stated that "wheel games, the game of three sevens painted on a white sheet, that known as 'under and over,' crap and poker games were in full blast before either craft were abreast Tenth Street. The play went on camp stools, on top of hatches, on the floor, and even on the plush covered seats of the main saloons."[28] Typically, the Big Feller and his coterie spent most of the day in the private suites on the steamers or at Donnelly's Grove gambling away. The favored game in the inner circle was poker and pots often reached a thousand dollars or more.[29] The gambling that characterized the 1909 chowder—the "talk of the town for weeks"—was too over the top for the city administration to overlook. Spirits at next year's chowder were damped by the presence of police who prevented any public gambling, though all other activities continued as usual. Big Tim and his colleagues remained sequestered on the boat, protected from the officious police and immersed in poker.[30]

Once they reached College Point the chowder goers were treated to more food, drink, and athletic competitions, such as foot races, baseball, and boxing. For the less athletically inclined, pie-eating contests were arranged, while those not into fitness might partake in the "fat men's race" with a minimum requirement of two hundred pounds for entrants.[31] For the 1903 excursion, the Sullivans handed out approximately one hundred thousand beer chits, which entitled each participant to about twenty-five glasses of beer apiece.[32] By 1909, the chits were dispensed with, and Tim's guests could have all the beer they wanted for the asking. When the played-out revelers returned to the Manhattan docks at night, they were treated to a fireworks display, which might be followed by a torchlight parade. In 1903, one man fell overboard as the boat was docking, but was fetched from the water unhurt. Under the circumstances, the wonder is that many more of the happy celebrants didn't end up floating in the East River.[33]

The chowders were not Big Tim's only activity as social director of the Bowery. Though perhaps not quite as memorable as the

11. Big Tim, second on left, enjoying the excursion boat during a Sullivan Association Labor Day Chowder. Tom Foley, Sullivan ally and mentor of Al Smith, stands at his left. Library of Congress.

Labor Day extravaganzas, the Annual Masquerade and Civic Ball held by the Timothy D. Sullivan Association was heralded as "one of the chief events of the East Side winter season."[34] On a smaller scale, Sullivan organized various "rackets"—balls thrown by the different civic and political groups that provided much of the social life in the Lower East Side—as well as a certain amount of profit for Tim.[35] Nor did the Big Feller forget the boys peddling newspapers in the streets. He always had coins in his pockets for the "newsies" and, at least once, treated two thousand of them for a day at Coney Island where he was part owner of the "Dreamland" amusement park.[36] Panhandlers patiently hovered along the route Tim took from his headquarters at the Occidental Hotel to Tammany Hall well aware that Dry Dollar never failed to make a contribution.[37] William Ellison once watched Tim hand something to every beggar who approached him as they walked across City Hall Park to the Astor House. When Ellison opined that 75 percent of those to whom he handed money were "not deserving," Tim smiled and replied,

"Well let's think of the other twenty-five percent."[38] Some observers estimated that Big Tim gave away $25,000 a year in his
district, while "[his] patronage amounts to seven or eight times
as much."[39] Critics charged he took a great deal more out of the
Bowery, but since much of that came from his illicit interests, his
overall role as the Bowery's benefactor is hard to dispute.[40]

Investor and Producer

By the late 1890s, Tim's interests in sports and recreation evolved
into yet another career—vaudeville and motion picture impre-
sario. The Bowery theater district, long famous for its impudent,
proletarian quality, attracted a large and diverse clientele who
often preferred it to the more respectable fare found on Broadway. Middle- and upper-class visitors from uptown and out of
town were drawn to the Bowery entertainments by their bawdy
and lively reputation. Tim became acquainted with theater
owners through his role as their protector from the city's Sunday
blue laws, which forbade performances on the Sabbath. But his
first real introduction to the theater world, and his initial investment, sprang from his friendship with Henry C. Miner, owner of
Miner's Bowery Theater. The Bowery Theater played a decisive
role in the shift from nineteenth-century variety to classic vaudeville, pioneering in such innovations as "Amateur Night" and the
use of the hook to drag failing acts offstage. The Bowery was also
the setting for the Sullivan Association's election eve rallies.

Miner introduced Tim to theater people in New York and
the summer resort/gambling circles at Saratoga. By 1896, Dry
Dollar had entered into a partnership with another entrepre-
neur, George J. Krause, who owned concert salons in the Bowery
and the vice-ridden Tenderloin district, which stretched from
Thirtieth to Fifty-ninth street between Sixth and Tenth Avenue.
In 1898, Sullivan and Kraus remodeled the "Volks Garden" on
East Fourteenth Street and renamed it the "Dewey Theater" after the Spanish-American War hero. Although—or perhaps
because—some critics denounced the performances of the scant-
ily dressed chorus girls as immoral, the Dewey became Union
Square's most popular theater, netting Sullivan $25,000 a year.[41]
The duo went on to open several other burlesque and music halls.

Big Tim's interest in vaudeville owed much to its pecuniary
awards, but it also dovetailed with his genuine concern for "his"

people. His obvious pride in his entertainment investments was heightened by the use to which they could be made when questioned about his sources of income. He raked in so much from his legitimate enterprises that he could plausibly deny he had no interests in gambling or any other forms of vice.[42] The benefits of local theater to Tim's constituents were real. Inexpensive amusements were highly popular among tenement dwellers, and the entertainment provided helped lessen the weight of poverty, six day workweeks, and twelve-hour or more workdays.

Out of self-interest and personal inclination, the Big Feller backed legislation greasing the operation of popular entertainment as well as boxing and thoroughbred racing. Tim had a good nose for which enterprises would become popular and profitable. After 1900, he extended his interests from sports and vaudeville to motion pictures and became a part owner of Coney Island's Dreamland amusement park.[43] His financial returns were matched by his satisfaction in providing cheap, easily accessible entertainment for the city's working classes. When a proposal was made in 1909 to close Coney Island on Sundays, Tim derided the measure as "the most ridiculous thing that I ever heard of. It is a case of 11,000 people trying to wag 2,000,000 and it can not succeed."[44] He was right.

Tim's two terms in Congress were barren in most respects, but they opened his eyes to the possibilities of bankrolling entertainment beyond the "Big Onion"—as New York was then called. In 1904, he joined with theatrical promoter John W. Considine to purchase vaudeville houses in the West. By 1907, the partners controlled about forty midsized theaters west of Chicago. Charlie Chaplin and Will Rogers were among the entertainers who honed their talents in Sullivan-Considine houses. The theaters were highly lucrative, and the Tammany politico took in about $200,000 a year from them.[45] Indeed, when his estate was later computed, the Big Feller's shares in the Sullivan-Considine Circuit comprised the largest percentage of his assets.[46] Tim also joined another Considine, George, no relation to John W., in opening a number of trendy clubs, among them the Metropole at Broadway and Forty-second Street, which became the Big Feller's midtown headquarters.

It was a short jump from vaudeville and burlesque to movie houses, and in 1908 Big Tim entered into a business/political alliance with William Fox, the Jewish movie pioneer. Their arrangement began when Fox leased two of Tim's vaudeville spots for $100,000, mixing live entertainment with movies.[47] In Albany, Sullivan threw his support behind efforts to repeal the blue laws, which made theater operations illegal on Sunday, even though he made money-protecting venues that did business on the Sabbath. In 1907 he attacked the Sunday restrictions, contending "the best way to ruin a cosmopolitan city like ours, which virtually lives off our visiting strangers, is to enforce or keep on the statute books such blue laws which don't belong in our age."[48]

Considering his close connection with popular entertainment, it is not surprising that songsters repaid the compliment. In 1905, just in time for the mayoral election, the team of Vincent Bryan and Gus Edwards wrote a satirical tune, *Tammany,* which they "Respectfully dedicated to the Hon. Timothy D. Sullivan." After playfully presenting Tammany's mythical American Indian origins, the verses got down to some unsophisticated, occasionally incoherent, but revealing political humor, bringing in many issues and personalities of the time. These included women's suffrage and William Randolph Hearst, whose third-party bid for city hall was Tammany's major threat that year.

Chris Columbo sailed from Spain, across the deep blue sea,
Brought along the Dagoe vote to beat out Tammany.
Tammany found Colombo's crew were living on a boat,
Big Chief said: "They're floaters," and he would not let them vote,
Then to the tribe he wrote
    Chorus
Tammany, Tammany,
Get those Dagoes jobs at once, they can vote in twelve more months,
Tammany, Tammany,
Make those floaters Tammany votes
    Verse
Fifteen thousand Irishmen from Erin came across,
Tammany put those Irish Indians on the Police force.
I asked one cop, if he wanted two platoons or four,
He said, "Keep your old platoons, I've got a cuspidor, What would I
    want with more?"
    Chorus
When reformers think it's time to show activity,
They blame everything that's bad on poor old Tammany.
All the farmers think that Tammany caused old Adam's fall, They
    say when a bad man dies he goes to Tammany Hall, Tammany's
    blamed for all.

Chorus
Tammany, Tammany,
When a farmer's tax is due, he puts the blame on you.
Tammany, Tammany, You're a devil Tammany.
  Verse
Doc Osler says all men of sixty we should kill,
That would give Tammany lots of jobs to fill.
They would chloroform old Doctor Parkhurst first I know,
After that they'd fix Tom Platt because they love him so, and then
  Depew would go.
  Chorus
Tammany, Tammany,
When you chloroform to kill, don't forget old Dave B. Hill.
Tammany Tammany,
Rope 'em, rope 'em, and we'll dope 'em, Tammany.
  Verse
If we'd let the women vote, they would all get rich soon,
Think how old man Platt gave all his money to a coon.
Mrs. Chadwick is a girl, who'd lead in politics,
She could show our politicians lots of little tricks, the Wall Street
  vote she'd fix.
  Chorus
Tammany, Tammany
Cassie Chadwick leads them all, she should be in Tammany Hall,
Tammany, Tammany,
Who'd get rich quick? Cassie Chadwick Tammany.
  Verse
Tammany's chief is digging out a railroad station here,
He shut off the water mains, on folks who can't buy beer.
He put in team shovels, to lay off the workingmen,
Tammany will never see a chief like him again. He's the poor man's
  friend.
  Chorus
Tammany, Tammany,
Murphy's your big chief's name, He's a Rothschild just the same.
Tammany, Tammany, Willie Hearst will do his worst to Tammany.

Though the lyrics were clumsy, and politically incorrect by twenty-first-century standards, the tune no doubt raised a smile in most New Yorkers, and there's no reason to think that Big Tim wasn't pleased by the dedication.

Big Tim wasn't a man of the written word, and his interests, political and economic, did not encourage record keeping. Nevertheless, despite his limited educational background, he commonly peppered his talk with references to Demosthenes, Lilliputians, and personages from American history. Though it may have confounded his many opponents, Tim enjoyed reading. His preferences ran toward Jack London, perhaps the most popular American novelist of the time, and Charles Dickens, whose human presentation of the poorer classes probably won Tim's approval. Victor Hugo's *Les Miserables*, with its theme of decent workers tormented by an unfeeling legal system, was a personal favorite, and there is no doubt who he would have identified with in the novel.[49] He had little use for the more adventuresome contemporary writers who pushed the envelope regarding sexuality. He once denounced Elinor Glyn's *Three Weeks* (1907), considered scandalously immoral at the time, by stating that anyone who read it should be sentenced to ten days.[50] The critique suggests he actually read the book, but disapproved of its theme. If so, Tim was simply following the orthodox "lace curtain" Irish attitude regarding public expression of sexual subjects, which was to avoid them whenever possible.

Tim was a member of any number of clubs and societies, some political, some not. He joined the Fraternal Order of Eagles, a charitable organization, after being introduced to it by John Considine. The society selected him as their "Grand Worthy President" for 1903–4.[51]

Ironically, for such a highly social man, and one who made the acquaintance of numerous women, Big Tim never established his own family. In 1886—or 1892—he married Helen "Nellie" Fitzgerald. She was a childhood friend of the Big Feller's and, according to some sources, took "an active part" in his early career. What that meant is uncertain as she was never mentioned in contemporary accounts.[52] They soon became estranged, though the circumstances of the break are unknown. A friend of Sullivan's explained, "Big Tim never discussed his domestic affairs with anyone, and we were all wise enough never to mention the subject to him."[53] Even the basic fact of their having children is clouded. Most accounts claim the marriage was barren, but after running a story to that effect, the *Times* corrected itself and reported they had a daughter, Ada Sullivan.[54] However, later reports maintained the girl passed herself off as Tim's daughter without being recognized as such by the Sullivan family.[55] In any event Big Tim provided a home for Nellie at 240 West Seventy-fifth Street where she lived until her death in 1912.

Though he seldom observed the rituals and strictures of the religion into which he was born, Tim remained loyal to the faith of his forebears. "I'm an Irish American," he once proclaimed conflating Irish and Catholic, "and we don't believe in divorce."[56] As unhappy as he was in his wedded state, divorce was out of the question. On the other hand, so was celibacy. An illegitimate daughter was born to him in 1896, but her existence, and that of another illegitimate child, only became publicly known during the legal wrangling over his estate following his death.[57]

Though failing at marriage, and enough of a Catholic never to seek a divorce, Tim was fortunate to have an extended family in the form of his brothers, cousins, and their children. These, along with a few close confidants, made up the small group—usually around twenty-five—that Tim invited to the annual birthday party he gave for himself.[58] Yet, especially in his time and place, the lack of a family of his own was probably a disappointment.

Nor did the Big Feller have a real home. He kept an apartment in the Occidental Hotel, his political headquarters, and he owned a house on East Fourth Street, but he never seemed actually "at home" in any place. The scene at the Occidental was one of continuous activity characterized by largely male jocularity. Its restaurant was frequented by most of the important politicians and businessmen, and the barroom's ceiling was covered with a huge painting titled *Diana Surprised*—a large nude—whose fame spread across the nation and whose memory was treasured long after its demise. But the clubhouse atmosphere was not the same as a home, and he had nothing like the domestic retreat Tammany leader Charles Murphy had in his East Side brownstone or his leisure home at Good Ground (Hampton Bays) Long Island.

A social animal, Tim enjoyed traveling. Trips to Democratic nominating conventions often took on the character of holidays— at least when he wasn't called upon to wheel and deal. He also visited Europe on several occasions. On May 26, 1909, for example, he left for the Continent aboard the liner *Mauretania*. On arrival at the pier, he was greeted by a twelve-foot-long model of the vessel constructed entirely from flowers, which was a bon voyage gift from the Sullivan Club. His itinerary included Ireland, Britain, Paris (where he expected to attend the Grand Prix races), Scandinavia, and then back to London and Ireland before returning home.[59] Ironically, William Randolph Hearst took the same liner for Europe. He boarded five minutes before departure time, possibly hoping to avoid Tim and his well-wishers. What, if anything, they said to each during the crossing was not recorded.[60]

Tim's largesse was well in evidence as the ship traversed the Atlantic. The flowers sent by well-wishers, which reportedly filled a lifeboat, were converted into bouquets for each of the four hundred saloon passengers. Big Tim handed $100 to a young man returning home to Ireland who had the good fortune to share his benefactor's name.[61] When Tim landed in Queenstown, Ireland (now Cobh), he found a "tidal wave of letters and telegrams" awaiting him. One of these may have been from Richard Croker, then living the life of a millionaire "returned Yank," whom Tim visited at his home outside Dublin.[62] The rest of the trip went largely as planned, but it was cut short on news of Little Tim's declining health.

Gambling was Tim's personal vice and he pursued it day and night at the poker table and racetrack. After he separated from his wife in 1905, he moved into the Occidental Hotel at the corner of Broome Street and the Bowery. The hotel was home to the Matamora Club, headquarters for the Timothy D. Sullivan Association, and it was here that Tim oversaw a poker game that reputedly ran for five years. The Big Feller always took care to place a poor onlooker in charge of the kitty, tipping him every time he folded his hand. Despite his love of the action, Big Tim was often unsuccessful in his wagers. According to contemporary accounts, professional gamblers "welcome him with open arms into the temple of chance. He plays high and he loses like a king."[63] Or, as an old friend put it, "He couldn't have won with ten cards to choose from."[64]

Next to cards, Dry Dollar loved horses and horse racing. He helped organize the Metropolitan Jockey Club and owned a stake in the Jamaica Racetrack. His equine interests led him to join with Frank Farrell and David Johnson to buy a stable of thoroughbreds.[65] One of Big Tim's horses won $100,000. This was offset by another of his racers, "Bowery," who proved to be a nag. Tim was a regular attendee of the track during the racing season, avoiding the clubhouse and sitting well back in the grandstand with his friends and confidants. As was the case with cards, Tim's luck with horses was spotty at best. He had the reputation for being a "nervy" bettor, but not a successful one. The Big Feller's love of gambling seems to have depended more on the conviviality and amusement involved rather than any strong interest in reaping more lucre. He always seemed to have enough of that, and considering his gaming record, he needed it.

While thoroughbreds and poker were Tim's personal gaming favorites, other sports events attracted his interest and his money. He put his cash behind those he favored in boxing matches and acted as stakeholder in the celebrated Jefferies-Johnson bout of 1910. To those who decried boxing as brutal, he countered, "There are more fatalities through American football in six months than there have been in the prize ring in 250 years."[66]

Sullivan took his losses in stride, but was quick to use his power if he felt he was crossed. In 1898 a boxing referee and gambling house owner named Honest John Kelly (not Croker's predecessor as Tammany boss), who had earned his name for probity in judging sporting events, called off a fight between Jim Corbett and Tom Sharkey. Big Tim had a large roll wagered on Sharkey and warned Kelly not to stop the fight. But Honest John stood true to his principles and halted the bout on suspicion of a fix. Sullivan honored his principles as well. The following day the cops raided and trashed Kelly's gambling house.[67]

Perhaps because his various interests generated enormous amounts of cash, Big Tim was always profligate with money. It was commonly stated that "Tim made millions and gave away millions."[68] Those who owed him, or wished to impress him, often sent him valuable gifts—expensive watches, diamond stickpins—which he commonly tossed over to his nearest lieutenants as if they were plastic Mardi Gras baubles. On the train taking Tim and his party to the 1904 Democratic Convention in Chicago, the group started a game of poker. With no chips available, $20 bills were pressed into service. When a new hand was started, someone realized that the pot was shy a $20. No one would confess to holding back and charges and counter-charges began to fly. As the argument grew heated, Tim grabbed the pot, tore the bills into pieces, and threw them out the window. "There boys, that ends the argument," he pronounced authoritatively. "Now let's put in again, and there won't be any misunderstanding."[69]

Most of Big Tim's spending went into his charities, and untold amounts were soaked up by his unsuccessful betting. If anything, his legendary generosity grew in his later years, when he sometimes gave away large sums so capriciously as to suggest his acts of philanthropy were intended to compensate for something missing inside him. On a trip to California he ran into a party of "sports" who claimed they knew him. Whether or not he really believed it, the Big Feller brought them back to New York in his private railroad car. When visiting Europe in 1909, where he found himself already famous as "King of the Bowery," he personally took charge of repatriating dozens of stranded Americans.[70] On a whim, he hosted a $3,000 dinner in an Albany hotel for a lame elevator operator named Conrad Kleinhans.[71] At Sullivan's invitation, assemblymen and judges arrived to celebrate the lowly hotel employee, who certainly treasured the event for the rest of his life. As Bowery historian Alvin Harlow observed, "The only return Tim got out of the affair was the joy of doing it."[72] Although conducted on a larger scale than most, the dinner was typical of the kindhearted gestures that won Tim the heartfelt support of his followers. Their loyalty was personal, transcending politics and leading many to overlook his flaws in other areas.

During his last few years, some claimed the Big Feller was "high-hatting" his old haunts and spending less time in the Bowery. It was claimed he had become "harder to see than the King of England." Though the statement seems exaggerated, Tim's partial withdrawal from the public was real, but it had nothing to do with putting on airs. Rather he—or his lieutenants—realized he had little ability to resist any plea for aid, so distance from potential supplicants became necessary.[73] Sullivan loved giving and took deep satisfaction in extending his hand to the less fortunate, but increasingly there seemed something manic about it. Or perhaps it was the onset of the affliction that led to his death.

6

No Final Victories

Politics Ain't Beanbag
—"Mr. Dooley" alias Finlay Peter Dunne

CONFIDENT THAT THE RETURNS FROM THE PREVIOUS YEAR'S ELECtions showed Tammany was back on track, Murphy readied his slate of candidates for the 1903 municipal contests. The grand sachem persuaded George B. McClellan Jr. to run for the key office of mayor. Possessing a famous name, and generally considered respectable, McClellan was a loyal Democrat who accepted the nomination even though he had been content in Washington. McClellan's opponent, Fusion mayor Seth Low, had worn out his welcome with much of the electorate. Widely considered stiff and puritanical, his determination to push Sunday closing laws evoked considerable resentment in many parts of the city.

The Sullivan clan began setting up the Low administration for defeat even before the fall campaigning season was under way. In June, Little Tim, who sat on the Board of Aldermen and "directed" it, deftly blocked an attempt by the Fusionists to make capital from what the newspapers referred to as "the Tammany methods of the old 98–01 days."[1] He turned enough members of the board against Low and for Tammany that they unseated Fusionist Herbert Parsons as chairman of the Finance Committee and replaced him with loyal Sullivan ally, John T. McCall. As the *New York World* put it, the Little Feller's "coup d'etat . . . landed a Tammany man where a Tammany man was most needed. . . . it took the breath away from the Fusion people."[2] Nor was Little Tim done. He proceeded to convince the president of the board, Fusionist Charles V. Fournier, to run on the Tammany ticket for the fall campaign.

Fournier was not the only conspicuous reform figure to convert to Tammany. In a maneuver the hostile *New York Times* pronounced "a deep political trick," the Democrats detached comptroller Edward M. Grout from Low to the Tiger.[3] The *Times* credited Murphy with the defection of both men from Low's team, though the Little Feller recruited Fournier earlier. Murphy may have been responsible for getting Grout to change affiliations, and possibly he and the shorter Tim worked together to detach the mayor's lieutenants from his banner. Timothy P. wasn't concerned who got the credit. He could have taken the position he arranged for McCall, but declined, stating, "No, I was not planning this for myself."[4] Both Tims knew that power and title were not necessarily the same thing.

Personal ambition probably loomed large in Fournier and Grout's decision to jump parties. They may have sensed the change in the political atmosphere and recognized that running on the Democratic line was the best guarantee for their continuance in office. The times were also changing. By 1903, much of the enthusiasm for third-force reform had abated, and its adherents returned slowly to their respective political parties. Members of the Good Government clubs or Citizens' Union increasingly tended to pursue their objectives through more narrowly focused special interest groups.[5] In the meantime, the defection of Fournier and Grout was a serious blow to the cause of reform—not to mention Low's own chances. Tammany's strategy, in the words of the *Times,* threw the Fusion forces "into a state of frightful demoralization which they do not attempt to conceal."[6] Indeed, many Fusionists denounced their erstwhile colleagues, demanding to know how they could remain principled reformers while running with the Tammany pack. In addition to the crippled Low, the Democracy faced one other candidate, William Deverey, who sought the mayoralty on the Independent People's Party line, a triumph of ego over reality.

The Democratic nominating convention met on the night of October 1–2, 1903, at Carnegie Hall. The building was jammed with delegates and observers while the crowds outside on the sidewalks were so thick and enthusiastic that Big Tim's coat was torn from his back as he pushed his way into the building.[7] Many expected to see Hugh McLaughlin's Brooklyn organization mount a challenge to Murphy's ticket over the nomination of the apostate Fusionists. It was understood that McLaughlin's dissatisfaction with the candidates stemmed more from his fear that Murphy would bring Brooklyn under Tammany's control than any substantive disagreement about nominees and electoral tac-

12. **The tiger crosses the bridge, 1903. A comment on Tammany's growing power in Kings County following the consolidation of the City of Greater New York.** *Glimpses of a Great Campaign,* **1903.**

tics. Indeed, from the moment he became the Hall's leader, Murphy had angled to unite all the Democratic clubs in the recently expanded city under Tammany leadership. With less to lose and much to gain, the Democratic leaders in Queens, Staten Island, and the Bronx made little complaint about folding their organizations into the Tammany machine. Brooklyn was another matter.

The Brooklyn Democratic organization, which McLaughlin had led for forty years, was accustomed to independence. McLaughlin's people followed the old motto "The Tiger does not cross the [Brooklyn] bridge." However, some in McLaughlin's club began to have second thoughts. Although he once said he would rather "be a serf in Russia than a satrap of Tammany Hall," Hugh McCarren, state senator, and McLaughlin, lieutenant, decided the Tiger could cross the bridge after all—if he paid a toll.[8] Consequently, the Brooklyn Democrats split. McCarren led a growing majority that accepted Murphy's leadership and supported the ticket entirely, while McLaughlin fought a rearguard action. By the end of the one-night convention, though some Brooklynites held out for Judge William Gaynor's nomination as mayor, Murphy's selections were approved.

Though a member of the privileged classes, McClellan proved a good campaigner, making a total of fifty-nine speeches, including three in Italian, five in German, and several in a combination of languages.[9] As usual, Tammany put on a more colorful and lively show than its opponents, complete with parades, rallies, thousands of banners festooned in the downtown neighborhoods, and billboard advertising. The Fusion campaign was less flamboyant, though they did manage to secure a caged tiger—perhaps the same cat that rode on the Tammany float after the 1898 election—which they displayed under the banner "Do You Want To Turn Him Loose Again?"[10] Fusion spokesman, Robert Fulton Cutting, affected unconcern about his team's prospects and guaranteed Low's reelection on the grounds that the people were tired of "Devereyism and the iceman [Murphy]."[11]

The most popular and effective campaigner in Low's administration was District Attorney William Travers Jerome, who was not up for reelection. Jerome, who especially despised criminality and low conduct in persons of wealth and education, concentrated his attacks on McClellan, even going so far as to contrast him unfavorably with the Big Feller. Addressing a Fusion rally in the final days of the campaign, Jerome declared

> I have many friends in Tammany, many in the rank and file and a few of the leaders, and some of them are good men, but McClellan stands as a tool of a little band of grafters . . . Look at Tim Sullivan. He was accused once of grave crimes and he stood up and told how as a boy he had been kicked about the streets, what his life and associations had been. He is not a good man, but he is a strong man. He is in some ways barbaric, perhaps, but he has his virtues, and he has not had half the chance McClellan had. I feel McClellan is false and treacherous to educated gentlemen, and I would rather by far entertain Tim Sullivan at my dinner table than Mr. McClellan.[12]

Big Tim, who was finding Washington a yawn, was in town for the election, no doubt working with Little Tim to ensure the "machine within a machine" again played its crucial role in the contest. The Sunday before the election, a large crowd turned out at a Tammany rally held at Miner's Bowery Theater, drawn by a rumor that the Big Feller would speak, but the congressman was a no-show, and the crowd had to remain content with Little Tim, who presided over the event. When reporters asked one of the Sullivan aides why Dry Dollar ducked the meeting, they were told he had gone uptown "to bet a million dollars on McClellan."[13] The million dollars was an exaggeration, but events would show the idea was right.

As election day dawned, each side forecast victory. Following a conference with the district leaders, Murphy predicted a Mc-Clellan margin of 86,000 in Manhattan and the Bronx. The bosses returned to their districts bearing bundles of campaign literature, buttons, and sample ballots, along with $1,000 in "walking around money." Fusionists, who had run a postcard survey, insisted that Low would be returned by 13,143 votes.[14] The survey was clearly unscientific. That evening, as word of a Tammany triumph buzzed through the city, the streets of the Bowery, Tenderloin, and Times Square filled with exuberant, rambunctious, but good-natured crowds celebrating the Tiger's dinner. The tune of the evening was a little doggerel that went

> There's a red light on the track for Sethy Low,
> There's a red light on the track for Sethy Low.
> There's a red light on the track,
> And we welcome Tammany back,
> There's a red light on the track for Sethy Low.[15]

McClellan took city hall with a 61,872 margin over Low—a little under Murphy's prediction, but solid enough.[16] Tammany candidates triumphed in all boroughs except Richmond, and secured the Board of Aldermen as well. Hugh McLaughlin's efforts to hold Murphy off at the East River also failed, and the old Brooklynite stepped into the political twilight while Tammany's allies across the river assumed control of the Kings County Democrats. Newspapers proclaimed Murphy the most important Democratic leader in the country, his strategy of co-opting the Fusionists hailed as a brilliant stroke. According to the *Herald,* "one lesson of the elections is that New York is not only still a democratic [sic] city, but a Tammany city as well. Deverey has ceased to be an issue, and the public have taken the view that Deverey was responsible for graft and blackmail and that Tammany, having thrown Deverey out, was entitled to another trial in managing the affairs of the municipality."[17]

Charlie Murphy congratulated his party on their victory, "by which honest democracy is returned to power," and pronounced himself satisfied that "indecent attacks upon decent men have been rebuked in the most emphatic way."[18] Jerome had a different take on the outcome. "The campaign resolved itself," he contended, "into the question of whether you could put up naked principle to be supported by an unlovable man."[19] Expanding on that reasoning, the magazine *World of Work* ascribed Tammany's success to "the feeling of the masses . . . that the Fusion administration was oppressive to them. It closed the saloons on Sundays. It enforced other laws that had never before been rigidly enforced."[20] Or as Croker observed earlier, the people can't stand corruption, but they can't stand reform either.

As Murphy and the other leaders prepared to sort out the city government and patronage according to their own liking, there was one last piece of business to attend to. The day after the election, bets on the contest were paid off on Wall Street for the brokers and financiers and at the Metropole and Hoffman House hotels for the politicos and gamblers. Big Tim was the second-highest winner among the latter group, scoring $62,000 from McClellan's victory. Others who profited from the election were Tim's old partner, Frank Farrell, with $58,000, and Charlie Murphy himself, who netted $46,000.[21]

Charlie Murphy was a Tammany boss, but he was no absolute monarch, and he knew it. In terms of personality and style, the Big Feller and Silent Charlie (never to his face) were polar opposites. At the very least, the Tammany sachem was probably uncomfortable with Sullivan's underworld connections. But the Sullivans were winners, their sway over the Lower East Side unshakable, and their influence extended well above Fourteenth Street. No Tammany victory was possible without their support, and at least until 1909, knowledgeable observers believed Big Tim and the "Wise Men" were more powerful than Murphy himself.[22]

Even as a congressman, Tim was seldom away from New York. Though his personal amusements and entertainment interests dominated his activities between 1901 and 1908, he and Little Tim continued expanding their network of alliances and the reach of the "machine within a machine." Battery Dan Finn's enthusiastic support for the Big Feller owed much to Sullivan's backing him in a contest with Colonel Murphy when Finn took over the First Assembly District. "Big Florrie" ruled the Eighth Assembly Distirct—"de Ate"—while Sullivan allies Julius Harburger and Charles Culkin headed the Tenth and Fifth districts, respectively.[23] In 1905, the two Sullivans did not hesitate to aid Thomas J. McManus against Murphy's choice, George Washington Plunkitt, as leader of the Hell's Kitchen District. McManus, known as "The McManus," as if he were a Gaelic chieftain, prevailed, and in the following year compounded Plunkitt's humiliation by defeating him for state senator.[24] All in all, the Sullivans controlled eleven of thirty-five assembly districts—including all the "gorilla territory" in and around the Bowery—making it impossible for Murphy or any other Democrat to attempt a measure they opposed. Although there is no evidence the issue ever came up between the two men, it was common knowledge that Charlie Murphy's reign would continue as long as he made no attempt to disturb Big Tim's arrangements.[25]

Placing his own allies and clients in control of assembly districts was a key to Sullivan's power, as district leaders could make or break aldermen, state senators, assemblymen, and even members of Congress.[26] But Tim's reach extended to other offices as well. After 1900 no one could hope for the Democratic nomination for mayor without Big Tim's approval. In the first decade of the new century, three of the city's sheriffs were Tim's men, who dutifully followed the Big Feller's suggestions for deputyships. He also placed three judges on the state supreme court. In one instance he selected a candidate for the court who "was so rank" that a public outcry was raised against him. Murphy asked him to get the candidate to withdraw from the election but, having given his word, Tim refused.[27] Fortunately for the Hall, when the nominee read the scathing denunciations of his candidacy in the newspapers, he decided to avoid further public embarrassment and backed out. "Remember," Tim told him after his retreat, "I didn't ask you to withdraw. If there's a bad smell around you it isn't of my making."[28]

Conferring nominations on judicial candidates was a revenue-enhancing operation as well as a political decision. Potential nominees seeking state supreme court judgeships were expected to feed the party's kitty, and those who wanted Tim's endorsement had to deal directly with him. William B. Ellison, an old friend and advisor, recalled the visit of a pompous lawyer who sought Tim's backing for a judgeship. After he finished delivering

a résumé of what he obviously thought were impressive credentials for the post, Tim smiled but said nothing. Flustered, the
supplicant "intimated" that he understood a substantial campaign contribution was expected. Tim continued to smile silently.
The would-be candidate then declared with "great confidence
that he would be willing to contribute as high as $10,000."[29] Tim
held his Mona Lisa smile a few seconds longer and then ended the
discussion saying, "It seems to me that you want to play the game
with white chips."[30]

The year 1903 marked Tim's fortieth birthday, and he celebrated the day "like that of a king." His office in the Occidental
Hotel was literally "smothered in roses and other flowers." Con-
gratulatory letters poured in and Tammany leaders, captains,
rank and file, plus ordinary supporters and admirers descended
on the hotel to extend personal best wishes to the "King of the
Bowery." Tim finally left his Bowery headquarters and made
something of a royal circuit of his domain, stopping at various
parks on the Lower East Side so well-wishers could greet him. He
ended his progress at an Italian club on Elizabeth Street where a
new oil painting labeled *Our Leader Timothy D. Sullivan* had just
been installed.[31] The painting joined the hundreds of pictures,
photographs, or lithographs of the Big Feller that gazed down on
his subjects from barroom walls, storefronts, and political and
social clubs all over his fiefdom.

Tim had every reason to feel satisfaction as he celebrated his
birthday. By age forty he had made himself and his extended
family a political power in the nation's greatest city. His legitimate investments and interests extended into a wide range of
exciting, lucrative, and prospering areas. He was probably the
best-known politico in New York—Murphy not excepted. He was
loved by tens of thousands for his charity and philanthropy. For
those who hated and despised him, they didn't count. "King of the
Bowery?" Of course. "King of New York?" Why not?

**

Of course, one can raise the question of what these titles meant
to Sullivan, his followers, his allies, or his enemies. "King of the
Bowery" and "King of the Underworld" were reverse caricatures
that came to define Tim Sullivan's public persona. The "King of
the Bowery" was the popular, street-smart politician, an affable
rogue, who by dint of a generous nature and two-fisted methods

made himself into the most powerful of the Tammany politicos. The "King of the Underworld" was the malevolent demagogue, master of corruption and chicanery, whose illegitimately derived power was a threat to the political and social order. Both images reflected common political—especially Irish political—stereotypes of the time. And like most stereotypes, they were based on truth, however distorted the final image might have become.

Newspapermen played a major role in fashioning both the negative and the more positive, if slightly disreputable, images. Reporters and editors recognized early on that the Big Feller made great copy. Drawing on genuine elements in his personality—the generosity, friendliness, wit, East Side argot, and political skill—they presented him as the outsized Irish proletarian-cum-political dynamo. Newspaper ethics were even less admirable than they are today, and many sayings and doings of Tim were hyped or exaggerated, some most likely invented. If they served his uses, Tim didn't care, spun them to his own advantage, or recognized there was little he could do about it anyway.

"King of the Underworld"—a label applied to him in print no later than 1907—was another matter.[32] Tim never hid his friendship with some members of the criminal classes, from the Whyos to Paul Vaccarelli, seeing them as products of bad luck and their environment. Sullivan was very much a "nurture" man when it came to assessing human character. He also participated enthusiastically in the traditional Tammany investment and protection of gambling—his own vice—if nothing else. Those in the press who loathed him, who included just about everyone connected with the *New York Times* and *Tribune,* used those activities to shape the portrait of the master criminal/politician—the spider in the center of the web. In doing so, they probably overstated not only Big Tim's criminal activities, but his control over gambling in the city, which was likely more diffuse and less organized than the published reports of all-powerful triumvirates. But assigning the role of vice lord to Sullivan gave Tammany's enemies a weapon to be wielded in every municipal election between 1886 to 1912. In truth, much of the popular perception of Tim Sullivan, especially among his critics, derived from press reports, a majority of which were hostile.

But the caricature was also a joint creation. Following a tradition extending back to Davy Crockett, Tim worked consciously to shape his own public persona. Based on genuine elements in his background and economic and political activities, Tim Sullivan made himself into Big Tim—the larger-than-life, charismatic, populist leader, the quintessential successful up-from-the-slums New Yorker—the anti-Knickerbocker. Much of what he gave and showed the press and public was real—he was the spokesman, exemplar, and protector of the downtown, heavily immigrant, working-class neighborhoods. On the other hand, there seems little doubt that the Big Feller could sharpen or mute his plebeian characteristics to suit his needs. His reading, vocabulary, investment interests, friendships, and ultimately political activities bespeak a more complicated man.

The incessant politicking, partying, and gambling suggest a fear of being alone. Sullivan's relationships with women, admittedly poorly known, seem transitory, providing short-term sexual satisfaction, but ultimately underscoring what was missing. For a late Victorian Irish Catholic, the lack of his own family—wife, children, and home—left a void not even his extended family could fill. When the glasses finally stopped clinking in the clubhouse below, and the cardplayers and hangers-on had departed or crashed into exhausted sleep, when Tim Sullivan at last entered his own bedroom alone to rest, what did he see when he paused in front of the mirror?

7

George and Charlie and Willie and Tim

William Randolph Hearst would run for anything. He'd run
for Alderman or President. It didn't make any difference.
　　　　　　　　　　　　　　　　—Big Tim Sullivan

WITH THE MAYORAL TERM OF OFFICE EXTENDED FROM TWO TO
four years, the municipal elections of 1905 were an even greater
prize for the parties and factions. Tammany was in good shape
for the contest as McClellan's term in office had gone reasonably
smoothly. The city's first subway line was opened and ground-
breaking had begun on a new Pennsylvania Station. The mayor,
however, was showing signs of becoming a problem. According to
his own account, McClellan's relationship with Murphy began to
deteriorate when the Tammany boss and Bourke Cockran came
to city hall for a meeting. Cockran, who did the talking, asked
McClellan to "throw the town wide open." The mayor asked if
that meant prostitution, liquor, and gambling. When Cockran
responded affirmatively, McClellan proceeded to tell him "exactly what I thought of him."[1] From this point on McClellan knew
that a complete break with Tammany was inevitable.

Under the circumstances, Murphy's decision to stay with Mc-
Clellan made little sense. McClellan claimed that Murphy offered to send him back to the House of Representatives if he
would bow out of the race. But although McClellan claimed he
did not find City Hall congenial, he feared being "nothing but
another Tammany mayor," and felt he needed another term to
"vindicate myself in the eyes of the people."[2] Consequently,
McClellan announced he would run for the nomination and re-
election. Faced with the prospect of his former ally running as an
independent and splitting the Democratic vote and losing the
election, Murphy had no choice but to go along. McClellan's recollections are feasible, but he wrote his account after his relation-

109

ship with Murphy, Sullivan, and Tammany was completely broken and poisoned. This may well have colored his account of events, which are impossible to verify.

The wild card in the contest was the presence of millionaire publisher William Randolph Hearst. Hearst had served as a Democratic congressman with Tammany's backing but sought a higher-profile office, and the position of New York City mayor, perhaps a stepping-stone to the New York State governor's mansion, provided such a place. Hearst was disliked by many for his forays into sensationalistic, distorted, and sometimes false stories—a practice that became known as "yellow journalism." But his wealth and possession of a major means of propaganda— his newspapers—made his personal aspirations dangerous to Tammany.

By 1905 Hearst had organized the Municipal Ownership League, a nascent political party that demanded that the city's transportation and utilities become public corporations. Though orthodox socialists disdained Hearst for his ego-driven politics, the Municipal Ownership League attracted considerable support throughout the city. It had particular appeal to those who were uncomfortable with Tammany while finding the Fusionists punctilious and puritanical. Hearst's urban populist stance posed a direct threat to Tammany by threatening its base—the Irish American vote. Hearst received the support from many Irish American labor leaders, and the press baron aggressively sought the Irish vote by portraying McClellan as an elite snob and castigating Murphy for his alleged aristocratic habits.[3] Tammany slowly began to realize that it faced a challenge to its major voting bloc as real as the one that had been posed by Henry George's Labor Party in the 1880s, and if it was to survive the Democracy, it had to deploy every weapon in its playbook.[4]

The Fusionists were deflated when William Travers Jerome declined to accept their nod for mayor. Republicans opted out of the Fusion alliance and decided to run a candidate on their own line, finally settling on William M. Ivins as their mayoral nominee. Hearst, who had been out of town, returned to the city on September 30, still acting coy about his intentions. Though the powers at the Wigwam had already determined on renominating McClellan, the formality of a convention, useful as a pep rally for the rank and file, was required for official candidacy.

The New York City Democrats assembled for their nominating convention at Carnegie Hall on the night of October 5, 1905. The Sullivan clan arrived en masse at the assembly, Big and Little Tim were joined by Florrie and another lieutenant, M. Clarence Padden, who had been give the nickname "Colonel" by Croker. Padden was known as the "Dude of the Bowery" for his extensive wardrobe, while some reporters, playing on his pseudorank, described him as "the aide de camp to the army of Sullivans."[5] Reporters covering the event noted that the Sullivan coterie "got the nosiest reception of any of the notables . . ."[6] The proceedings went off smoothly with Murphy and the Sullivans working together harmoniously to ensure the Tammany slate was accepted without dispute. Big Tim himself introduced a resolution commending President Theodore Roosevelt for negotiating the Treaty of Portsmouth, which ended the Russo-Japanese War. Accepting the nomination as mayor, George McClellan Jr. stated he did so "without pledge to any man or set of men."[7] Such a statement was often a pro forma device intended to deflect charges of bossism, but the mayor's sinking alliance with Murphy gave the words extra bite. Events would reveal that McClellan, with his eye on greater prizes, meant what he said, setting the stage for a confrontation between city hall and Tammany, which the Sullivans would attempt to exploit for their own advantage.

A week later the Municipal Ownership Party held their own convention at Carnegie Hall. Reporters from the *New York Times* noted the crowd was larger and more enthusiastic than those at either the Republican or Democratic conventions. Hearst received the mayoral nomination, pledging municipal control over the city's transit and gasworks, which he argued would reduce costs and prices. As a portent of things to come, the crowd booed loudly whenever Murphy's name was mentioned. Indeed, as the campaign developed, Hearst, his writers, and cartoonists virtually ignored McClellan—both sides ignored Ivins—and ran directly against Murphy as a symbol of Tammany corruption. Hearst slammed Murphy as the "Colossus of Graft," while his artists turned out cartoons picturing the Tammany boss in convict's stripes. The caption accompanying one such drawing read, "Look out, Murphy! It's a short lockstep from Delmonico's to Sing Sing."[8] Murphy also took jabs from Jerome, who kept asking, "Where did he get it [his money]? Where did

Good Ground and the automobile and the liveried servants come from?"[9]

Hearst's challenge left some in a quandary. The *Tribune* argued that with Tammany and Hearst splitting the vote, a Republican like Ivins could win. The *Times* contended that anti-Tammany candidates were only successful when political scandals became so great that the citizenry was outraged. No such sense of discontent existed in 1905, the *Times* observed. Dismissing the possibility of a Republican victory, the *Times'* editorialist discounted the "Hearst Scare." The voters of New York, he trumpeted, had "not gone down to that ignoble depth of degradation." But it was obvious that Hearst was exactly what the newspaper feared. The *Times* writer went on to declare "that a candidate of his character, antecedents, occupation and principles, or want of them, should cut any serious figure at all in a campaign, or receive more that a mindless 'crank' vote supplies an argument to those who are skeptical about the advantages of popular suffrage."[10] Yet as election day neared, it seemed increasingly possible that the press lord might triumph. At the end of the campaign, the *Times,* finally discovering a political organization it loathed more than Tammany, ran sample ballots showing voters how to split their ticket for both McClellan and Jerome, who was running for district attorney independently. The *Tribune* instructed its readers how to split a vote for Ivins and Jerome.

Tammany responded by pulling out all the stops, sending two hundred street-corner and "cart-tail" orators into the city's thirty-five assembly districts, while the "dough committee" dispensed the "mother's milk of politics"—cash. McClellan opened German, Italian, Jewish, and Latin American "bureaus" to get his message out to the polyglot neighborhoods.[11] Tammany ripped into Hearst as a socialist and supporter of anarchy. The Democrats printed posters featuring Hearst in a yellow suit fleeing from a bomb labeled "Czolgosz," the name of McKinley's assassin. This alluded to an editorial which ran in Hearst papers before the president was killed that seemed to support assassination as a political act. The Hall also began urging Republicans to vote for a candidate who could win—McClellan—as the only way to block Hearst, widely viewed as a dangerous demagogue in GOP ranks.

The Democracy called upon its most prestigious speaker, Bourke Cockran, to ratchet up the tone against Hearst. On October 29, Cockran addressed a Democratic rally in Carnegie Hall attacking politicians who preached socialism—a term used to describe Hearst's agenda. Four days later Tammany staged a massive torchlight parade in support of their ticket. At about 9:30 PM, twenty thousand marchers from all eleven districts south of Fourteenth Street began to file past the Wigwam, where inside a hundred more heard Cockran assail Hearst for "promoting anarchy."[12] Reporters described the downtown neighborhoods as "ablaze with lights from red fire-sticks [flares], calcium lights, and torches . . . Nothing like it has been seen in the City since the famous sound-money parades when McKinley was a candidate for the presidency."[13]

All the Democratic clubs and their allies filed past Tammany Hall, led by their luminaries. Murphy himself marched, and McClellan, arriving late from a campaign event in Queens, strode up the steps of the Wigwam to acknowledge the cheers of his supporters. Bands continually thumped out "Tammany," the campaign song of the season, though some occasionally broke out with "There'll Be a Hot Time in the Old Town Tonight." But the Sullivan organization bands tramping up from their headquarters seemed to know only one tune—"The Bowery." The mass demonstration on the outside, and Cockran's bitter denunciations of Hearst on the inside, struck some reporters as an indication of Tammany's fear of the publisher's following.[14]

Hearst's supporters held their last rally at Madison Square Garden two days before the election. Twelve thousand Hearstites jammed the building while an additional twenty thousand supporters filled the streets outside.[15] Hearst and his lieutenants stoked up the crowd with their rhetoric, while the audience took up a popular tune, "Everyone Works But Father," changing the last word to Murphy. The Hearst extravaganza was the last major event of the campaign. Murphy took the threat from Hearst seriously enough that he distributed $225,000 for election-day expenses, an unusually high amount, attesting to the perceived danger.[16]

The Democratic campaign ended with the Sullivans' traditional Sunday before Election Day rally at Miner's Bowery Theater. A host of Democratic speakers, including Senator Tom Grady, Thomas F. McIntyre, Maurice Blumenthal, and corporation counsel John F. Delany, roused the audience with tales of their opponent's infamy and shortcomings. One of the high points was a bit of doggerel composed by Dan Boland, the "Bowery Bard," titled "Big Tim."

Who is the idol of the "boys,"
and revels in election noise—
to him the sweetest of all joys?
  "Big Tim!"
Who, when the "banner" looms in sight,
will pay your doss on a winter's night,
and now calls you in his fight?
  "Big Tim!"
Who, on own old Bowery here,
where foams the great, big scoop o' beer,
has proved himself true and sincere?
  "Big Tim!"
Who, when the foes of liberty,
invade this "garden of the free,"
comes out and says, "We'll let 'em see"?
  "Big Tim!"
Who when your rent is overdue,
and troubles manifold accrue,
takes out his roll, a helper true?
  "Big Tim!"[17]

The preliminary speakers spent more time bashing Jerome than Hearst, although Grady opined that the newspaper tycoon had as much chance of becoming mayor as he had of becoming head of the "Irish Republic"—at the time only a dream of hard-core Irish revolutionaries. Little Tim then took the stage and presented the man who "needs no introduction," the Big Feller himself. For fully five minutes the crowd roared its approval with cheers, applause, and shouts of "Hello, Tim," "How's the old sod?" and "You're de lad."[18]

When the audience finally quieted, the Big Feller went right to the issue at hand. "Here we go again, like the clown in the circus. But we are better off than the Republicans who will vote for a Democrat next Tuesday, while we will vote for a Democrat who is bred in the purple. Hearst is running to destroy the party that gave him political life."[19] Tim assured his audience that he was not going to orate à la Demosthenes, but give them "plain Bowery talk"—as he always did. He ripped Hearst's gathering at Carnegie Hall, stating "ladies" couldn't go there because of all the nasty things that were spoken, while the gentle sex was safe to attend Democratic rallies in the Bowery "without fear of being shocked. We might have eaten with our knives at one time, but that was many years ago and we have improved. And it all gets down to next Tuesday; that's our chance. We are going to vote for George B. McClellan. . . ."[20] Tim closed with the admonition to keep intraparty disputes in the family and out of the general election and took his seat. The theater again erupted into cheers, after which most of the crowd headed for the exits, a deflating, if expected, experience for those scheduled to speak after the Big Feller. Reporters on the scene noted that the mayor's name— which Tim mispronounced as "McClennan"—received nothing like the enthusiasm they showered on Tim.

The mayoral election of 1905 was the basis for a key scene in Orson Welles's classic *Citizen Kane,* whose title character was a thinly disguised version of Hearst. In the movie, Charles Foster Kane/William Randolph Hearst's political nemesis is "Boss Jim Gettys"—no ethnic element there. Gettys destroys the seemingly unstoppable Kane by revealing his affair with a singer when Kane refuses to bow out of the race. In the actual mayoral election of 1905, made the gubernatorial contest in the film, Tammany beat Hearst the old-fashioned way—fraud and street muscle.

When the votes were finally tallied on election day, McClellan held city hall with a margin under four thousand votes. The Democrats also took the presidency of the Board of Aldermen and comptroller. As expected, the maverick Jerome was reelected. According to the *Times,* all that saved McClellan was the "effectiveness of the Tammany organization in Manhattan and the Bronx" and thousands of Republicans crossing over to prevent Hearst's election, "which they believed would be a calamity to the City."[21] That was true enough as far as it went, but there was more to the Tammany victory than that. Amid rumors of numerous floaters and repeaters, the returns from the downtown districts came in so slowly that the situation, in the words of one reporter, did not "look healthy."[22] Additionally, the *Tribune* reported that "all evening there was a procession of [poll] watchers, many of them bruised and battered with tales of illegal voting" making their way from polls in the downtown wards.[23]

Convinced he had been cheated from his victory, Hearst declared the election was stolen through "Tammany trickery."[24]

The press baron and would-be mayor asserted that "We have won
the election . . . the recount will show that we have won the
election by many thousands of votes."[25] Most observers believed
Hearst was right. But they also doubted that it would make any
difference. "There is a well-founded suspicion," the *Tribune* commented, "that to make McClellan's election sure Tammany election district officials took the benefit of the doubt in thousands of
[voters'] cases, and they will follow up their advantage when the
Board of Aldermen, in control of the Sullivans, comes officially to
canvass the ballots."[26] The *Tribune* understood the realities of
New York City politics as Hearst did not. Though his papers
bellowed about the fraud, Hearst's confident expectations that
the election would be reversed went unfulfilled.[27] As days turned
into weeks, then months, William Randolph Hearst resigned
himself to licking his wounds and preparing for the next election.

McClellan's second term was marked by a complete split from
Murphy. Partly this resulted from McClellan's aspirations for
higher office and the paradox of Tammany support. He needed
the backing of the Hall to prevail in contests in the city, but a
close connection with the notorious Democracy made him suspect
in national contests. Consequently, McClellan was determined to
prove his independence. The mayor's course of action may well
have been determined by the nature of his narrow victory. He
concluded he had been saved by Republican votes, and that Murphy was weaker than presumed.[28]

The crucial confrontation between the mayor and the Tammany boss took place shortly after the 1905 election. Murphy
arrived at McClellan's house to discuss patronage and positions.
Although Murphy had the reputation of being the most modest of
drinkers, the mayor claimed the Tammany boss "had evidently
been drinking and was in the condition that is known colloquially
as 'fighting full.'"[29] Murphy presented a number of men for key
positions and McClellan declined them all. After each name was
offered, the mayor asked for another candidate, and Murphy replied that the rejected nominee was the only one he had. Finally
the Tammany leader announced, "That's my slate. Take it or
leave it. I got no other candidates."[30] When McClellan showed no
intention of changing his stance, Murphy left. In the mayor's
posthumously published autobiography, McClellan claimed that
the Tammany boss was so intoxicated that as he tried to stand,

"his legs had gone back on him. I was obliged to help him up and support him to his cab. . . ."[31]

The now-open feud between McClellan and Murphy boiled over after the Tammany boss surprisingly agreed to support Hearst for governor in 1906. McClellan had been hoping for the nod and was bitter about Murphy's choice. For his part, Murphy believed Hearst was popular in some Democratic circles and backing him for governor might defang him in the city. McClellan, who despised Hearst, determined to take on Murphy once and for all and break his power in Tammany. As the election season neared in the autumn of 1905, McClellan conceived a three-part plan. First, he would block Hearst's nomination by the Democrats, handing Murphy a defeat in the process. Second, he hoped to engineer the nomination of William Travers Jerome for governor and see him elected. Jerome, often a tough opponent of the Hall, was a Democrat, even if an idiosyncratic one, and McClellan thought it possible for him to get the gubernatorial nod. Last, having succeeded with parts one and two, McClellan would depose the weakened Murphy when the Tammany Executive Committee met in December. The agenda was ambitious and risky. Much rode on the mayor's relations with the Sullivans.

To execute his plan, McClellan needed allies among the city's Democrats, and the Sullivan clan appeared to fit the bill. For their part, the two Tims appreciated the value of working with the mayor to promote their own followers and strengthen their overall position. As is true in much of the political machinations involving Tammany, the steps in the minuet between the Sullivans and the mayor are obscure. Big Tim was not a man to leave a paper trail, and in his own account, composed after events had embittered him, the mayor presented himself as a straight-arrow opponent of graft and corruption. However, contemporary newspaper accounts consistently stated that McClellan regularly placed Sullivan men in city jobs. As the *Herald* put it, "They have had practically everything they asked at his hands."[32]

McClellan's view of the Sullivans is hard to evaluate. His own recollections are unlikely to be a totally reliable guide to his feelings at the time. He later stated that Big Tim repeatedly told him that he disliked both Hearst and Murphy and would support his efforts to defeat them both.[33] At any rate, it is clear that McClellan believed he had the backing of the Sullivans as the Democrats prepared for the election season that got under way in September 1906.

Though it seems indisputable that the Big Feller gave McClellan some reason to count on his support, he had not cut his ties to Murphy. Moreover, he was determined not to make a choice on candidates until events forced his hand. On September 15, Little Tim met with Fire Commissioner John H. O'Brien, McClellan's major agent. The conference was widely interpreted as an attempt to discover the Sullivans' intentions.[34] The following day, Big Tim declared his support for his old ally, William Sulzer, for governor. Some observers pronounced the move a masterful strategic stroke, saving the Sullivans from a difficult political position. By declaring for Sulzer, they avoided coming out in the open against the mayor and jeopardizing the considerable patronage they had received.[35] At the same time, their influence in Tammany was expanded since they held a balance of power in the Democratic civil war. Other voices argued the move helped McClellan more than Murphy, as it gave the Sullivan clan the option of throwing support to Jerome—McClellan's choice—if the convention began to pull toward him. In any event, it was taken as a signal Big Tim opposed Hearst.[36]

The first collision between McClellan and Murphy took place in the Democratic primaries of September 18 when party voters elected district leaders. Basically, it was a matter of choosing Murphy's or McClellan's man in the district—except the ones under Sullivan clan control. When the ballots were tallied, Murphy controlled seventeen districts, McClellan nine. The Sullivan clan held seven, "where they have always held their strength."[37] Assuming the Sullivan block would join the mayor's forces, the *New York Herald* pointed out that the results gave Murphy a one-vote majority in the Executive Committee. Should two "doubtful" districts join him, McClellan "could carry out his promise to depose Mr. Murphy" in December.[38] But others weren't so sure. The *Times* counted the Sullivan bloc with Murphy's districts because the Sullivans "have always been with 'the organization,' and Mr. Murphy appears to be 'the organization' still."[39] Since convention delegate strengths were based on district numbers, Murphy would head into the convention with fifty-seven votes to McClellan's twenty-seven. The Sullivans controlled twenty-one.

As the six trains bearing 1,800 Tammany members headed for the New York State Democratic Convention at Buffalo, the out-

come seemed in doubt. Charlie Murphy was still disingenu-
ously—and unconvincingly—declaring that he had no personal
choice for governor, though it had been open knowledge that he
had been pushing for Hearst's nomination for months.[40] Murphy's problem was that many Democrats loathed Hearst, who
had consistently employed his papers to excoriate Tammany and
regular Democratic organizations statewide. Certainly Murphy
had felt the sting of Hearst's editorialists and cartoonists, and
many were puzzled by his seemingly perverse support of the
newspaper tycoon. Murphy professed to believe that the Democrats could only win with Hearst on the ticket. "Why, you know
we can win with no one but Hearst. Why can't you take a common
sense view of the situation?" he asked at a meeting with Erie
County Democrats after he reached Buffalo and finally dropped
his feigned neutrality.[41] Murphy's real game was to distract
Hearst from further attacks on Democrats and split him off from
his Independent League power base, thereby neutralizing that
threat, and using the campaign to advance Democratic gains in
the city. Not incidentally, he intended to defeat McClellan by
blocking his choice for governor, William Travers Jerome.

The Sullivans were a major problem for Murphy. The Tammany boss's ability to control a majority of the delegates was
uncertain without their support. Newspapers continued to report
that both the Murphy-Hearst and McClellan factions had been
persuaded that Big Tim sided with them. On September 20, as
the smoke was clearing from the primaries and Tammany prepared itself for the trip to the state convention at Buffalo, a friend
asked Little Tim if their support of Sulzer was serious or whether
it was just a ploy to buy time before they came out for Hearst or
Jerome. "What would we want either Hearst or Jerome for?" the
Little Feller snapped. "What has either of those fellows done for
the Democratic Party in this city? Both have been fighting the
organization these many years." When asked who the Sullivans
preferred for governor, Little Tim snapped, "What's the matter
with Sulzer? Isn't he alright?" The questioner pressed Little Tim
about their plans in Buffalo and whether they would stick by
their endorsement of Sulzer at the convention. "Well, Buffalo
isn't my district and I'm not interested in anything outside my
own district. But Sulzer is alright."[42] Little Tim's answers satisfied no one and gave nothing away—as intended.

Nevertheless, most reporters continued to believe the Sullivan clan would ultimately throw in their lot with McClellan and endorse Jerome's nomination. McClellan certainly thought so. In his autobiography he stated that Big Tim met him the morning before he left for Buffalo. "Mr. Mayor," the Big Feller affirmed, "if I am in the meeting of the [state] committee I swear to you, so help me God, I shall stand behind you to the finish."[43] Control of the state committee meant control of the convention—and nominations—and the mayor believed that with Big Tim and one other delegate pledged to him, he could command the process.

The "machine within a machine," comprising the second wave of Tammanyites, arrived in Buffalo on September 24. The Sullivan Association required two trains with each district being assigned a car for delegates, alternates, and friends. The Sullivans' trains were deemed "by far the most joyous," and Big Florrie confessed that his car was supplied with 200 bottles of whiskey, 100 cases of beer, and five cases of "soft stuff." Supplementary provisions included 1,000 ham sandwiches, 500 assorted sandwiches, ten boxes of cigars, and twenty-five packs of cards, which were broken out the moment the train left New York.[44] Big and Little Tim's underlings may have been able to enjoy the party, but for the leaders, some very somber work had to be done. The time had come for them to climb down off the fence and join one side or the other.

Upon arrival at Buffalo, Big Tim went directly to the Iroquois Hotel where most of the Democrats were staying. His first stop was McClellan's apartments on the ninth floor. After he concluded his meeting with the mayor, he ran into Hugh McCarren, the Kings County leader, who was angling to give the nomination to Judge William Gaynor. A meeting with Murphy in his apartment followed, after which Sullivan and McCarren returned to McClellan's suite. By that time Murphy had gone to the room used by the state committee, where he was again joined by McCarren and Sullivan. The three leaders whispered intently to one another, but onlookers and reporters were unable to tell what was going on. But the wheeling and dealing was apparently just the last steps in settling the decisive events of the convention.[45]

In fact, Big Tim had made his choice even before leaving New York. He telegraphed his proxy to Murphy, who handed it over to one of his followers to use.[46] While the sequence of events is confused, Big Tim apparently informed McClellan of his intentions when he met him at his apartment in the Iroquois. Upon leaving the mayor he was asked how events were going and replied, "It looks as if Tammany was going for Hearst."[47] Shortly after, ignorant of the situation, John H. O'Brien, McClellan's floor manager, asked for Tim's proxy at the state committee in the event he was not there. The fire commissioner also asked for Battery Dan Finn's as well. Reportedly, Big Tim "fidgeted" and mumbled something about going off to Niagara Falls with Finn and quickly broke off the conversation. But he never made the visit. Instead he went into the state committee and voted with Murphy.[48]

About the same time that the *New York Times* let its readers know that the Sullivans and Murphy "are fully agreed," the Murphy-Hearst forces took control of three key committees: the Committee on Contested Seats, the Committee on Platform and Resolutions, and the Committee on Permanent Organization. The Committee on Contested Seats then proceeded to expel all of McClellan's delegates, O'Brien included. In order to make it easier for regular Democrats to swallow Hearst, the Platform Committee devised a highly conservative agenda that repudiated virtually everything Hearst claimed to stand for. The Democrats accepted Hearst for governor and took former Independence League candidates for lieutenant governor and secretary of state. Having no further use of the organization he founded to further his career, Hearst acceded to the removal of every other Independence League candidate from the ballot. All that was left were the formalities.

On September 26 the New York Democracy—Tammany Hall—held its caucus. The only real issue was to vote up or down on the unit rule—meaning that whatever the majority decided would be converted into one bloc vote that would be delivered by Murphy. In the voting, only two of McClellan's stalwarts sided with the mayor, though there were a number of absentees who apparently gagged at the prospect of voting for Hearst. Big Tim looked glum, an unusual expression for him. Already, he was being attacked by the McClellan delegates and excoriated by some of the newspapers. "Big Tim who has always been known in gambling circles . . . as a man who never broke his word, is pointed at and gazed at" in the hotel.[49] The *New York Herald* declaimed "political history records no story of deeper disloyalty and double dealing than that of the Sullivans desertion of Mayor McClellan and their alliance with Charles F. Murphy."[50] During the debate on the unit rule, the Big Feller rose to speak. Delivering what some called "the most remarkable speech probably that he ever made," tears filled his eyes.

> I vote aye. A great deal has been said about me being a traitor, and being treacherous, and I want to say right now that I have never bid to any man and have never broken my word. That is the secret of my success. In all the years I have been in public service there is not a man living who can say I ever deceived him, and any man with whom I have ever had any dealing will tell you that I never went back on my word. I have never been against the organization and never will be. I have never told anyone I was against it, and I want to deny all those allegations of treachery. I don't know what started them. I am an organization man. You all know it, and I am glad to vote for the enforcement of the unit rule and abide by it. No one can ever make me break it.[51]

The unit rule was adopted sixty-three to twenty-six. When names of candidates were placed in contention, Julius Harnsburger, representing the Sullivans, placed Sulzer's name before the caucus. The outcome was preordained. Sulzer was voted down and Tammany voted for Hearst.

The mood at the next day's convention was sullen. Hearst was in; only the nicety of counting the votes remained. But the Democrats, Hearst's supporters excepted, were clearly unhappy with the candidate that had been foisted on them. The only enthusiastic moment came when Sulzer's name was placed in nomination. "Riotous" applause broke out for five minutes with cries of "Sulzer," "Billie Sulzer," followed by "Come on Sullivan! You're for Sulzer you know." But Tim had made his choice. "Not a Sullivan stood up," the *Herald* reported. "Big and Little Tim sat indifferent."[52] When it was all over, Hearst had 809 votes to 124 for Sulzer.

After the balloting, a series of speeches on the Democratic platform denounced socialism—a code word for Hearst's objectives—and municipal ownership, the centerpiece of Hearst's political program. As the *Times* observed, "the organization has no use for him personally and is supporting him only because it needs him in its business."[53] Indeed, word soon circulated that, whatever public face he put on it, Murphy did not expect Hearst to win, "and he would be entirely satisfied if [he] lost, provided it enabled [him] to carry his ticket in New York."[54]

Trying to make sense of Tammany-Sullivan clan politics is much like peering through a fogged-over window. The players can be identified, their movements noted, but the voices are muffled, the gestures indecipherable, and the motives hidden. In the end, the observer sees who stays and who goes, but why the principles acted as they did remains uncertain. In no situation was that more true than Big Tim's role in the McClellan-Murphy-Hearst struggle in the autumn of 1906.

The cumulative evidence leaves little doubt that Tim had made some kind of commitment to McClellan, though perhaps he did not use the iron-clad language McClellan later recorded. In his own mind he may have been more tentative than McClellan and his followers perceived him. But though it was amusing and lucrative to play both sides, the feat could not be extended indefinitely, and the two Tims had to make their decision as the convention opened. Whatever he had said to McClellan—and Sullivan no doubt despised Hearst—Murphy spoke for Tammany. Tim may not have wanted the job of boss, and was impregnable within his bailiwick, but in the end, as the *Times* had pointed out, he was an organization man. At least that part of his speech at the Tammany caucus was honest. But the Big Feller knew, somewhere, that he had led McClellan on, and his subdued and somber mien at Buffalo reflected his discomfort over his own duplicity as much as it did disgust at voting for Hearst. For his part, McClellan had no doubt what had happened. "I think that Big Tim was the slickest crook who ever sold me out," he later wrote.[55]

In October a periodical called *Outlook* published a piece stating that after Sullivan had promised to stand with McClellan, Hearst's *New York American* lashed him in articles and cartoons, damning him as the "dirtiest crook in the City." Shortly after, the attacks ceased because the Big Feller had gone over to Murphy.[56] The account is unconvincing. Big Tim had taken a lot of condemnation and excoriation from Hearst and others—as had Murphy—shrugged it off, and kept going. It seems hard to imagine such an assault motivated his choice of sides. One unanswered question is the price he received for finally standing with Murphy. Part of it was getting a commitment that no Hearst candidate would oppose his choice to replace him in Congress, but this hardly seems sufficient compensation for his sullied reputation and the crucial nature of his support.[57] Whatever he got from Murphy remains hidden behind the frosted glass of time. Hopefully, for Tim's sake, it was considerable, as things did not get easier as the campaign progressed.

The shotgun wedding arranged at Buffalo lasted through election day with the major players exhibiting poorly concealed mutual loathing. In early October, it seemed that Hearst would break his pledge to support local Tammany candidates for state and local offices. Hearst publicly backed off, but his Independence League then insisted it would field its own slate of nominees. In short order the Independence League candidates were dropped or forced off the ballot by legal maneuverings.[58] But one thing Hearst did insist on—he would not run on the same ballot as Big Tim Sullivan.

It was understood that when the Big Feller left Congress, he wanted to resume his seat in the state senate. Hearst, however, despised him, possibly for his role in defeating his mayoral campaign in 1905. He may have swallowed an alliance with Murphy to attain the governor's chair, but he was determined to thwart Big Tim. It was even claimed that Sullivan knew it would be impossible for him to run if the party nominated Hearst, which made his final decision appear all the more odd.[59] Nevertheless, when the city's senate districts held their nominating conventions there was a massive show of support for the Dry Dollar. The convention was held at Battery Dan's Huron Club on Hudson Street. A steady stream of Bowery supporters descended on the club, and the Big Feller was escorted into the room by Tom Foley and his lieutenants. Tim, however, was uncharacteristically hesitant and subdued, and the convention adjourned without making a nomination. As the crowd filtered out, the throng gathered around Tim, shaking his hand and wishing him well. "They want me to run, but I don't want to run and don't think I will run," Sullivan told reporters.[60] Asked if it was true that Hearst had ordered him off the ticket, Sullivan scoffed. "Forced? Me? I guess not. If I decide not to run, Hearst will have had nothing to do with it." He then quickly added, "But if anyone says I intend to denounce the Democratic candidate for governor he tells a lie."[61] After Tim left, Battery Dan boldly told the newsmen that everyone "below the line" wanted Sullivan, but if the Big Feller declined, another suitable candidate would be found. Experienced observers noted that the adjournment without a nomination left the ball in the court of Hearst's Independence League, who had the weekend to name its own nominee or back off.

The next day, Little Tim signaled the way the wind was blowing. Claiming that his older cousin's business interests mitigated against his going to Albany, the Little Feller announced that the Big Feller was not running for the state senate. There was no outside pressure in the decision, Timothy P. insisted. "It's business, nothing but business."[62] Like everyone else he went out of his way to say that Hearst would be supported downtown.

The drama ended on October 10 when the Eleventh Senate District nominated Dominick F. Mullaney for the position. Although his numerous supporters still wanted him to run, the Independence League threw down the gauntlet with their own nomination for the seat. There is no doubt that Sullivan could have prevailed in the district, but his candidacy might have led to other challenges and split the vote, jeopardizing the city seats, which was the reason Murphy decided to harness the newspaper tycoon in the first place. So, again, Tim sided with the organization and, like a fighter taking a dive in a bout with a lesser man, gave up his chance to return to Albany in 1906. Indeed, he did not appear at the convention, sending a letter pleading the pressure of business interests prevented his running. Mullaney himself was a placeholder. "A faithful adherent of the Sullivans," he publicly conceded that he was only running because the two Tims had asked him to do so.[63]

The campaign ran on to its inevitable conclusion. Despite attempts to gag the widespread distaste for Hearst among Tammanyites and other Democrats, the veneer of unity began to crack. Hugh McCarren publicly denounced Hearst and was congratulated by Richard Croker, who wired him his commendation for his "manly" attack on the official nominee.[64] Nevertheless most of the district leaders trudged on to the end, following the glimpse of light thrown off by the probability of sweeping most of the city and state offices.

Whatever their personal disgust, the Sullivans held their standard Sunday before Election Day rally at Miner's Bowery Theater. The Big Feller was present, but said nothing. It was left to Bourke Cockran to go through the motions of a rally. Well aware of what was on everybody's mind, Cockran reminded the gathering that Big Tim had not turned on the Democratic candidate.

"Never has his loyalty been so tested," Cockran proclaimed with massive understatement, "and never was it so triumphant as today. He has refused himself to be a candidate, but he has promised the largest majority ever returned for a Democratic candidate. I make this promise on his behalf."[65]

Whether Tim had made any such promise to anyone is debatable. Before the state convention in Buffalo, he declared, "If they nominate this fellow [Hearst] they can all go plumb to hell as far as I am concerned."[66] Things changed after he threw in his lot with Murphy. But his public professions of support rang hollow, and while he did nothing to impede the Hearst campaign, he certainly did little to promote it. When Tim declined the state senatorial candidacy, some papers noted the Sullivans were in a splendid position to defeat Hearst. They didn't knife the yellow press baron, but they dragged their feet. When the polls closed on election day, Charles Evans Hughes, the Republican candidate, won by 63,338 votes. Hearst took the city by 71,644 votes, far fewer than Coler four years previously.[67] Despite Hughes's victory, the Democrats triumphed in almost every other state and city position. It was a dirty job, but the Murphy-Sullivan faction, as the papers called them, got most of what they wanted without being saddled by Hearst.

None of the principals in the 1906 election emerged from the contest with their dignity and reputation intact. Murphy achieved his major goals. He neutralized an independent Hearst and used him "as a club to destroy McClellan."[68] The price he paid was publicly "fawning at the foot that kicked him, and licking the hand that had so mercilessly applied the scourge to his back."[69] The price Hearst paid for his nomination was abandoning both his own political movement and every principle he had ever espoused. Though he might not have known it, his political career in New York was over. He would run for office again, and remain a nuisance, but as far as Tammany was concerned, he had been defanged and ceased to pose a menace.

Big Tim, who had always prided himself for standing by his friends, was believed by many to have sold McClellan out. The New York Herald, a McClellan supporter, was almost beside itself, predicting how McClellan would wreak revenge on the perfidious Sullivans. The city "will be closed up tighter than it ever has been before," the paper proclaimed, promising tough times for Tim's saloons, poolrooms, and gambling spots.[70] The attacks on his political integrity made during the convention were only the beginning of the price he paid for staying loyal to the Tiger. To assuage the Democrats' gubernatorial candidate, he put his own desire to return to state office on the back burner, and—however hollow the declarations—professed support for the man who insisted that he do it.

As the *Herald* predicted, McClellan sought payback for his humiliation at Buffalo. On October 26 eighty-five out of eighty-six police captains were transferred to different precincts. The *Herald* saw the move as "an absolute scattering of the Sullivan men, and the politicians declare that it was inspired from the City Hall to make it difficult to carry out 'deals' with police on election day."[71] The seething mayor then unleashed his commissioner of accounts, the capable and scrupulous John Purroy Mitchell, who found millions in city funds had been wasted through various kinds of fraud.[72] Mitchell then sought indictments against the borough presidents of Manhattan, the Bronx, and Queens—all Murphy allies—who were removed by Hughes. If that wasn't enough, McClellan cut Tammany off from any part of the patronage from the $100 million Catskill Water Supply project and rejected Murphy's candidates for city jobs.[73]

Displaying the type of aggressiveness in political combat that his father conspicuously lacked in the real thing, McClellan pursued his attempt to unseat Murphy as Tammany boss at the December 27 Executive Committee meeting. But Murphy proved to be as shrewd against the son as Robert E. Lee had been with the father. As he did with Deverey, "Silent Charlie" changed the rules of Tammany's Executive Committee, allowing outgoing members to determine the qualifications of newly elected members and permitting the committee to enlarge itself at its own discretion. Consequently, when McClellan attempted to induce some board members to turn on Murphy, the wily leader enlarged the group from thirty-five to forty-three—the newcomers being his supporters, who easily repulsed McClellan's attack.[74] Though he might not have known it at the time, George B. McClellan's political career would end with his mayoralty. Without Tammany support he could not receive the Democratic nomination to any post in New York. And Charlie Murphy had determined never to give him the nod again.

Possibly encouraged by representatives of the national Democrats, an attempt was made to heal the breach between city hall

and the New York Democracy. In spring 1907, Big Tim, representing Tammany—and certainly his own interests—met with
William B. Ellison, the city corporation counsel, fellow Democrat,
occasional advisor, and personal friend. The two men discussed a
pact in which McClellan would keep out of Tammany Hall matters, including primary fights, and the mayor would be left to run
the administration. Ellison would be on hand to prevent the appointment of anyone anathema to the Hall.[75] Ellison apparently
had McClellan's approval to negotiate with Tim, but when he
announced that a compact had been secured, the mayor told reporters that he had made no deal affecting his position in any
way.[76]

The situation hung fire for a month while rumors flew. Some
claimed Murphy would be forced to resign in order to repair Tammany's clout at city hall. McClellan's denunciation of Murphy
during the convention the previous autumn was not retracted
and, in fact, restated. The mayor, it was held, would deal with
Tammany, but not Murphy. Anticipating a future president, Mc-
Clellan declared that any rapprochement must be concluded on
the basis of "peace with honor."[77] Treating with Murphy was out,
but McClellan agreed to enter into a compact with "men whose
opinions he respected."[78] Murphy wasn't moving and informed
the press that the talks between Ellison and Sullivan in no way
involved his stepping down. Unsurprisingly, many believed the
Sullivans were angling to gain every possible advantage from the
maneuvering between Tammany and the mayor. They were probably right.

The drama came to an end in July. Ellison, whose role was key
from the Sullivan-Murphy perspective, had been undercut by the
mayor's partial disavowal of any peace settlement. McClellan
finally discharged him and began putting anti-Sullivan men in
the Street Cleaning Department, where the Big Feller had provided "hordes of men"—largely Italian—with jobs. Exactly what
the two sides were willing to discuss privately is not known. The
Times opined that if Ellison had not disclosed his discussion with
Sullivan before he briefed the mayor, a settlement would have
been reached.[79] Whether a rapprochement could have been made
with Murphy in the boss's chair is hard to see. Still, McClellan's
recent experience with Big Tim had been unhappy, yet he was
willing to let Ellison try to reach some sort of agreement with
him. Quite possibly it was dawning on the mayor that his break

with Tammany jeopardized his future political prospects. But, in the end, the wounds were too fresh and too deep to heal.

Despite the denouement, stories circulated that the Sullivans played "Murphy and McClellan against each other for all they could get out of it."[80] Exactly what that was remains, as usual, unknown. In any event, McClellan could fire Big Tim's lieutenants from appointive posts, but there was a limit to how many of Tim's plebeian followers he could dismiss from city jobs without hurting himself. The Sullivans had survived hostile administrations before, and with their grateful followers remaining in key positions throughout the city, they would again. They could also reward followers with jobs provided by their businesses' allies, who fully expected that Tammany and the "machine within a machine" would prevail over their opponents. In the meantime, the chowders, Christmas dinners, and shoe distributions were held as usual. By 1907, from Big Tim's standpoint everything was status quo ante Hearst, and the world was his oyster.

Despite the switching of the police captains, the Big Feller's gambling interests continued largely unabated during McClellan's time in city hall. The mayor's police commissioner, Theodore Bingham, reported the operation of both gambling houses and "disorderly hotels" by Tim's captains in the Lower East Side.[81] In the election year of 1909, Bingham started to clean up the area around Chatham Square, starting with a dive run by Paddy Mullin at Six Mott Street. Knowing Mullin's connection with Big Tim, one politician asked Bingham if he had cleared the arrest with the Sullivans. "The Sullivans!" Bingham exclaimed, "They can't even get the time of day from the department." A few weeks later Bingham was replaced.[82]

Throughout the cold war with city hall, and the scouring of the political landscape by Mitchell, the Sullivan clan's power battened during the McClellan's last years in office. Big and Little Tim actively supported and won yet more allies—"Boxing Bill" Frawley, Thomas McAvoy, Ross Williams, and Percival Nagle—extending their influence up the length of Manhattan and even into the Bronx.[83]

Though the Big Feller stayed in the background, allowing Little Tim to run the Sullivan Association, his pattern of operations—political, entrepreneurial, and criminal—remained essentially as they were from the time he began his career. But much else in the city was changing with increasing speed.

8

The Progressive

All Politics is Local.

—Thomas P. "Tip" O'Neill

EXCEPT FOR WINNING THE PINOCHLE CHAMPIONSHIP IN CONgress, Big Tim found Washington a disappointment and left after a second term in 1906. The rules in the House of Representatives were tight, and with the Republicans in control, there was little scope for the kind of action that engaged Tim, and he spent most of his time back in New York enjoying himself and looking after his interests. His few personal accomplishments in Congress consisted of introducing bills for private pensions. Referring to his time in the House, Sullivan dismissively snorted, "It's a piker's game. There's nothin' to this Congressman business. They use 'em for hitching posts down there."[1] Bored with Washington, unfulfilled by his extracurricular activities, the Big Feller decided to get back in the game he knew best—the New York state senate. The Hearst imbroglio delayed his return, but with the ambitious newspaper baron dispatched from the political scene, Big Tim received the nomination for the state senate from the Twelfth District on October 2, 1908. The outcome was preordained. His placeholder, William Sohraer, who had replaced Dominick Mullaney, "drop[ed] out without a whimper."[2]

The Lower East Side that Tim would represent again—his expressed desire for the office was all that was necessary for election—had been changing rapidly in the years since the new century began. The Irish and German sections of Tim's youth were now reduced to a few relict neighborhoods, their inhabitants having largely relocated to mid- and uptown areas on the West and East Side. In the Lower East Side, the area west of Broadway was turning Italian, while the streets to the east of the thoroughfare became home to one of the largest Jewish communities in the world. Between them, the Eastern European Jews and their Italian neighbors made up 85 percent of the Lower East Side by 1910.[3] The Italians tended to be indifferent to politics, but the East European Jews, who made up 50 percent of the Lower East Side by 1910, were politically involved, volatile in their interests, and attracted to socialism.[4] Many had been drawn to Hearst's popular quasi-socialistic platform, and it took all the Sullivans' best (or worst) efforts to hold their districts in the downtown areas.

Some researchers have argued that Tammany did not work hard to organize the new immigrants the same way they had labored to naturalize and register Irish newcomers ca. 1870–90. Furthermore, it was charged that Tammany distributed its spoils unevenly, with the Irish being awarded most of the public service jobs while the later-arriving Jews and Italians received various services, homeless shelters, police protection, business licenses, and new precinct houses, all of which were supposedly less valuable than employment. Jews, being more politically active, were given some jobs and political positions, though these tended to be relatively few and disproportionately minor.[5] This argument appears to undervalue the costs of the various services—charitable, social, and recreational—which were considerable. Nevertheless, it was true that Tammany did not have unlimited patronage, and there were just so many jobs to be distributed. The Irish were the best organized and most politically active of the various ethnic groups in New York before the First World War. By 1890, when they were 25 percent of the population, they made up a third of the voters,[6] and their political activism continued to exceed that of other ethnic groups into the 1920s. While Tammany's predominantly Irish leadership may have enjoyed distributing patronage plums to their fellow Celts, it was equally the case that the Irish provided the core of the reliable, manageable vote that Tammany needed to win—what today's political parties call their "base." Keeping their base satisfied was a prime consideration in Tammany calculations, and if that meant public sector jobs went disproportionately to Irish job seekers, so be it.

In contrast to the Irish, the Italian population, which included the largest percentage of return migration of all immigrant groups at the time, tended to be apathetic. Many downtown Jews were more interested in labor reform than voting, as upper-middle-class reformers discovered to their chagrin during the unrest in the garment trade, 1909–13. It was also true changes in federal and state law made it more difficult to naturalize and register new immigrants than it had been before 1890. If many Tammany politicians showed less interest in organizing the new immigrants, it had less to do with ethnocentricism—though that might play a role—than practical politics. But even if he were so inclined, Big Tim could ill afford to behave indifferently to the Jews in his district, which was the epicenter of Jewish life in America at the time.

Despite the demographic changes "below the line," Big Tim Sullivan remained personally popular in the Bowery and adjacent areas. His personal magnetism, concerned politics, and practice of dispensing rewards, promotions, and favors regardless of ethnicity stood him well. While the leadership of the "machine within a machine" remained predominately Irish—and family—he had long extended a welcome to Jewish advisors and captains. Indeed, Big Tim started many successful Jews in their careers. He is often credited with bringing Max Steuer, who became Tammany's and New York's most successful attorney, into the Democratic system.[7] After 1909, Henry Appelbaum became Tim's personal secretary and one of his closest political operatives. It was clear to most that the Big Feller liked Jews generally, thought they were smart, and admired their energy. For the most part, the downtown Jews returned the compliment. Tammany, however, was another story, and whether any other Tammany leader could do as well with the Lower East Side Jews was increasingly an open question.

It wasn't just the ethnic makeup of New York that was changing in the early years of the twentieth century, but the city's economy was changing as well, with the Lower East Side becoming the center of the nation's "rag trade"—clothing apparel. By 1909, manufacturing in Manhattan alone employed more people that the mills of Massachusetts, and most of these were in the clothing and needle trades.[8] The manufacturing sites were changing as well. While sweatshops still operated, most clothing was produced in specially constructed multifloored factory buildings. The factories may have been more spacious, but the legacy of the sweatshop lived on in long hours, low pay, and poor safety standards.

One result of the rapid expansion of clothing manufacturing was the growth of unions. Between 1909 and 1913 the number of unionized workers jumped from 30,000 to 250,000.[9] The larger proportion of workers in the garment sector was made up of women, primarily young Jewish girls, though a significant minority of Italians was involved as well. The Jewish women gravitated toward socialism or like-minded organizations. One of the largest unions in the city, the Women's Trade Union League, began to agitate against specific firms, especially those producing blouses—called shirtwaists. Their goals were typical of early twentieth-century unions—shorter hours, more pay, better conditions, and, of course, recognition of the union and collective bargaining. The rising militancy of the largely female garment workers would prove a challenge for Tammany in 1909. Despite its self-proclaimed role as voice of the masses and workers, Tammany, which received considerable campaign support from business interests, was a bulwark of the status quo. When labor agitation exploded in the autumn, Charlie Murphy would be scrambling to construct an effective response. Big Tim would prove more politically astute—and more compassionate as well.

Though the placement of the Big Feller's name on the ballot guaranteed his election in November 1908, his return to city and state politics was greeted with less enthusiasm by the reformist press. The following year, prostitution became front-page news again, as a grand jury headed by John D. Rockefeller heard evidence about police involvement in the sex trade. Perhaps inevitably, the old charges of Big Tim's supposed connection with commercial sex were revived. In June 1909, as the parties began to prepare for the fall elections, *McClure's Magazine,* a progressive, muckraking publication, ran what would later be called a "hit piece" on Tim and his allies under the guise of a report on the "Lawrence Mulligan Civic Ball." The writer, George Kibbe Turner, excoriated Tammany in general, the Sullivans in particular, and repeated the charges that had dogged Big Tim since the 1890s—his alleged connections with crime and, most explosively, prostitution. On the night of the ball, Turner wrote,

> The streets of the tenderloin lie vacant of its women; the eyes of the city detective force were focused on the great dancing hall—stuffed to the doors with painted women and lean-faced men. In the center box, held in the name of a young Jewish friend, sits "the Big Feller"— clear-skinned, fair faced and happy. Around him sit the gathering of his business and political lieutenants . . . the rulers of New York; Larry Mulligan, his stepbrother, head of this pleasing association;

Paddy Sullivan, his brother, president of the Hesper Club of gamblers, business associate, owner of the Metropole Hotel, where the "wise ones" gather; Big Tom Foley and—an exception to the general look of rosy prosperity—Little Tim Sullivan, the lean little manager of the old Third District and leader of the New York Board of Aldermen.

The council unbends; it exchanged showers of confetti; the Big Feller smiles gaily upon the frail congregation below him—the tenth short-lived generation of prostitutes he had seen at gatherings like this since, more than twenty years ago he had started his first Five Points assembly—he himself as fresh now as then. In the rear of the box a judge of the General Sessions Court sits modestly, decently, hat in hand. In the welter on the slippery floor, another city judge, known to the upper and under world alike as "Freddy" Kernochan, leads the happy mazes of the grand march of a thousand pimps and prostitutes to the blatant crying of the band:—"Sullivan Sullivan, a damned fine Irishman."[10]

The charges attracted the attention of Charles Whitman, running for district attorney on the Republican ticket, who set up a satellite office on the Lower East Side to rein in the prostitution and other vice operations that Big Tim was supposedly running.[11] Sullivan held his fire until October 31, 1909, when the traditional end of the campaign rally was held at Miner's Bowery Theater—of which he was part owner. After word had spread that Big Tim was going to speak, a sizable chunk of the Bowery's population filled up the building and spilled out onto the sidewalks. As usual, a panoply of Democratic politicians was in attendance, including Congressman William Sulzer, who helped warm up the crowd. He was followed by James J. Hagan of the Fifteenth Assembly District, who tore into the Goo-Goos. "Reformer!" he sneered, "These people don't know anything about reform. The real reformers are the thirty-five district leaders who were ordained by Christ himself."[12] Following this assertion of divine sanction, Sullivan's political and show business partner stepped forward. "No introduction is needed for the next speaker," George Kraus proclaimed. "I only need say that it is Big Tim."[13]

At the mention of the Bowery monarch's name, the crowd burst into such enthusiastic cheering that the building itself seemed to shake, and several minutes passed before Tim could begin. "I want you to bear with me while I try to make a speech," he told his assembled supporters. Then, affecting a debutante status in speech making at odds with his history, he declared, "I never made one in my life, but with the way things are going in this campaign, with the vilification of everyone and the degradation of good men for the sake of a few offices I want to make a speech."[14] The Big Feller took out a sheet of paper on which he listed the charges made against him and proceeded to refute them one after the other. He started with the allegation that he had made himself a millionaire on a salary of $1,500 per year. As he had done in the past, Sullivan attributed his wealth to his theatrical investments, stating that his partnership with Kraus never netted less than $55,000 per anum. He also declared that he and Considine owned "more theaters than any two men in the world," and he was afraid to reveal his share of those profits for fear his "friends would be around in the morning to borrow money."[15]

"I'm worth something," Tim admitted, "and there's no reason why I shouldn't be. I'm an average downtown boy, with a good clear head, for I don't drink or smoke. But I haven't changed my residence since I got my money, and I ain't going to. I was born among you and I'm going to die among you."[16] Tim then admitted that he had provided bail for some toughs on the East Side, including Paul Vaccarelli, gang leader and master repeater, a practice he defended as aiding friends in trouble with the law.

Tim then began to hit his stride. "The trouble with the reformers is that they don't know our traditions down here. That's why they think because I've got a little money there must be something wrong, that I must be getting the money in some crooked way or I wouldn't stay here. I'll tell you why I stay here." The Big Feller then related the story of his hardworking mother and her struggle to keep her brood going, feeding them even if it meant she herself went hungry. "That's the kind of mothers that bore us down here," Tim declared, his voice rising in emotion and his face wet with tears. "If we can help some boy or father to another chance then we are going to give it to them. The thieves down here ain't thieves from choice, they are thieves from necessity and necessity don't know any law. They steal because they need a doctor for some dying one, or they steal because there ain't enough bread in the house for the children."[17]

Tim then turned to Turner's piece in *McClure's*. "I've been looking Turner up. He's got three children and a wife, and they might

13. The de facto "official" portrait of Timothy D. Sullivan which was widely reproduced and displayed throughout the Lower East Side. *Munsey's Magazine*, 1901.

have been starving, and a man who has children starving will do anything," he suggested with facetious understanding. "Now we come to the last of all—the white slave talk. My God, they have put me in [with] thieves, and I'm not the first man who has been pilloried between thieves." The crowd either missed or agreed with the Big Feller's appropriation of Christlike martyrdom and he quickly went on.

> In the article [Turner] wrote about the Lawrence Mulligan ball, and he said the women were of questionable virtue and the men worse. Now I've got right here in hand a list, and the reporters can take it and look up the names, and I'm here to say that they will find that every woman is a virtuous woman and every man a decent man . . . I've been living here all my life, and I never knew a man engaged in this business, and I won't stand for this. I'm not going to say anything but this man Turner had better keep out of this district. I've never professed to be more than an average man. I don't want you to think I'm very good for I've done a lot of wrong things. I'm just an average man, but I've told you of that old mother of mine and what she did for me, and I want to say here before you all that there is no man on earth who believes in the virtue of women more than I do.[18]

Having indignantly denied the charge of complicity with vice, in a manner—despite his protest that he never made speeches— similar to previous rebuttals, Sullivan took the offensive against Whitman and his proposed office on the Bowery. Again, not for the first time, Tim played the class card. "He don't have to do that," Tim explained to his receptive audience. "He better start one up by the [reformist] Union League Club and get after people who's tryin' to form blind pools and shove up the price of meat a cent or two a pound."[19] Satisfied with verbally smacking Whitman, Sullivan next defended his philanthropy against those who had heaped negative connotations on it. "Someone has said the Sullivans give the people a little turkey and a pair of shoes and rob them the rest of the year. As I'm the Sullivan that does this they must mean me, and I'm goin' to tell you how I got the idea of giving away the shoes."[20] Tim again reached back into his childhood and repeated the tale of how he had arrived at school in dilapidated shoes and his teacher sent him to the local Tammany captain to a get a chit for a new pair. "[A]nd I thought if ever I got money I would give shoes to people who needed them," he said reaching his conclusion, "and I'm going to buy shoes for people just as long as I live. And all the people on earth can't stop me from doing what I think is right by calling me names."[21]

Tim stopped, his face red with emotion, and sat down. The crowd hesitated a few seconds and then erupted in enthusiastic applause. Newspaper accounts related that "men and women stood in their seats and shouted and men rushed across the stage to grasp the hand of the speaker. The Band played 'My Country Tis of Thee' and the cheering continued as everyone stood and gave the Bowery leader the greatest demonstration he ever received."[22]

The performance at Miner's was Tim at his best—of course, he had been refining the same basic speech for twenty-five years. As political theater it was superb, and as a way of stoking the zeal of his troops, it was magic. In case anyone missed reports of his performance, he introduced a bill in the senate the following January—designed for publicity—that called on a state committee to investigate prostitution in the city and imprison those involved.[23] But regarding his complicity with the purveyors of commercial sex, Sullivan's impassioned rebuttal at Miner's was partly dishonest. Tim may have mentally compartmentalized his operations to the extent that he succeeded in convincing himself that he had no pecuniary interest in prostitution, and he may have personally kept his distance from it as well, but his statement that he never knew a man engaged in it was patently false. If many of the rank and file chose to believe the assertion, certainly the political operatives knew better. So did Tim. So did his enemies.

For his mayoral nominee in 1909, Charlie Murphy tapped Brooklyn supreme court justice William Jay Gaynor. Although a Democrat, if an idiosyncratic one, Gaynor had the reputation of being a Fusion sympathizer with a strong ethical sense. Murphy chose him because he thought he could win, and saw no other option. For his part, Gaynor accepted the nomination because he knew Murphy could deliver. Visiting the Wigwam shortly before the election, Gaynor delivered a statement that was a portent of things to come. "So this is Tammany Hall," he said looking around. "It is the first time I was ever here. I did not even know where it was. . . . But if this is Tammany Hall, where is the tiger—the tiger which they say is going to swallow me up? If there happens to be any swallowing up, it is not at all unlikely that I will be on the outside of the tiger."[24] Murphy may have smiled tight-lipped, but the remark was less than encouraging. Gaynor was opposed by Hearst, a slow learner who ran independently, and Republican Otto Bannard.

The election was thrown into greater confusion by an outbreak of labor strife. In October, garment workers were locked out of the Triangle Shirtwaist Factory, one of the largest in the city, after they refused to join a company union. Locked-out strikers, mostly young women, picketed the factory and were set upon by whores and pimps hired by the Triangle's owners, Max Blanck and Isaac Harris. Tammany, still tacitly allied with business interests, ordered its cops to intervene against the workers, hauling off the young strikers. The situation escalated at a mass labor rally held at Cooper Union on November 25. At the urging of socialist firebrand Clara Lemlich, a general strike of all garment workers was declared. The workers received unexpected support as well. Socialites Alva Vanderbilt and Anne Morgan, JP's daughter, brought money, support, and publicity. Soon young college girls from the "Seven Sisters" traveled to the Lower East Side to help the strikers and picketers, a move that intimidated both police and judges.

Along with business interests, politicians of major political parties, including the Democracy, were apprehensive at the alliance of wealthy uptown women and struggling women workers downtown. But the unlikely alliance could not hold. The college girls and upper-class socialites hoped to use the strike to launch the larger cause of women's suffrage, which found little resonance in the Lower East Side.[25] On the other hand, the strike leaders, primarily socialists, disliked the attention given to the wealthy women who had intruded into the strike. When Local 25 of the International Ladies' Garment Workers' Union (ILGWU) refused arbitration with Triangle—the backbone of the industry's resistance—many of the socialites began to drift away. At a mass rally held at Carnegie Hall on January 2, 1910, the strident socialist rhetoric offended the remainder, who withdrew from the effort, taking newspaper coverage with them.[26] Shortly after the workers settled with Triangle and the other large garment producers. They had gained in wages, slightly shorter hours, and agreements that union membership was not prohibited. The unions remained unrecognized, however, and the major outstanding issues continued unresolved. Hours were still long, pay low, and safety standards, not directly addressed in the strike, had not been improved at all.

Most investigators believe that Murphy, cautious and conservative, was shaken by the emergence of a major workers' movement that could challenge Tammany's hold over the downtown districts. He was also strongly opposed to women's suffrage and feared that the alliance between working and socialite women would expand the feminist movement. What Big Tim thought is not precisely known. He and Little Tim probably had a better grip on the sentiments downtown and were more inclined to do something to support the workers out of self-interest. Additionally, Tim's fond gratitude and respect for the work of his mother and sister was not merely an act he dusted off for public consumption when attacked politically. The plight of the strikers, mostly girls and young women, genuinely affected him deeply, as events would tell.

But in the meantime, ordinary politics continued. The municipal elections took place even as the tide of labor unrest, the "Revolt of 20,000," gathered momentum. Tammany did not do well. Although Gaynor won city hall, the Democracy was turned out or back in almost every other position. Even the personal backing of Big Tim could not help Christy Sullivan win the post of sheriff. Gaynor soon proved as difficult as predicted. He ignored Murphy while making appointments and even abolished some positions held by Tammany men. When asked what he intended to give Murphy, Gaynor sarcastically replied, "Suppose we give him a few kind words."[27] Tim revealed the prevailing attitude in the Hall, when a reporter inquired if Gaynor might be the Democrats' next presidential candidate. "I am saying nothing, but we will make no mistake next time," he replied.[28] The new mayor might have been even more of a disaster for the organization that put him in office had he not been badly wounded the following April by a discharged Docks Department employee. Gaynor completed his term, but he was never the same thereafter. Nevertheless, his administration, though nominally Democratic, was a hard one for Tammany loyalists.

The year 1909 was a bad one for the Sullivan clan as well. In June Florrie Sullivan died. He had begun showing signs of mental instability two years previously and was taken to Europe in the hope that a cure could be found. He was insane when he returned home.[29] Then came Christy's defeat for sheriff. An even greater blow fell on December 22, 1909, when Timothy P. "Little Tim" Sullivan, majority leader of the Board of Aldermen and district leader of the Third Assembly District followed Florrie to the grave. Little Tim had long been the Big Feller's closest and most trusted advisor. While Tim was dabbling in Washington and enjoying his recreational and entertainment interests, Little Tim kept the "machine within a machine" well oiled and running smoothly. Less flamboyant than Big Tim, some claimed that in the years immediately before his death, "it was the smaller Sullivan who furnished most of the brains and least of the talking of the Sullivan clan."[30] The Big Feller did not dispute the contention. "He had the brains," he remarked simply.[31]

Little Tim's death was not entirely unexpected. In January he was sent off to Hot Springs, Virginia, with a $100-a-plate dinner attended by virtually every politician or politically connected lawyer in the city.[32] Recuperative trips to the Adirondacks were also tried. But despite such attempts to restore his health, papers reported that he "had been failing for more than a year and . . . sinking fast for three months."[33] Though whispers of consumption spread through the city's political class, it was also known that the Little Feller had spent time in the psychiatric ward of Bellevue hospital.[34] When the end came, the cause of his death was publicly reported as Bright's disease and endocarditis.[35]

Little Tim's last request to his cousin was that he preside over the Sullivan Association's traditional Christmas dinner at the Bowery.[36] Though the Big Feller had begun the celebration many years previously, Little Tim ran it after Big Tim went off to Washington. Of course, Big Tim promised to fulfill his cousin's dying request and the Sullivan Association Christmas dinner fed 5,000 men with 10,000 pounds of turkey, 500 loaves of bread, 200 gallons of coffee, 5,000 pies, 100 kegs of beer, plus pipes and bags of tobacco for every diner. Tickets were distributed entitling the bearer to a pair of shoes and socks. The entire holiday event cost Tim $13,750.[37] The dinner was a fitting tribute to Little Tim's memory, but it probably did little to assuage the loss caused by his passing. For the Big Feller, Little Tim's early demise was a personal and professional body blow.

The Republicans gave Murphy the opportunity to mount a comeback in the state elections of 1910. The incumbent governor, Republican Charles Evans Hughes, had alienated the business community by favoring regulation of banking and utilities. Republican politicians were also caught in a bribe-taking scandal. Murphy ran John Alden Dix for governor, who triumphed in the polls. Dix proved a loyal subordinate to his Tammany master. At the same time, two of Murphy's most effective young protégés, Robert Wagner and Al Smith, became majority leaders of the state senate and assembly, respectively. Dubbed the "Tammany Twins" by the press, Wagner and Smith pushed through the so-called "Murphy Charter," which weakened New York City's civil service system, opening up thousands of patronage jobs for the Tiger's followers.[38] Though at first they followed Murphy's policies to the letter, Wagner and Smith were far more attuned to the demands and needs of the toiling poor in the larger cities and over time would carve out enduring reputations as defenders and proponents of the rights of labor. But in 1910 that lay in the future.

The only problem Murphy encountered was over his backing of "Blue-Eyed" Billy Sheehan for United States senator. The endorsement brought an insurgency of reformist Democrats, led by Duchess County legislator Franklin Delano Roosevelt. The Roosevelt faction lacked the numbers to win the nomination for their choice, but by boycotting the Democratic caucus, they could prevent the selection of another candidate. As the impasse continued, Big Tim proposed that the Democrats nominate Isodore Straus, a philanthropist and part owner of Macy's department store.

Ultimately, on March 31, 1911, Murphy and his aides made the trip to Albany to settle the matter. Meeting with the Democratic leaders in Room 201 of the Ten Eyck Hotel, Murphy announced that he had dropped Sheehan's nomination in favor of state supreme court judge James O'Gorman. Sullivan vocally argued against the choice and pressed his support of Straus. Some suggested that he simply wished to shore up his support among Lower East Jews with his pro-Straus campaign, but his pushing for a Jew was in keeping with his known policies. Murphy, taciturn as usual, let his lieutenants voice his arguments. Silent Charlie believed that Tammany could ill afford a defeat, and a Jew was unelectable. Sullivan groused to reporters about Murphy's decision, but went along with it, and voted for O'Gorman's candidacy.[39] So did Roosevelt, who bragged about what he termed "that final Murphy surrender" over the Sheehan candidacy. In reality, O'Gorman, a former Tammany grand sachem and personal friend of Murphy, was even more congenial to the Tammany leader than Sheehan.[40] In any event, he was a good choice, going on to win the senate seat.

Despite his personal philanthropies, employment measures, and overall social welfare activities, Big Tim's career as a state senator before 1909 followed the standard Tammany line. Essentially conservative, as such things were measured at the turn of the nineteenth century, Tammany's legislative stance was generally pro-business, and generally suspicious, when not opposed, to protections for organized labor or the implementation of state-mandated social services. In turn, many businesses and investors readily contributed to the Hall's war chest during the election season. Even when out of power a large number of firms contributed to Tammany's kitty as insurance, for although it could be wounded, the Tiger never died.

Stories had long circulated about the infamous "Black Horse Cavalry"—legislators who took bribes for pushing or killing bills, including laws which aided striking workers. Some counted the Big Feller in the horsemen's ranks, and in 1910 the president of an insurance company dredged up such a charge. According to George F. Seward, president of the Fidelity and Casualty Company, in 1892, a man claiming to represent Sullivan offered to defeat a bill that was inimical to the company's interests for $10,000.[41] Seward, who was testifying before a committee of the New York State Insurance Department, told the investigators that he sent a telegram telling Sullivan to "go to hell."[42] Big Tim quickly rebutted the allegation, charging that "Seward tells a blank lie." He denied having anything to do with insurance legislation in the 1892 session and dismissed the whole affair as an attempt to "drag a Democrat" into a scandal.[43] The truthfulness of Seward's allegations is difficult to ascertain. He himself admitted he never had any contact with the Big Feller himself, only someone who claimed to be an emissary, and Tim might have been entirely innocent in this instance. On the other hand, if he could have arranged payment for supporting a proposal that was not against his personal interests, he probably did it.

Early in the 1910 session, Sullivan introduced a bill into the senate that was clearly beneficial to his constituents. The measure, which he had introduced previously in 1899, 1900, and 1901, would put private bankers under the control of the New

York State Banking Commission. In a period before banks were brought under the purview of the Federal Reserve System, the small private banks, mostly in Italian and Jewish neighbor- hoods, were the least controlled of all, often with disastrous con- sequences for the poor workers who resorted to them. Tim argued that dishonest policies by such bankers had ruined many emi- grants—"the poorest people in the world have lost half a million dollars"—and he asked "every member to look into this matter and give our people in the lower part of New York some protec- tion."[44] The bill passed and became law.

At the beginning of the 1911 senate session, Big Tim intro- duced a measure designed to address a lethal and growing prob- lem in the city—especially downtown. The statute, still known as the "Sullivan Law," was Tim's response to the increasing gun violence on the Lower East Side. Guns had long been familiar to New York's gangs, but their use seemed on the increase after 1910, another symptom of the declining conditions in the Bowery. In contrast to earlier gangs who had used any variety of lethal weapons, but generally avoided guns, the new gangs, particu- larly the crews led by "Big Jack" Zelig and Jack Sirocco, were quick to pull triggers, and the number of shootouts and deaths reached troubling proportions.

During the city Democratic convention in autumn 1910, the Big Feller announced his intention to introduce a bill to regulate the possession of concealed firearms. He told the assembled poli- ticians and supporters that he knew some of them were carrying revolvers, and if they had any objections to his course, they could tell him so there and then.[45] No one said a word. Tim made good on his promise and introduced his bill in February 1911. The proposed law mandated police permits for concealed weapons, and unlawful possession of a firearm became a felony. Gun deal- ers were required to ask for such before selling a good and were to keep records of those purchasing pistols. On April 25, as the senate weighed placing the measure on the calendar for an up or down vote, Tim agreed to consider reasonable amendments, "but [did] not want any offered in the interests of the manufacturers who place the money they get from the sale of dangerous weapons above the value of human life."[46] "This bill," he went on, "is in- tended to cut down on the murder and suicide statistics in New York City by at least fifty. No man knows more about the situa- tion with which this deals than I do, and you must take my word for it that I know what I am doing."[47] The senate concurred, and Tim's bill went forward.

The measure to control guns won Tim some unexpected—and surprised—allies. "Chances to commend the bills of Senator 'Big Tim' Sullivan have not come to us very frequently," the *New York Times* conceded, "but that is the more reason for utilizing any that do arrive, and therefore we say again that if his unquestionable legislative efficiency has the result of decreasing the number of revolvers owned . . . he will have used it to good purpose. And we won't spoil the praise by adding 'for once.'"[48] But, of course, they did. Apparently they just couldn't help themselves.

The "Sullivan Law" came up for a formal vote of the senate on May 10. Senator Ferris from Oneida County, the only senator publicly opposing the bill, argued that the licensing provision "would prove a hardship to those who desired to have pistols in their homes for their own protection."[49] "Have you a gun factory in your district?" the Big Feller demanded. When Ferris admitted so, Sullivan asked if he would oppose the bill if such were not the case. Ferris denied the presence of the gun manufacturer in his district had anything to do with his position and charged that Sullivan's bill would not stop murders. "You can't force a burglar to get a license to use a gun," he insisted. "He'll get it from another state." Tim responded quickly, emphasizing his primary motivation in the matter. "I want to make it so the young thugs in my district will get three years for carrying dangerous weapons instead of getting a sentence in the electric chair a year from now. The manufacturers oppose my bill because they know that if we pass it other states will follow suit."[50] When Ferris pointed out that Alabama had had a similar law but repealed it, Big Tim dismissed the point, saying, "Alabama is too far away from the Bowery for me to talk about it."[51]

Tim then ticked off the organizations and individuals who had supported his bill. These included old enemies such as the City Club, the Merchants Association, and the Association of Magistrates. "The only thing they found bad about the bill was that Tim Sullivan introduced it," he noted wryly.[52] The number and caliber of prominent individuals who joined him in his fight to regulate pistols were equally impressive. Supporters included District Attorney Whitman, Jacob H. Schiff, John Wanamaker, and John D. Rockefeller Jr., whom Tim intriguingly described as "a social acquaintance of mine." Tim concluded his appeal, predicting that "if you pass [the bill] I believe it will save more souls than all the preachers in the city talking for the next ten years."[53] The senate believed him and the measure passed overwhelmingly with only five votes against. Although Sullivan feared heavy opposition in the assembly, it passed readily on May 15. Governor Dix signed the law fifteen days later, and the Sullivan law came into effect of September 1.

Cynics suggested that Big Tim pushed through his law so Tammany could keep their gangster allies under control. Hoodlums who forgot who really ran things in the city could be easily arrested if found with a gun—or if one was slipped into their pocket. The Big Feller surely heard the charges and likely shrugged them off. If there were political benefits from doing the right thing, what was the problem? But all the available evidence indicates that Tim's fight to bring firearms under control sprang from heartfelt conviction.

Then, as now, arguments arose about the efficacy of the handgun restrictions. Some, including police officers and judges, contended that the law had little effect on criminals, while it made it harder for citizens to obtain protection by owning a pistol. The law's defenders countered that the statute provided a useful tool in the city's monitoring and identification of dangerous weapons. "Well enforced," the *New York Times* believed, "it leads to the identification of murderers and other felons."[54] In any event, the law remains on the books, and as Tim predicted, was widely copied in other areas as well.

9

The Last Hurrah

It's all right, me girl! The bosses thought they was going to kill
your bill, but they forgot about Tim Sullivan
—Big Tim Sullivan

IN THE SPRING 1912 ALBANY SESSION, AS IF HE SENSED HIS TIME
was running out, Big Tim Sullivan threw himself into a variety of
initiatives intended to improve the lot of New Yorkers—especially those downtown. His right-hand man in his final session
was his cousin, Christy Sullivan, who had shaken off his defeat in
the 1909 sheriff's election and become a state senator. In Albany,
the two were commonly called "The Sullivans," though there was
no doubt who the senior partner was. Frances Perkins, working
energetically as lobbyist during the period, remembered that
"Christy used to follow Tim around like a little white rabbit. It
was like *Harvey,* the play."[1]

In January Big Tim reintroduced a bill that would reduce the
tax rate on buildings by stages, until after five years improved
property would be taxed at half the rate of undeveloped land.[2]
The idea was to discourage land speculation, expand the city's
housing stock, and lower rents. Real estate interests were not
enthusiastic. Later he proposed legislation that would limit
the commissions paid to fire and casualty insurance agents at
15 percent, and cap administration expenses in liability and
casualty companies at 32.5 percent.[3] Price control of the insurance industry was the obvious intention. But Tim's energy, ex-
pertise, and clout were primarily, and enthusiastically, centered
on another area—workers' and women's issues, especially the
combination of the two.

In January 1912 Big Tim lent his support for legislation that
would permit women to serve as sheriff's deputies in New York
County (Manhattan). His old friend and ally John Harsburger,

147

then sheriff, had named two women to the posts, only to be informed that the law forbade female appointees. Shortly afterward, an unnamed "woman lawyer" drafted a new statute opening deputy positions to females and sent it to Tim requesting he introduce it in the senate.[4] Tim's well-known sympathy for women's rights led to his being chosen to present the bill. When Tim made no reply to the proposed bill, the lawyer, without having her name divulged by the press, accused the Big Feller of "a lack of courtesy."[5] Tim's response was to introduce the bill on January 24. The new law allowed the sheriff to appoint anyone over twenty-one as deputies. With Tim's support a small, if visible, barrier to women's employment fell.

Sullivan was an early supporter of women's suffrage. To a large degree this was based on his enduring appreciation of his mother and sisters, and respect for the work women did. "If women are going to be the toilers," he declared, "I'm going to give them all the protection I can."[6] His support of women's issues led him into another unexpected friendship, this time with feminist/suffragist Harriot Stanton Blatch, daughter of pioneer women's rights advocate Elizabeth Cady Stanton. Blatch had formed the Equality League of Self-Supporting Women, which actively tried to attract poorer, working-class women to the cause of women's suffrage. She was also a leader of the Women's Political Union and was frequently in Albany leading lobbying efforts for women's suffrage. Blatch and Sullivan became allies, and the feminist leader made free use of Tim's name and arguments in her own letters and statements to the press.[7] She also arranged for Tim to speak before women's groups on suffrage and related topics. The Big Feller's appearances before the largely upper-middle-class Anglo-Saxon feminists must have been an exotic experience on both sides.

Big Tim's support for women's voting rights sprang from his personal political philosophy. Sullivan was an instinctive Democrat with both a small and capital D. When the question of women's suffrage came up late in the 1911 session, the Big Feller threw his weight behind it. His arguments were based partly on the increasing presence of women in New York's workforce, but he also acted on a more fundamental principle. "I think that this proposition independent of that [women's role in the labor force] ought to pass. Just recollect that fifty years ago you would not let a man vote on account of his color; because his color was not right

14. Big Tim in formal attire, c. 1905. Courtesy of the Library of Congress.

he could not vote."[8] For his part, Tim pledged to keep pushing for the right of women to vote "as long as I had a vote in this legislature."[9] "[Women's Suffrage] is going to come," he concluded, "and you can't stop it. I don't look to have to wait for our grandchildren to have it. I think in a year or two we will have it."[10] But not that year. The suffrage bill failed 17 to 16.

The issue came up again on March 19, 1912. When the amendment was brought to the floor of the Senate, Senator McClelland led the opposition, launching into a long-winded speech whose theme was that "motherhood is the true mission of womanhood today in this country."[11] Blatch and her allies were beside themselves in the galleries, both amused and incensed, but were constrained from making any demonstration or rebuttal. Not so Big Tim. As McClelland reached the end of his bloviation and "nearly wept over the surcharged emotional nature of women, [and] her preordained lack of self control," he confessed that thirty years previously, as a young and inexperienced assemblyman, he had voted for women's suffrage. "You had sense then," Big Tim retorted getting to his feet and launching his counterattack.[12]

Tim explained he had been in Albany for twenty-six years and from his earliest days to the present had been a supporter of the vote for women. He quickly reiterated the role of women workers as a justification for suffrage, and then took on the anti-suffrage charge that voting and politics were too vulgar and rough for feminine sensibilities. The Big Feller related that he had been "out in Los Angeles the day of the last election, and the ladies went up to the booths without any fuss and cast their ballot. The day is past now of scrambling at the polls and pulling and mauling. Any lady could go if she had the franchise and could vote without any interference. And I don't think woman will turn out to be any less intelligent when she has the vote than now when she is not a voter."[13] But despite the best efforts of Sullivan and other suffrage supporters, the measure again failed, 19 to 21.

On March 30, 1912, shortly after the suffrage amendment was defeated, Big Tim attended a meeting of the Women's Democratic Club held at the Hotel Astor, where he expounded on his reasons for joining the suffrage crusade. Although the Democratic women hosted it, the gathering attracted suffragists of various political persuasions, and Tim was introduced by Republican Mary Garrett Hay of the State Federation of Women's Clubs. "I am a suffragist and I am glad of it," Hay began, "and I want to say that there is one man whom we suffragists honor and respect because he has always stood for us, and he is the Honorable Timothy D. Sullivan."[14] At that point the previously sedate audience burst into cheers, some shouting, "Speech! Speech! Sullivan! Sullivan! Tim! Tim! Big Tim!"[15] Big Tim rose as suffragists and their supporters continued to shower him with applause. He likely broke into a pleased and bemused smile as the middle- and upper-class reformers gave a good imitation of a preelection crowd in the Bowery. As usual, Tim denied he was much of an orator and warned his listeners that they would have to take him as he was. "I've always been a woman suffragist," he began, and then continued:

> I've been a suffragist from the first day I ever went to the Legislature, and I have voted for every bill for women, whether it was for suffrage or for labor—every thing that would help the ladies, even giving them preference over the men.
>
> In the lower part of the city where I was born most of the people were Irish, and the Irish tried to keep their girls at home. They would send out the boys and we would sell papers and do what we could, but unless there was sometimes a very good place in a family the girl would stay at home.
>
> Years ago you wouldn't see one girl to twenty-five men going out to work, but now there are all the nationalities of the earth down there, and there are about as many girls starting out to work that day as there are men. And the men will always have the advantage of the women, and the working women will have the worst of it.
>
> I never listened to a suffrage speech in my life, but I can see that without the vote, especially in the lower walks of life, the women don't have a chance. If any one wants anything it is the man who gets it, because he has the vote.
>
> And the thing that keeps suffrage down—the thing that has kept it down this year—is that the politicians of both parties are afraid of you woman—we're all afraid you will take the easy jobs away from us.[16]

With that Tim sat down to another burst of applause. In addition to elucidating his commitment to suffrage, the speech provided sound sociological insight. The Irish did generally keep their daughters at home until they were older and positions as maids and cooks could be found for them. The prevalence of Irish girls and women in such jobs helps explain their being more widely dispersed throughout the city than most other ethnoimmigrant groups in the decades just before the Great War. The boys, as Tim stated, were sent out into the world earlier. The one thing missing from Sullivan's presentation was that the Irish pattern disintegrated in broken families like his own. As he remarked on other occasions, his sisters had to go out into the working world at a young age.

Though Tim continued to do his best for the cause of women's franchise, it failed in 1912 as it had the year before. The Big Feller was right when he told his fellow legislators that votes for women could not be stopped. But Charlie Murphy, by nature more cautious and conservative, could delay it. In 1917, after Tim was gone and women's suffrage had become indeed unstoppable, Murphy reversed gears, backed it, and won Tammany some credit for its passing.

While Big Tim was lending his muscle to the cause of women's voting rights, he played a decisive role in securing some real protections for the largely female workforce in one of the state's industries. Sometime around 1910–11, the Big Feller made the acquaintance of a young woman whose political efforts led to his finest—certainly his most dramatic—hour as a state legislator. Frances Perkins was a bluestocking reformer who had gone into social work after graduating from Mount Holyoke. By 1910 she was in New York, completing a master's degree at Columbia and becoming executive secretary of the Consumer's League, an organization dedicated to improving working conditions. Her work often took her to the teeming downtown streets where she conducted a study of cellar bakeries. In addition to her investigations and social welfare efforts, she became increasingly involved in trying to move the state government to improve the hours and conditions of the working poor.

Perkins's first up close encounter with a Tammany politician was probably with "The McManus," Big Tim's ally and boss of Hell's Kitchen—the heavily Irish section of the mid-Forties and Fifties west of Broadway. Perkins took up the case of a penniless woman with two daughters, one of whom was illegitimate. The woman was an alcoholic, and she and her girls had been supported by a son who had landed in jail. Perkins first turned to an established private charity, hoping to find aid for mother and daughters, and help in getting the son released. The institution described the mother as an unworthy, promiscuous drunk, and refused to step in.[17] Somewhat in desperation, not having developed a high opinion of Tammany politicians from her studies and conversations with her progressive colleagues, she went to McManus, in whose district the woman lived. The district leader was not interested in the morality of the situation, but he did want to be sure that the woman was indeed a resident of his bailiwick. "Well, I'm always glad to help anybody in trouble," he told the young reformer, and in hours the son was released from jail.[18] Frances Perkins had just received her first lesson in practical politics.

Before long, Perkins, later Franklin Roosevelt's secretary of labor and the nation's first woman cabinet member, would meet a variety of Tammany men, some of whom she would find quite supportive. Indeed, she often found them more sympathetic and helpful to her efforts than politicians of her own class and background. Looking back on her experiences in New York in the years just before the First World War, Perkins wrote

> I was tremendously interested and intrigued by politicians like Tim Sullivan of the Bowery and his cousin, Christy; Senator Grady, the great orator who was nearly always slightly intoxicated when he made his orations in the senate of New York, The McManus called by a columnist of his day "The Devil's Deputy from Hell's Kitchen." The warm human sympathies of these people, less than perfect as I examine their record, gave me insight into a whole stratum of American society I had not known. In contrast to these roughnecks, I don't hesitate to say now, Franklin Roosevelt seemed just an ordinary, respectable, intelligent and correct young man.[19]

The youthful Roosevelt was also condescending, narrow-minded, and sanctimonious. "Awfully arrogant fellow, that Roosevelt," Tim confided to Perkins after a verbal dustup with the supercilious senator from Duchess County.[20] In another instance, Roosevelt turned down a small appropriation for his district on the grounds that it was unnecessary, and he would not dirty his hands with any kind of pork. "Frank, you ought to have your head examined," an exasperated Sullivan declared.[21] The differences between the two Democrats were a matter of class and environment. FDR was born to wealth and status and felt the need to distance himself from what he deemed vulgar, horse-trading politics. Tim had grown up poor and in a hurry. He had learned to take his opportunities for himself—and his constituents—as best he could. Time and experience would transform the disdainful young legislator from the Hudson Valley, who later admitted "I was an awfully mean cuss when I first went into politics."[22] Perkins gave some credit for Roosevelt's evolution into a more humane, generous, and effective politician to his years in the state senate where he "had learned from rough Tammany politicians like Tim Sullivan and The McManus."[23]

Silent Charlie pursued his own agenda. Naturally mistrustful of unpredictable change, the Tammany boss was always mindful of the financial support sent the Hall's way from business interests. Despite appearances, rhetoric, and misconceptions, the Democracy and the business and financial sectors usually saw eye to eye. As early as the 1890s, a number of business trade journals declared that only a tough, organized group could run a city like New York.[24] The New York-based *Banker's Magazine* explained that a "system of bosses in politics"—a machine—"has its usefulness and reason for being."[25] Among the benefits of a strong machine dominating the ethnic-immigrant neighborhoods was its role in providing the propertyless classes with employment and a "friend in court." As a result, the machine kept the lower classes from revolting or joining a more radical, hard-core redistributionist movement, as Tammany had done in blocking Henry George in 1886.[26] Under pressure from George, Tammany adopted pro-labor rhetoric and vocal support for labor reform, but did little to see it implemented in a significant way. Likewise, after the Hearst challenge of 1905, the Hall sponsored municipal ownership of utilities, deflating Hearst's appeal while providing jobs for their followers. But, in general, Tammany adopted labor reform only under duress. Going his own way, with his finger on the pulse of the most diverse and potentially volatile part of the city, Big Tim Sullivan would prove an exception to the generalization.

Beyond the usual policy of trying to work with business leaders—which made sense not only from a political but a practical point of view—Murphy devised his "Businessmen's Plan" intended to provide the Democracy with both money and jobs to reward followers and provide a cushion during the times the Hall was out of power.[27] Cash and jobs came from contractors working for the city, while the municipally regulated utility and transportation firms were "tithed" for campaign war chests.[28] What businesses got in return was a generally well-run city. Whatever the kickbacks and honest graft involved, the Tammany-connected firm did the jobs contracted for (unlike the situation under Tweed), while the Hall stifled any serious challenge to the laissez-faire status quo.

Unsurprisingly, Murphy was generally unsympathetic to those pleading the case of the working classes. During the 1909 general strike, he used Tammany's power over the police against the striking women, moderating his policy only when it seemed to threaten a backlash. But such a stance was detrimental to the Sullivans' hold on the Lower East Side, and the "machine within a machine" struck a contrary course.

For openers, Big Tim genuinely wished to lighten the burdens of the downtown poor as his charities and employment services attested. It was simple evolution to proceed from personal and organizational support to ensuring state protections and entitlements by statute. As Sullivan himself once put it, "I've been against radical legislation in the past. On the other hand, I have been for liberal laws."[29] He seems to have meant he did not wish to challenge the prevailing socioeconomic structure, but would push legislation designed to improve it and open it up for the workers and poor. And so he did.

Those were the positive—and personal—motivations driving Sullivan in his last senate term. There were coercive factors as well. Sullivan knew better than most how close the fight with Hearst had been, and how the press lord made deep inroads in many East Side districts by advocating government-owned transportation. He also saw the attraction socialism held for many Jews. If he could not deliver—or at least support—pro-labor legislation, his reign as "King of the Bowery" would be jeopardized. And there was one last factor. The "machine within a machine's" leader would demonstrate a delight in tweaking Charlie Murphy's nose when the time came.

It took a major tragedy to alter the state government's attitude toward labor reform from indifferent to supportive. On March 25, 1911, a fire broke out at one of the city's largest garment manufacturers, the Triangle Shirtwaist Company on the northern border of Washington Square. Lacking fire safety equipment, and with some doorways locked shut, a flash fire lasting thirty minutes led to the deaths of 146 workers, 123 of them women and girls.[30] Some of the workers were killed by smoke inhalation or burning; others perished when they jumped from the windows to escape the flames. The fire and the toll shocked and angered the city.

Although Max Steuer, generally regarded as a Tammany lawyer, got the owners off, other Tammany men were shaken by the catastrophe. Al Smith was among them. Tim's thoughts are unknown. Considering his record, he was surely outraged.

The Triangle fire galvanized the movement for safety and labor reform. On April 2, 1911, the cream of progressives and socialists assembled at the Metropolitan Opera House. Members of the Consumer's League and the Citizens' Union were prominent, as were members of the city's social elite, such as Henry Stimson, Henry Morgenthau Sr., Anne Morgan, and Robert Fulton Cutting. The meeting at the Metropolitan led to the creation of the Committee on Safety, whose mission was to pressure the state to pass the kind of laws that would make a tragedy like the Triangle fire unlikely if not impossible. Frances Perkins was appointed lobbyist for the committee's agenda.

About two weeks after the Committee on Safety was founded, Perkins met Al Smith. Smith, a good Tammany man and Murphy loyalist, but highly sympathetic to Perkins's efforts, gave her another lesson in practical politics. There had been no politicians at the Metropolitan meeting, politics being considered dirty by many progressives and their allies. Smith told Perkins the committee would fail unless its objectives were adopted by legislators. "It isn't the first people of the state that have the most influence in the legislature," the downtown assemblyman told the social worker cum lobbyist. "If you want to get anything done, you got to have this be a legislative commission. If the legislature does it, the legislature will be proud of it. . . . These fellows in the Assembly are good men at heart. They don't want to burn up people in factories. They just don't know anything about how to prevent it, and they don't really believe that there is any hazard until you show them. And they'll be more impressed if it is shown them by their own commission and own members."[31]

Though initially skeptical, Perkins later conceded that Smith's arguments were "the most useful piece of advice, I guess, we've ever had."[32] Perkins and most of her associates came to realize that Tammany had the power, and that if anything were to be accomplished, it had to be done Tammany's way. The question was how. Charlie Murphy kept a close watch on developments, consulting with Smith and Wagner at his home at Good Ground or the famous "Red Room"—Murphy's private office on the second floor of Delmonico's Restaurant on Forty-third Street decorated totally in scarlet. In devising the strategy for initiating factory reform, it is likely that Smith took the lead, with Murphy dragging his feet.

In the end a Factory Investigation Commission was authorized on June 30, 1911. The commission, co-chaired by Wagner and Smith, consisted of nine members, five from the state legislature and four appointed by the governor. The commission had extensive powers of subpoena, could select its own members and employees, and even revise its own charter. Wagner and Smith appointed a member of the International Ladies' Garment Workers' Union as their lead investigator. Progressive reformer Belle Moskowitz joined the team as Smith's advisor, a position she would keep throughout his long and productive career. Between 1911 and 1913, the Factory Investigation Commission sent teams of investigators into forty-five cities. Ultimately its work led to laws mandating fire safety measures, factory inspection, and laws concerning the employment of woman and children.

The culmination of the reform activity in the 1912 legislative session was the 54-Hour Bill. The bill took its name from its key provision—the limitation of the working week for most women to fifty-four hours. The bill had great support from the Factory Commission, the reformist groups, and many legislators. There was, however, a hitch. Charlie Murphy did not want to see the law passed. Murphy's opposition was based on his reluctance to alienate the Democrats' business contributors. The 54-Hour Bill was opposed by a number of cannery companies whose work was largely seasonal. The Huyler Brothers' Candy Company, another mostly seasonal concern, also leaned on Murphy to block the bill. Not wanting to show his hand and alienate the growing labor movement, Murphy directed Smith and Wagner to use parliamentary proceedings to make sure a bill did not get out of the legislature. Smith, who was highly sympathetic to the cause of labor reform, candidly explained to Perkins that Murphy had taken steps to ensure that the bill would never get out of committee.[33] Perkins was initially incredulous, but when Smith's warning was borne out, she redoubled her lobbying efforts before the 1912 session ran out.

The political situation had shifted during the 1912 legislative session. The Democrats still held the senate, but the Republicans had retaken the assembly. The 54-Hour Bill was presented for passage on March 27, just two days before the legislature was to adjourn. If not passed in the brief forty-eight-hour window, it would be dead for another year. The McManus, chairman of the Committee on Labor and Industry, presented the bill for a debate and a vote. Senator Victor M. Allen of Troy led the opposition, trying to gut the bill with three amendments that were rejected. In the course of his arguments, Allen declared the factories in Troy were bright and airy and the women workers would rather labor in the factories than remain at home.[34] At this absurdity, Big Tim rose to his feet and responded facetiously. "Mr. President, I wish to endorse everything my honored friend, the Senator from Troy, has just said. I've seen the shirt factories in Troy, and I want to tell you it's a fine sight, too, to see them women and girls working in those bright, airy places the Senator has so eloquently described. But I also want to tell you that it's a far finer sight at noontime to see the fine, big, up-standing men fetching around the women's dinner pails."[35]

Most of the senators burst into laughter, and the 54-Hour Bill was passed 32 to 15. Even Wagner and Murphy's son-in-law and de facto representative, James A. Foley, voted for it. Perkins assumed this meant Murphy supported the bill. She was wrong. The canning and candy interests had put their muscle in at the assembly, which passed an amendment exempting canneries on the grounds that it was a seasonal industry that required longer hours to prevent spoilage. The Assembly Rules Committee then had two bills before it—the straight 54-Hour Bill passed by the senate and its own amended bill. Despite Perkins's lobbying, the Rules Committee reported out the amended version. Perkins went to Smith, now minority leader, to voice her dismay. "I'm afraid that was intended," he told her.[36]

The next day the amended bill passed 104 to 26. With one day left in the legislative session, two differing bills were in contention. Only one could pass. Since the assembly had overwhelmingly voted for the amended version, only that had a chance to become law—if the senate approved it. There was one bit of good news. The noon adjournment time was set aside, and the legislature would supposedly continue until the work was completed. But each minute worked against Perkins. Part of her problem was that the Consumer's League had consistently declared it would never accept a bill exempting the canneries. Perkins went to Big Tim, who in her eyes was the "only politician who accepted the principle of the [54-Hour] bill and was willing to see it through."[37] Like Smith, he was frank about the politics of the bill. "Me girl," he began in what Perkins described as "his rich Irish brogue,"

> I seen you around here and I know you worked hard on this and I know you done your duty and I know it's very hard for a young lady like you to work away from home. I'll tell you; it's the truth. Murphy told them to go ahead and put out the bill, but the idea is that the Assembly will pass a different bill. They say, of course, you can't accept it—you're under instructions not to accept it. They don't mean to put it through though. They don't mean to let you get that law this year because they know you won't accept the bill that's over in the House [assembly] with the canners' amendment on it. That's the idea.[38]

Perkins was stunned by the slickness of Murphy's ploy. In an election year when the Republicans could claim that they tried to do something for most workers, the Democrats could proclaim that they tried to aid all the women workers. But there would be no law, and Tammany's big bucks contributors would be satisfied. But Sullivan, McManus, and Smith had been good teachers, and Perkins was an apt pupil. She decided to ditch the Consumer's League demand for a bill with no exemptions. There were about 400,000 women working in the state. The assembly bill denied protection to about 10,000. Perkins decided to take protection for 390,000 and work on covering the remaining 10,000 later. Otherwise she would achieve nothing. Acting on her own, Perkins went to her senate allies, telling them they could vote for the assembly bill. Wagner seemed surprised but agreed to report it out. Then with the clock ticking and some senators leaving, Wagner took over as presiding officer of the senate after the lieutenant governor left for a meeting. A minimum of twenty-six votes were necessary to pass the bill.

Big Tim and his cousin Christy were putting on their coats to catch the eight o'clock boat to the city. Perkins pleaded for them to stay, explaining that Wagner had promised to have the Rules Committee release the assembly bill for vote. The Big Feller then taught his student another lesson in hardball politics. "Wagner's the chairman of the Rules Committee, and you'll have to have a rule. He's now temporary president of the Senate so he can't call the Rules Committee together to pass a rule. That's the plan," he told her smiling.[39] "Oh, Mr. Sullivan," she exclaimed, taken aback by the duplicity of it all. The Big Feller was moved by the

earnestness and disappointment in the eyes of the young lobbyist. "Me sister was a poor girl," he explained, "and she went out to
work when she was young. I feel kinda sorry for them poor girls
that work the way you say they work. I'd like to do them a good
turn. I'd like to do you a good turn. You don't know much about
this parliamentary stuff do you?"[40] Perkins shook her head no.
But Tim did. "Well I'm the ranking member of the Rules Committee. Wagner is presiding officer, and his orders are not to recognize anybody to move for reconsideration. If you don't believe me,
you just try it."[41]

Quickly falling in with the Big Feller's plan, Perkins collected
supporting signatures from a majority of the Rules Committee
and sent two junior members, Josiah Newcomb and Mayhew
Wainwright, down the senate aisle to get Wagner's recognition.
Standing directly in front of Wagner they called "Mr. President,
Mr. President," but Wagner studiously refused to look at them,
and the two men finally returned to their seats. This was just as
Big Tim expected, and he seized the moment, striding theatri-
cally down the aisle to Wagner shouting, "A report from the Rules
Committee. A report from the Rules Committee!" Seeing the Big
Feller lumbering down the senate aisle, Wagner turned white
and desperately grasped at legislative technicalities to avert
defeat. "I can't receive any additional rules. No rules to be given."
Tim was not to be put off. "I am the acting chairman of the Rules
Committee," he retorted, "and I de-mand a vote on whether I can
make a report or not."[42] Sullivan remained at the foot of the aisle,
positively "beaming" as the besieged Wagner called in the senate
parliamentarian, who ruled in Tim's favor. Wagner then sent for
the lieutenant governor to return and take over the senate so
that he could resume his position as chairman of the Rules Committee and block Sullivan's report. But Tim was way ahead of
him and dispatched some of his men to keep the lieutenant governor out of the way as the senate prepared to vote on the House
version of the bill. Perkins, who was now getting a graduate-level
education in practical politics, described Tim's performance as
"smart parliamentarianism as well as politics."[43] As Wagner
fumed helplessly, the Big Feller personally set up the amended
bill for a seemingly successful vote.

Checking the numbers, and thinking all was safe, Tim and
Christy, still dressed in overcoats, voted first and headed for the
boat back to the city. However, after their departure, two wave-

rers, most significantly James Foley, reversed their votes and it failed 24 to 14. A frantic Perkins told McManus she would get the Sullivans back and that he must call for a reconsideration of the bill, which, under senate rules, he could do as one who had voted for it. McManus agreed. "We'll make you eat crow," he hissed at one of the vote changers.[44] The atmosphere in the senate chamber was electric as all involved realized that the climax of the legislative session was upon them. The bill's opponents, supported by Wagner, called for a "closed call of the house," meaning that the senate doors would be locked during a roll-call vote. If Big Tim and Christy did not return before the doors were locked, they would not be admitted, could not vote, and the 54-Hour Bill was doomed.

Each senator was entitled to a five-minute explanation of his vote for the bill, and most of the bill's supporters used their allotment to buy time for the Sullivans to return. McManus, effectively the bill's floor manager in Sullivan's absence, later recollected that he spent his time spouting "drivel."[45] Tim and Christy had received a phone call from Perkins telling them what happened, but the cab she sent for them failed to find them. Without transportation, the two senators rushed up the hill from the Hudson and burst into the senate chamber, "one [Big Tim] red-faced and puffing, the other [Christy] white-faced and gasping." "Record me in the affirmative," the Big Feller shouted as he stormed through the door.[46] The senate and galleries "broke into roars of applause," Perkins later recollected. "The Sullivans were heroes. I got some of it . . ."[47] Basking in the cheers and congratulations of the chamber, a smiling Big Tim went up to Perkins. "It's all right, me girl. We is wid [sic] you. The bosses thought they was going to kill your bill, but they forgot about Tim Sullivan. I'm a poor man meself. Me father and me mother were poor and struggling. I seen me sister go out to work when she was only fourteen and I know we ought to help these gals by giving 'em a law which will prevent them from being broken down while they're still young."[48]

In many ways, Big Tim's dramatic intervention to save the 54-Hour Bill was the crowning event of his political career. His motives were simple but several. For openers, it was good politics. His crucial support of the bill could only strengthen and extend the popularity—and power—of the Sullivan Association among the citizens of the Lower East Side. Probably, he also enjoyed stiffing Murphy in much the same way he tormented Croker. While never as hostile toward Silent Charlie as he became toward Croker, he may well have thought it useful to repeat the lesson that Tammany's boss ruled only with the consent of Big Tim.

But beyond that, Tim cared about the welfare of the "his" people—the workers, the poor, the troubled. He had spent much of his life providing support for his constituents through his personal activities. Now he took steps to ensure that such protections became a matter of law. It was a natural progression. Certainly Perkins understood and appreciated the man who had given her the bill, and contrasted the Sullivans' support with the tepid performance of young Franklin Delano Roosevelt. "I took it hard," she later wrote, "that a young man [Roosevelt] who had so much spirit did not do so well in this, which I though a test, as Tim Sullivan and The McManus, undoubtedly corrupt politicians."[49] But abler and more compassionate, she might have added.

10

Decline and Fall

Big Tim, let me say now, was an innocent sufferer. He was one
of God's noblemen. . . .

—Bald Jack Rose

They . . . went away to think of him, not as he had been in the
last two years, but as they had always seen him at the curb in
front of his clubhouse, a great, blue-eyed, pink-cheeked boy,
with his hands in his pockets and a smile on his round face.

—Oliver Simmons

As Big Tim was winding up his most productive session in
Albany, the scene was shifting in the city. During the mayoralties
of Seth Low and William Gaynor, the police presence increased
downtown and overt vice became harder to operate. Charlie Murphy continued to nudge Tammany away from the "police graft" in
which Sullivan, with his gambling establishments and underworld connections, was still involved. In addition, the environment—social and economic—on the Bowery was declining. The
area always had its destitute and criminal classes, but the nature
of the neighborhood coarsened after 1909. The rowdy and bawdy
recreational spots were replaced by the tawdry and dangerous.
The small businesses that catered to the working classes began
to abandon the Bowery, as flophouses and cheap drink dives
proliferated in their place. While gang violence had always been
part of the downtown scene, the newer manifestations were more
lethal and more likely to use guns, their depredations spurring
the flight of those with upwardly mobile aspirations.

Big Tim himself sensed the new winds blowing through the
Lower East Side. Though he never abandoned his Bowery headquarters, he began establishing outposts in the Tenderloin,
spending more of his time in midtown, where the Metropole
Hotel became a de facto headquarters. But, for all his power,

clout, alliances, and satellites, Big Tim Sullivan had no defenses against the calamities that struck in 1912. Even as he proudly basked in the cheers and accolades of the 54-Hour Bill's supporters, both he and his world began to unravel.

Among the gamblers given a start by the Big Feller were Herman Rosenthal and Arnold Rothstein. Tim described the two as "smart Jew boys. They're gonna go places."[1] He was half-right. Rothstein became a major-league gambler and underworld fixer, but Rosenthal could never quite make it despite Sullivan's backing. Some accounts maintain that Rothstein first drew Sullivan's attention by hanging around the Big Feller's Bowery headquarters and making himself useful.[2] Others contend that Tim first noticed Rothstein as a teenager "shooting stick" in one of Florrie's poolrooms. Whatever the case, the future underworld leader made a favorable impression. Sullivan reportedly encouraged the ambitious youngster to "stick with gambling. Gambling takes brains, and you're one smart Jew-boy."[3]

The Big Feller monitored Rothstein's progress, and a few years later put him in charge of the gaming room at the Metropole Hotel, a Times Square spot he owned with the Considine brothers. By 1901, Sullivan had arranged for Rothstein to run a gambling house with William Shea, a former ward leader and foreman with the Department of Water Supply, Gas, and Electricity. The two never got along, and in the wake of an argument over profits, a drunken Shea signed over his half of the casino to Rothstein. When Shea sobered up and realized his blunder, he entreated Tim to put him back in the operation. "Nothing doing," the Bowery leader reportedly replied. "You thought you were putting one over on Arnold. Well, now you know you got to get up pretty early in the morning to do that."[4] By 1912 Rothstein was a high roller in New York gambling circles, his way to the top greased by Big Tim's benevolence.

Rosenthal was another story. Like Rothstein he began his association with the Big Feller by hanging around the Bowery headquarters, and soon became a runner for the Sullivan Association. For reasons unfathomable to many of Tim's associates, and which some considered an early sign of mental instability, Big Tim took a liking to the ingratiating Jewish kid and made a special pet of him.[5] A heavy gambler himself, Rosenthal was often found sitting in at Tim's marathon poker parties, strengthening the personal relationship between the two.[6] Herman also made himself useful politically and served for a while as the effective leader of the Nineteenth Electoral District in the Third Assembly District.[7] After the Sullivans withdrew active interest from the Hesper Club, Rosenthal ran it as a concession, but he had famously bad luck, and despite his connection with Sullivan it folded. He then decided to move uptown to the Tenderloin, and in November 1911, with Tim's aid, Herman opened a new establishment at 104 West Forty-fifth Street.

Sullivan's assent to the relocation was crucial. By 1912, gambling, especially in the Tenderloin, was controlled by another triumvirate. This version included two members of the 1901 syndicate, Frank Farrell and Big Tim. The police were represented by Winfield Sheehan, chief assistant to Commissioner Rhinelander Waldo "who, it was understood, had no idea what was going on right under his nose."[8] The triumvirate's headquarters was the Metropole Hotel at Forty-third Street just off Broadway, jointly owned by Big Tim and the Considine brothers. Anyone wishing to open a gaming house in the Tenderloin needed the syndicate's approval. The de facto "license" fee could reach $1,000 for a choice location, plus monthly protection. A piece of the proceeds went to the neighborhood police captains and inspectors, but the bulk was distributed among the triumvirate according to a system called "the Great Divide."[9]

Despite his connections, Rosenthal ran afoul of the police, especially Lieutenant Charles Becker, head of the Special Squad Number 2—the "Strong Arm Squad." Becker was the most recent in a line of corrupt, brutal cops extending back into the nineteenth century. By the time the dilettante Waldo placed Becker in charge of the "Strong Arm Squad," he had already won an unsavory reputation as a shakedown artist and woman beater. The purpose of the "Strong Arm Squad" was to control gambling. Becker, who received his first appointment to the force in 1893, thanks to Tammany, used his job to extort a cut from the gamblers, sending his bagman "Bald Jack" or "Billiard Ball" Rose (née Jacob Rosenzweig) to make the collections. For hard cases who refused to cough up Becker's tithe, the lieutenant would send in Big Jack Zelig's crew.[10]

Rosenthal's problems grew from his refusal to make the requisite payments to the local police, a course of action that was rooted in his now-chronic shortage of funds. In any event, he was subjected to repeated raids in the spring of 1912, which led him to publicly complain that he was being persecuted by "the System"—an ill-defined combination of politicians and police. Although Rosenthal later claimed that Becker received 20 percent of the profits of his gambling house—whose fourth floor was his residence—Becker raided the place on April 15, and by placing a permanent guard around its entrances effectively shut it down.[11] Rosenthal continued to wail to all who would listen about his unfair treatment at the hands of the police, a course of action that drew even more attention to the gambling scene in the midtown area. Rothstein was the recipient of an unannounced and unwelcome police visit in April. He reopened in a week but was incensed at having his operations interrupted. He and other gamblers, and their politician backers and police connections, were infuriated at Becker, but increasingly concerned about Rosenthal, whose actions kept drawing attention to the midtown gambling scene. Rosenthal's fellow gamblers were made even more unhappy by the growing recognition that their loudmouthed fellow was supplying the police with information about competing gaming operations and they soon found themselves face-to-face with the "Strong Arm Squad."[12] By summer 1912, Rosenthal had put himself in a dangerously isolated position, despised by the police, and mistrusted by the gambling interests and those who staked them.

Oblivious to the precariousness of his position, Rosenthal became more brazen in attacking the police. After failing to get an appointment with Mayor Gaynor, he went to Herbert Bayard Swope, the star investigative reporter of the *New York World,* and soon to be its editor. Swope was hardly scandalized by Rosenthal's charges. A gaming man himself, Swope was a familiar figure in New York's sporting circles and was a close personal friend of Arnold Rothstein. He was also on good terms with the Big Feller. But Swope knew a hot story when he heard one and encouraged the babbling gambler to spill his guts—or exercise his imagination.

Swope, who had Rosenthal dictate his story in an affidavit form, began running with the story on July 12, when Rosenthal's charges about his oppression by the "System" and his sharing 20 percent of his profits with an unnamed police lieutenant ran on page one. Two days later in another large-point headline complete with photographs, Rosenthal named Becker as his police accomplice.[13] The growing publicity forced both Commissioner

Waldo and District Attorney Charles Whitman to respond. Waldo stated the matter would be investigated. Whitman agreed that Rosenthal was describing the overall situation accurately, but that no action could be taken until legal corroboration was supplied. In a further statement on July 15, Whitman again insisted Rosenthal supply evidence to support his allegations. "Charges do not constitute truth," he pointed out.[14] Becker denied any connection to the gambler.

Rosenthal's accusations threatened nearly everybody involved, and pressure was immediately applied to shut him up. Big Tim's ally and Al Smith's mentor, Big Tom Foley, allegedly contacted Rothstein and ordered him to "Get that stupid son of a bitch out of town."[15] Another account claimed Rosenthal visited Rothstein, who also advised him to keep his mouth shut and cancel the meeting with Whitman. According to this story, Rosenthal pleaded that he would only talk about Becker. Rothstein countered that Whitman was a Republican out to "crucify" the Big Feller, who would also tell him to keep his mouth shut if he were there. Rothstein then supposedly offered the desperate gambler $500 to leave New York. Rosenthal refused.[16] If the offer was indeed made, Herman would have been well advised to take it.

At 2:00 AM on the morning of July 16, 1912, Rosenthal was cut down by four gunmen in front of the Metropole on West Forty-third Street. A passerby remembered the license plate of the car used by the shooters. This led back to Bald Jack Rose, who had hired the car. Rose, along with two other passengers, Bridgey Webber and Harry Vallon, claimed the hit had been ordered by Becker, with the actual murder carried out by yet another group, Lefty Louie Rosenberg, Whitey Lewis, "Gyp the Blood" Horowitz, and "Dago Frank" Cioffi. All the suspects accused of the shooting were subsequently arrested, tried, convicted, and executed.

The day after Rosenthal was shot, a famous name was introduced into the case when Swope printed the entire text of the dead gambler's statement. "There is only one man in the world who can call me off," Rosenthal had written,

> that is the Big Fellow, "Big Tim" Sullivan, and he is as honest as the day is long, and I know he is in sympathy with me. He don't want to see anybody else hurt, and I don't want to hurt anybody. My fight is with the police. It is purely personal with me. I am making no crusade and my friends know all about it. . . .

The police know that I think more of "Big Tim" Sullivan than I do of anybody else alive. They know that the only way they can hurt me is to involve him with me—by trying to show that he is, or was, my partner in the gambling business. They know this is not true—that it is a dirty lie. He is not and never was invested with me to the extent of a penny. I hope his name will not be brought out in this connection.

Tim Sullivan and myself have been friends for many years. I knew him as a boy. I would lay down my life for him, and on more than one occasion he has proved his friendship for me. I believe that I could get anything he's got, and if I need money I can go to him for it and he will give it to me or get it for me. It is purely a matter of friendship, and he never expects to make a nickel profit out of it. He is the only man that could call me off, and he has told me that he believes I am doing right in trying to protect myself and my home.[17]

Whatever Rosenthal intended in his rambling statement about Sullivan is not entirely clear. Possibly he felt invoking the Big Feller's name would add some weight to his story. He may have also gone out of his way to clear Tim from any connection with his problems to keep in the good graces of the Sullivan clan, whose aid might be needed later. His contention that he had the Big Feller's full support in his public campaign was clearly false. Big Tim's affection for the doomed gambler was real, but it would have been sorely tested by Rosenthal's blurting out his charges to the papers and potentially Whitman.

In the uproar following Rosenthal's murder and the publication of his full statement to Swope, rumors swirled about the Big Feller's possible role in the shooting. Sullivan's friendship with Rosenthal was well known, as was his own abiding interest in gambling.[18] Contrary to what he told Swope, Rosenthal had succeeded in getting past the cordon of Sullivanites determined to protect Tim from spongers and loan seekers, and wheedled a $2,500 note from the Bowery boss. Any number of people had seen the note, since Herman repeatedly displayed it in his attempts to raise cash for his new gaming room.[19] That Sullivan was acquainted with Charles Becker was no secret either. Many wondered what Becker might have to say about Big Tim's connection with Rosenthal as well as the larger issue of Tim's involvement with gambling throughout the city. The police lieutenant was increasingly suspected of complicity in Rosenthal's murder. On July 17 Whitman declared that the police "through certain members are responsible for killing the man who threatened the system, and who had shown he had nerve enough to make good his threats."[20] Few doubted the identity of the "certain" member Whitman had in mind.

Newspapers ran several stories alleging that in the days before Rosenthal's murder the entire East Side underworld expected the shooting. According to the buzz, Big Tim knew on Monday night, July 15, that Rosenthal was to be killed. Sullivan tried to protect the loose-tongued gambler but to no avail. "Even [Sullivan's] influence was unequal to the task of reaching those bent upon removing the man who threatened the gambling fraternity," the *Herald* informed its readers. "He did the best he could. He telephoned to Rosenthal to get out of town at once and stay away for a short time. Rosenthal ignored the warning. Similar warnings came from other sources. He ignored them."[21]

Like reports appeared in other New York papers. The *Tribune* ran a piece claiming that two or three hours before he was killed, Rosenthal "received a summons to appear before one of the highest politicians of Tammany Hall who had been his friend for years, 'Herman, you have gone too far' said the friend. 'It's time you pulled in your horns. You're spoiling things.'"[22] Hearst's *American* informed its readers that a "very well known East Side politician" told Rosenthal that if he did not shut up, "I wash my hands of you."[23] Of course, the identity of the unnamed East Side politician in the stories was obvious to all. Larry Mulligan quickly dismissed the stories. "Everytime anything comes off they have to drag 'Big Tim' or someone close to him into it," he commented derisively.[24] The details in the various accounts may be suspect, but many reporters maintained close contact, even friendships, with members of the political and gambling classes, and the overall message of the reports seems accurate enough.

Despite the initial interest, steps were quickly and effectively taken to keep Big Tim's name out of the investigation and subsequent trials. The Big Feller himself left town for the Catskills sometime during the evening before Rosenthal's murder.[25]

On July 18, two days after Rosenthal fell before a hail of bullets, a man described by the *New York Times* as "a very well known gambler of the Broadway tribe" visited Whitman's apartment to "take up the story where Rosenthal left off."[26] The description best fits Rothstein, who was probably acting as an emissary from either Murphy or the "machine within a machine." Tammany would raise no objection to the prosecution of Becker, whose position deteriorated by the day, but there would be no wider investigation—no pursuing the Sullivan connection. Credence for this interpretation was provided by Whitman, who was milking the case for all political advantage. When reporters asked him about Tim's involvement in Rosenthal's gambling house, the district attorney snapped that he was "investigating a murder, and not conducting a sociological investigation."[27] In short, Whitman revealed an unwritten contract with the Tiger— he could make political hay from the lurid underworld assassination with Tammany's passive consent, but the political angle would be left alone.

In the meantime, Tammany lawyer Max Steuer, another former newsboy given a helping hand by the Big Feller, entered the case. Steuer quickly won plea bargains for Rose and his nonshooting associates in return for their testimony against the hitmen and Becker himself. When first approached about taking part in the defense Steuer demurred, but later changed his mind "yield-[ing]," as the papers phrased it, "to the persuasion of friends who felt the interests of someone whose name has not been mentioned in the case would not be safe unless a lawyer of Steuer's ability was on hand to represent them."[28] The "friends" were no doubt Larry Mulligan and Patrick Sullivan, now the effective heads of the Sullivan clan. In any event, whatever the rumors and speculation, Big Tim's name would remain unspoken at the ensuing trials. Becker, a grafting cop but probably innocent of Rosenthal's murder—he had nothing to gain and much to lose from it—was indicted on July 29.

The exact role played by the Big Feller in the Rosenthal-Becker affair remains murky. Much of this is due to the onset of mental illness, which first manifested itself in 1911. His psychological condition deteriorated rapidly in 1912, coinciding with the uproar over the Rosenthal-Becker case. Some light was shed on Tim's actions when Becker, twice convicted and facing the electric chair, released statements that he hoped were either exculpatory or supportive enough to win him a stay of execution and, maybe, a new trial. His first attempt came in the form of a story he told "to several persons, including his lawyers and his spiritual advisors."[29]

According to the published accounts, obtained from "a man who had seen Becker in the death house on many occasions," the disgraced detective maintained that the night before Rosenthal was gunned down he received a phone call from Big Tim and agreed to meet him at a Broadway theater in which the Big Feller had an interest. When Becker arrived, he found Tim, Bald Jack Rose, and another man whom he did not know. Supposedly, Sullivan was terrified about Rosenthal's potential revelations. "He's going before the grand jury," Tim wailed, "and I'm afraid we'll get mixed up in this."[30] Becker tried to calm Sullivan down claiming "all the witnesses were fixed and that Whitman could not corroborate Rosenthal's story." According to Becker, the still-agitated Big Feller suggested giving the gambler five or six thousand dollars to buy his silence. Becker said he advised against it, arguing that Rosenthal "could say nothing that would hurt any of them," and repeated his opposition after Rose pressed for a payout. Becker then left the conference.[31] As recounted by Becker's emissary, the cop later heard that Rose had received the $6,000 and made an appointment to meet Rosenthal at the Metropole, where he intended to bribe him to leave the country.

According to the *New York Times,* this was all Becker himself had said about the case. However, the paper's informant "learned from other sources" that when Rose and Bridgey Webber went to a Forty-second Street gambling house on the night of July 15, they met Harry Vallon, and the four gunmen. Plans were changed and Rosenthal was to be kidnapped, with Rose and the others pocketing $5,000 of Sullivan's money. Rose, Webber, Vallon and the other gangsters then went to the Metropole, stopping for a few drinks along the way. When Rosenthal emerged, Vallon started firing, and the other gunmen followed suit.[32] Becker could have told his story during his second trial, the *Times'* source alleged, but his lawyers felt the jury would disregard it and he'd never get another. In the meantime, Becker's legal team was seeking witnesses to support his account.

Though the convicted cop's story, as published in the *Times,* reported that Becker and his supporters believed Big Tim's 1913 death was murder, they did not explain what the connection would have been between the Rosenthal case and his death. If Becker's tale is taken at face value, it simply demonstrates Sullivan was unreasonably anxiety ridden. As Becker himself contended, Rosenthal's accusations were legally valueless without corroboration, of which there seemed little or none. Moreover, the most that could be asserted was that the Big Feller wanted Rosenthal out of town, not dead. A curious element in the story is Tim meeting Becker with Rose and the unidentified man. By this point, the Sullivan clan was keeping close tabs on its shaky leader, and Becker knew most of Tim's entourage. It seems unlikely Sullivan could have gotten away on his own with a second-rate hood like Rose.

The day after the first Becker story appeared, the former detective's attorneys released a lengthy statement resembling a deposition, in which Becker putatively told everything he knew about the Rosenthal case. In this more formal, written account, Becker claimed he first met Tim in January 1912, at Sullivan's midtown office in the Shanley Building on Forty-third Street. By this time, Rosenthal's gambling house was up and running, and Tim stated that he was invested in the operation to the tune of $12,500 and wanted to help him avoid raids. The Big Feller advised Becker that he had spoken to Commissioner Waldo and understood that Rosenthal could operate if he did so quietly. He then came to the point of the meeting, and said he wanted to make sure Becker would not raid Rosenthal. The detective replied that if he had Waldo's word, "he need not worry about me, as I only raided when and where Waldo ordered me to, and that if Waldo did not order me to raid Rosenthal, I would not do so."[33] Tim seemed satisfied and Becker left the building. On the way out he ran into Rosenthal, who anxiously pressed Becker as to whether he had seen his protector. Rosenthal also produced a note for $2,500 signed "T. D. Sullivan," which the nervous gambler said proved that the politician was his "friend."[34]

A few weeks later, Waldo ordered Becker to raid Rosenthal, setting off the chain of events that drove the frustrated gambler to go to Swope. According to Becker's final declaration, about a day after Rosenthal's first edited story appeared in the *World,* Sullivan's secretary, Henry Appelbaum, arranged a meeting between the Big Feller and the now-threatened leader of the "Strong Arm Squad." The two discussed matters at another of Tim's offices at Sixtieth and Broadway. Becker described Tim as "worried to death about what Rosenthal was doing." Specifically, he was terrified that Rosenthal would connect him with his club as well as "some election frauds on the east side."[35] As Becker recollected it, Tim virtually pleaded with him not to mention his dealings with the unstable gambler. "Now I want you to assure me you won't bring me in[to] this," Tim asked, "If you don't I am alright."[36] The policeman pledged he would keep the Big Feller out of the investigation regardless of what Rosenthal said. Becker also claimed that Tim told him he had sent Appelbaum to give Rosenthal $5,000 to get out of town and offer $100 or $200 to Mrs. Rosenthal if she would persuade her husband to stop making accusations.[37] This meeting ended with Becker once again assuring Sullivan that he would not mention his name in any police inquiries. It was 1:30 AM on July 15.

On July 27 Henry Appelbaum made another visit to Becker on Big Tim's behalf. Discussing the situation in a room at the Sixty-Fifth Precinct house, the Big Feller's secretary described his boss as "nearly insane about Rosenthal's murder," and was terrified the increasingly beleaguered cop would mention their previous contacts concerning the dead gambler.[38] Appelbaum and Becker met one last time at 1:30 AM on the morning of July 29. Sullivan's secretary informed Becker that he had received assurances from Rose and his confederates that they wouldn't mention Tim in any way. Becker agreed to stand by his promise and keep Sullivan's name out of it.[39] He was arrested later that day.

Though Becker's final testament was self-serving, he had indeed made no mention of his contacts with the Big Feller during the trial and up to the brink of his execution. Becker's allegations that Tim wanted Rosenthal out of the way suggested that a desperate Sullivan was capable of ordering a hit, but by 1915, no one was listening. Whitman dismissed the affidavit as old news, and most of the parties mentioned in Becker's version of the case denied any statements that implicated them.

Even so, parts of Becker's testament were undoubtedly true. Police Commissioner Waldo, for example, confirmed Tim's attempts to intervene in matters on Rosenthal's behalf. Waldo remembered that Sullivan had approached him and asked if Rosenthal was being singled out for police attention. Waldo replied that the gambler would be shut down with everyone else. Tim, who spoke casually, "neither pleading nor in anger," then tried to turn the commissioner by implying political benefits if Waldo were "good to his friends."[40] Waldo said he dismissed the suggestion. Tim, who had referred to Rosenthal as a "friend" during the conversation, seemed satisfied that he had done what he could. According to Waldo there was no mention of money during their talk.[41]

Henry Appelbaum confirmed Becker's story of meeting with Tim at various junctures regarding Rosenthal. But his recollection of events differed in key respects. Tim's old secretary denied his boss was invested in Rosenthal's operation. Appelbaum related that early in 1912, Sullivan told him he had given $2,000 to Rosenthal for a "bank roll." The needy gambler returned a few days later begging for more money, and the Big Feller gave him two notes for $2,500 each. Rosenthal repaid the $2,000 cash, but then asked for another $2,500 note from the Bowery leader. "Now, does this look as though Senator Sullivan was in any way interested in the gambling house?" Appelbaum asked referring to the relatively small amounts involved.[42]

Appelbaum explained that Tim's subsequent actions were driven by his mental difficulties. In April 1912, shortly after the close of the 1912 legislative session, Tim was taken to Europe, probably in hopes of finding some relief for his problems. A month later when Appelbaum saw him in Paris he found his boss "a very sick man in a terribly unsettled mental condition. He was worrying over everything, and everything seemed to worry him. He made mountains out of molehills."[43] Nor was Sullivan any better when he returned to New York, a fact that was apparent to all who had contact with him. Appelbaum pointed out this was well before Rosenthal's situation reached the crisis stage, discounting rumors the unfortunate gambler's confession and murder had pushed Tim over the edge. According to Appelbaum, the Rosenthal-Becker case "affected him so far as to aggravate the disease," but it did not cause it.[44] Tim's old confidant corroborated Becker's assertion that Big Tim was distraught over Rosenthal's affidavit and murder. Sullivan was worried that his loan would be seen as evidence that he had set up Rosenthal in his sporting club, and he had Appelbaum get him in touch with Becker as the cop had stated. But Appelbaum denied that either he or Tim had attempted to induce Rosenthal to leave town or offered any money toward that end.[45]

All the principals in Becker's trial, including the defendant, honored their commitment to remain silent on any connection between Big Tim and the dead gambler. Becker's belated sixty-page testimony did him no good. The governor who held the power of reprieve was the same Charles Whitman who had prosecuted Becker in 1912. Having ridden the sensational case into the governor's office, Whitman was not about to grant any clemency. Becker was electrocuted July 31, 1915.

Though Big Tim's name had been kept out of the hearings and trials, there had been some talk of subpoenaing him to explain the $2,500 note that Rosenthal was trying to negotiate just before his death. In August 1912, as rumors of a subpoena surfaced, Tim "disappeared." It was later discovered that he had headed west to Hot Springs, Arkansas.[46] Whether his family and advisors were hoping to find a cure in some spa or hospital or just get him away from New York is hard to judge. Probably both. Under the circumstances, the stress of giving evidence would have inflamed Big Tim's demons, and he was probably in no state to provide it anyway. In any event, on September 20, 1912, Frank Moss, who was helping Whitman prepare the case against Becker, declared no subpoena for Big Tim was or would be issued.[47]

Considering that most of those involved had no interest in revealing all they knew, Big Tim's exact role in the Rosenthal murder will never be completely clear. Tim's friends and associates moved decisively to keep his name out of the mess, a course of action that reflected concern to avoid wounding Tammany as much as sensitivity about Tim's mental state. Without the psychiatric factor, there is no obvious reason for Sullivan to have been so discombobulated by Rosenthal's affidavit. He often lent money to those he liked, and it was well known that he had taken a liking to the ill-fated gambler. The Big Feller's own mania for gambling was common knowledge, and no one would have been shocked that he had invested in a gaming house. It is also unlikely that Rosenthal—or Becker—knew much more about political operations downtown than could be read in the papers.

Yet, in his condition, which included symptoms of paranoia, the Big Feller was clearly terrified by Rosenthal's going public about his dispute with Becker. Worried to a frazzle—making mountains out of molehills—he might have pressed Becker to remove the source of the agitation from the stage. If so, others would have been involved, since he was seldom, if ever, alone after his deterioration became manifest. Such a conspiracy would have been hard to keep secret, though perhaps a few close lieutenants could be trusted to remain silent. Of course, there was no advantage to Becker in accusing Sullivan of ordering—or paying for—a hit if he was the one who arranged it. Besides, his silence regarding the Big Feller, like that of Rose and those who took a plea bargain and turned state's evidence, might have been bought with the promise of Tammany support. Rose and company got it through Steuer. Tammany stalwart Bourke Cockran, always close to the clan, took part in Becker's defense, especially the attempt to win a reprieve, and he might have been acting for the Sullivans. Intriguingly, as Cockran desperately searched for anything that might halt the convicted cop's execution, he received an unsigned letter alleging that Big Tim had made middle-of-the-night phone calls to Whitman's assistant district attorney, asking them to help Becker.[48] Unfortunately, the anonymous nature of the letter made it useless in a legal proceeding. If the letter was genuine it suggests that Tim knew Becker was innocent and sought, even as he descended into the pit of mental illness, to save him. If so, Big Tim probably knew who did murder Rosenthal, but if he revealed it to anyone else they—like him—took the secret to the grave.[49] Of course, that might have been the point. If Tim did, indeed, know who had organized Rosenthal's murder, his mental problems might have become a matter of concern. In sound mind, the Big Feller might be counted on to keep his mouth shut. Beset by monsters in his own head, his silence might have become problematic, requiring a permanent solution. At this remove, the true sequence of events, and the motivations of the major protagonists, are unknowable.

Exactly when and how Tim's mental problems first appeared is not precisely known. Reading into the evidence, it seems his psychiatric difficulties, once they arrived, did so with increasing frequency, pulling him further and further into mental confusion and decline. Whenever the symptoms first showed up, by 1911 they were serious enough that a Fire Department doctor, Herman L. Reis, was brought in to examine the Big Feller.[50] Reis's diagnosis has not survived, but from his later comments, he probably determined that Big Tim suffered from "melancholia"—an early term for depression. By 1912, the Big Feller's slide became precipitous. He was reportedly beset by delusions and hallucinations in March of that year, making his final performance in Albany even more impressive.[51] More surprising, he decided to return to Congress, and was—as usual—easily elected. The triumph was a hollow one, as he proved incapable of taking his seat.

Although Sullivan's family was careful to avoid any public revelation of his disintegration, it did not go unnoticed. Leeches took advantage of Big Tim's clouded faculties to get him to sign promissory notes, while others began forging his name on various

IOUs.[52] Remarks made by observers about Tim's "high-hatting" the Bowery during his last few years may simply reflect the efforts of family and friends to keep him away from the public and out of trouble. Tim's family, led by half-brother Larry Mulligan and younger brother Patrick Sullivan, searched desperately for a cure for their sibling and leader. Trips to Europe in April 1912, and California and Hot Springs, Arkansas, that August enabled him to seek relief at spas and sanitariums. The uproar over the death of Rosenthal fed whatever demons raged inside his head, but some claimed he was better after his western sojourn. Tim was brought back to New York in September so he could visit the deathbed of his long-estranged wife. The Big Feller's attendance at her September 13 funeral wrenched him so emotionally that he suffered a relapse and fell into a decline from which he never really recovered.[53] At this point, his problems, mental and financial, became front-page news.

On September 20, 1912, the *New York Times* ran a story detailing Big Tim's condition. According to the paper, Tim's finances were undone by his legendary generosity. In recent years "men of big affairs . . . in danger of financial ruin have come to him by the score, and he has helped them out, often taking merely their promise as security."[54] An anonymous friend told reporters that Tim had signed notes amounting to $400,000 in 1911, and an additional $300,000 in 1912.[55] "His friends welched on him and Big Tim had to make good," the unnamed source stated. "His own friends have driven him almost to despair."[56] In a letter to a friend dated April 2, 1912, Tim complained he had been "robbed of $350,000."[57] Tormented by mental and financial difficulties, the Big Feller had dropped sixty pounds in three weeks. The *Times* added that ten years previously the Big Feller "was a very rich man, but these losses . . . have considerably lessened his fortune."[58] And exacerbated his mental difficulties, they might have added.

Observers noted that Tim appeared agitated at Nellie's funeral, and he had to be assisted to his carriage. He was immediately driven to the St. Denis Hotel, owned by Larry Mulligan, where he was guarded by Mulligan, Christy Sullivan, and Dr. Reis, who was acting as Tim's personal attendant. Tim's afflictions gave him no peace, and when he came downstairs to report he could not sleep, he was taken to the sanitarium of Dr. G. M. F. Bond in Yonkers. The family sought to keep his whereabouts

15. Big Tim Sullivan near the end of his life. *Munsey's Magazine,*
December 1913.

secret and maintained the fiction that he was still in his room
and not to be disturbed. Larry Mulligan stationed himself by the
elevator and intercepted anyone who attempted to visit his half-
brother. Among would-be callers was a woman dressed in mourn-
ing clothes who asked to see Tim. "Show him this picture," she
said reaching into her pocketbook, "and then he will let me see

him." One of the pages took the picture to Tim's watchdogs. But the man returned and told her no one could be admitted to his room.[59] The woman's identity was not revealed, but her dress suggests she was a relative of Nellie's, and her actions that she was close to Tim as well.

Confined to the sanitarium, Big Tim missed the traditional pre-election Sullivan rally at the Bowery Theater. It was the last ever held there, as the building was torn down soon after—fitting symbolism for the end of an era. Though the Big Feller's condition was common knowledge by this time, such was the spell of his name and reputation that he won his congressional seat by a margin of 1,857 votes.[60] Only five days later it was admitted that he could not take his seat, and "political and business associates" privately conceded "that no hope was entertained for his recovery."[61] Finally, on November 21, Patrick Sullivan and Larry Mulligan issued a statement about Tim: "Senator Sullivan is now staying at the private sanitarium where he went some time ago, in an extremely serious condition, brought on by overwork, this condition being aggravated by a slight attack of diabetes. Dr. Bond's diagnosis of the case is neurasthenia. We are pleased to say the Senator is improving daily. Dr. Bond's orders of absolute rest and quiet are imperative."[62]

Tim had his good days, which the family seized upon to proclaim improvement and predict eventual recovery. Nevertheless, their course of action disclosed the overall trajectory of their famous relative's illness. On January 11, 1913, the Sullivan family and their legal counsel had Tim committed to Bond's sanitarium, where he had previously been a voluntary patient. The order permitted the Big Feller to be kept in physical restraint if necessary.[63] On January 18, William Ellison, acting for Tim's family, petitioned the supreme court to authorize a committee to oversee Tim's person and property. The application was made on behalf of Tim's surviving family, brothers Patrick and Larry Mulligan, sister Margaret Hickey, and the children of his deceased older sister.

On January 23, 1913, a sheriff's jury and three commissioners met to determine the merits of the petition. The courtroom was packed with those "who seemed to take the affliction of Sullivan as a personal sorrow for he had a strong hold on his friends."[64] William Ellison introduced the family's case by explaining, "We are here to save a man from himself."[65] Larry Mulligan, the only petitioner to testify, fought back the tears as he related his brother's decline and broke down in the jury room after giving his evidence.[66]

Mulligan was followed by a succession of doctors and psychiatrists testifying to Big Tim's condition. Tim's physical ailments were confined to "foot drop extension paresis of recent origin," but his mental problems were several and severe. According to one of the alienists (psychiatrists) who had examined him, "[the] patient showed intense anxiety and seemed filled with forebodings; He insisted that conversations should be in whispers; his voice was in whispers; he insisted that he was being doped by his enemies, that dope was put in his food and forced into the air of his room; was disconcerted as to time, but showed quite some insight."[67] The doctor went on to say that the Big Feller's present condition began in March 1912, and "was characterized by alternate excitement and depression, threats of suicide and, less often of violence, delusions of conspiracy and persecutory delusions not systemized, almost continuous olfactory and gustatory hallucinations, has less of visual hallucinations."[68] The other doctors provided similar evidence. Dr. John Herrity, on the staff at Dr. Bond's sanitarium, diagnosed Tim as suffering from "manic depressive insanity."[69] After visiting Tim at the sanitarium, Dr. Herman C. Hoeffling, Tim's personal physician for twenty-five years, found his patient "utterly and absolutely incompetent."[70] Dr. Bond concurred with the diagnosis. William B. Pritchard, an expert witness who examined Tim, was asked by a juror if it was possible Tim might recover. "Yes it is possible," the psychiatrist responded, "but I do not think it probable."[71] In the weight of such evidence, the jury took just five minutes to declare Big Tim Sullivan incompetent to run his own affairs.[72]

The privately written opinion hinted that tertiary syphilis was at work, though the charge was not made publicly, nor was any supporting evidence presented in support of the allegation.[73] No insinuation of syphilis is found in the published statements of the doctors, and it might have arisen from prejudice and the belief that the Big Feller's presumed involvement in prostitution led him to dally with the wrong woman. Recorded evidence suggests depression, paranoia, and possibly schizophrenia. At any rate, on January 30, the person and estate of Timothy D. Sullivan were entrusted to a committee consisting of Larry Mulligan, Frank Farrell, described as "a business partner . . . and owner of the New York baseball club of the American League [Yankees],"

Emmanuel Blumenstiel and Patrick H. Sullivan.[74] Former corporation counsel, and one of Tim's longtime informal advisors, William B. Ellison, stayed on as the group's lawyer and official spokesman. Despite the well-publicized losses, Big Tim was still considered to be worth close to a million dollars, and some estimates ran higher. Some observers believed Tim's estate actually grew as his mental capabilities worsened. The close guard his family and doctors kept over him prevented him from signing any more notes.[75]

On April 1, 1913, Tim was taken to his brother Patrick's house in Eastchester. The family and friends attributed the move to Tim's supposed improvement and publicly claimed that a complete recovery was expected. Yet only three days before the Big Feller "had a severe setback. For a time he became violent and had to be put in a straitjacket."[76] Perhaps grasping at straws, Tim's family argued that the Big Feller was generally better except when he became depressed at being confined, and hoped the less-institutional setting of Patrick's house would prove beneficial to Tim's condition. According to the press, Big Tim himself resisted going to his brother's house but was finally convinced it might be better for him.[77]

But the familial surroundings did not have the intended effect. Once again the family looked to Europe for help. On June 6, Tim, accompanied by Patrick, sailed for Europe from Boston with a large delegation of Tammany braves on hand to see him off. The family once again released a positive report, asserting that Big Tim was "rapidly recovering from long illness and [he] hopes that a few weeks at the baths in Europe will bring about a complete recovery."[78]

Following Tim's return to the United States, he was provided with an apartment at the Hotel St. Denis, which was managed by Larry Mulligan. On August 21, 1913, he gave his nurses the slip and headed for his old haunts downtown. He was soon returned unharmed and taken to his brother Patrick's home in the then sparsely developed Eastchester section of the Bronx, near Pelham Bay Park. Ten days later, after an all-night card game, Big Tim walked away from his slumbering nurses and disappeared into the night.

For fourteen days the Big Feller's whereabouts were unknown. The family, led by Mulligan and Ellison, appealed to the public for help. Photographs of Tim were distributed—though his face peered down from nearly every bar in the city and was frequently reproduced in newspapers—but the family cautioned that his appearance had changed. Under the burden of his affliction, Tim had dropped about thirty pounds—he was down to about 190—and had become "a bit stooped." He had also lost some teeth from both sides of his jaw.[79] Though obviously frantic, the Sullivans and Ellison attempted a facade of confidence, maintaining that the Bowery leader was in no danger. "He's all right," Mulligan told the press. "He just got tired of his nurses and slipped off to have a good time by himself."[80]

Despite the Sullivan clan's best efforts, reports of their forebodings began to circulate. Some relatives expressed fears that Tim would die of exposure, since he had almost no money when he left his brother's house. Others began to whisper about the possibility of suicide, "since he had been suffering from melancholia brought on by illness."[81] "Alienists"—today's psychiatrists—offered their take on the Big Feller's disappearance. Herman Reis, the Fire Department doctor who had first treated Tim, "gloomily insisted" that the missing politico had killed himself in a relapse of melancholia—depression.[82] Psychiatrists at Dr. Bond's sanitarium, where Tim was confined in 1912, agreed the possibility was "tenable." Dr. Foster Kennedy, the Big Feller's current physician, was not quite so pessimistic. Accepting the belief that his charge was still alive somewhere, he expressed regret that Tim had "indulged" in such an escape as "we were just beginning to think that he was well again."[83]

Mulligan, Ellison, and most of Tim's friends and family reacted with anger that anyone would suggest suicide. They clung to the story that the Big Feller was hiding out with a misguided friend. Nevertheless, newspapers reported that "all of 'Big Tim's' friends and relatives [feel] more anxiety than they betray." Moreover, "those who felt that he would never be seen alive again said everything was being done to make it appear that the Bowery leader was sane enough to maintain his prestige, while his condition was in reality most discouraging."[84] But as the search for the missing leader continued, stories and rumors spread and faded of his surfacing in various parts of the metropolitan area. Someone said they saw him in Smithtown, Long Island. Others claimed they saw him in Harlem, Broadway, or the Bowery itself. But if they did, it was only his shade.

On September 13, 1913, at the East Twenty-sixth Street morgue in Manhattan, a cheap city-supplied coffin was about to be
sealed and shipped to the potter's field on Hart Island. Peter
Perfield, a patrolman on duty, took the last legally required look
at the body in the coffin. It was the corpse of a man who had been
hit by a train near the Westchester freight yards in the early-
morning hours of August 31. Though the body had been severed
at the trunk, the face was unscathed. Taking a second, closer
look, Perfield exclaimed, "Why it's Tim! Big Tim!"[85] Big Tim's
family was quickly notified, and Mulligan, Patrick Sullivan, and
Alderman Johnny White rushed to the scene. Patrick caught
sight of Tim's blood- and cinder-stained coat and ran from the
room sobbing, "It's Tim's coat. I can't look at him," leaving Mulligan with the unhappy task of making the official identification.[86]
"Yes, it's Tim. Poor Tim! Poor Tim!" Mulligan moaned gazing into
his dead half-brother's face. After initial plans to have Tim
waked at a funeral home were rejected, the Big Feller's body was
conveyed to the clubhouse of the Timothy D. Sullivan Association
at 207 Bowery.

Tim's coffin was set on two stools in the assembly room on the
fourth floor of the building. Placed next to the bier was a large
leather rocking chair White had given the Big Feller which was
now conspicuously and symbolically empty.[87] Twenty thousand
people turned out to pay their last respects to the Big Feller. The
doors to the clubhouse opened at 5:00 AM and from then until
midnight, downtown New York paid its last respects to the Big
Feller. The mourners who filed past the bier came from all walks
of life, "rich and poor, old and young." According to the *New York
Times,* "behind the Irishman walked the Jew, the Italian, the
Frenchman, the Scandinavian, the Chinese, the Spaniard and
even the Turk. It was, in fact, a procession of all nations."[88] The
large room where Tim was waked was illuminated by a twenty-
four-candle candelabrum. Large and expensive floral pieces, trib-
utes from Tim's friends and allies, surrounded the coffin. A news-
paperman judged the flower arrangements "fit for the bier of a
king, which was proper enough, for 'Big Tim' was a king in the
Bowery view of kingship and down here, where for years his regal
sway had been unquestioned, they were paying reverence to a
ruler dead."[89]

Of Tim's closest survivors, Larry Mulligan was most visibly

distraught. Before it was finally identified, Sullivan's body had gone from a Bronx police station to the Fordham Morgue, the Harlem Morgue, and finally the central morgue at Bellevue. Mulligan was tormented by the knowledge that there were people in all these places who had known his brother. Throughout the wake, Mulligan clung to the tag that the Fordham Morgue had attached to the corpse: "August 31. Received the body of an unknown man killed in the New York, New Haven and Hartford Railroad near Pelham Parkway."[90] Venting his grief, Big Tim's half-sibling repeatedly unraveled the crumpled tag and pressing it on passing mourners asked how such a fate could befall a man that "even dogs in the streets know . . ."[91] It was a question that would be asked many times in the succeeding weeks.[92]

Big Tim's funeral began at 10:00 AM the following morning. The service was held at Old St. Patrick's Cathedral. To prepare for the event, Mott Street, which runs in front of the cathedral, was scrubbed for the occasion. Among the dignitaries attending were three United States senators and twenty members of the House of Representatives, as well as justices of the state supreme court and judges of the city court. Charlie Murphy and his doomed mayoral candidate, Tim's old client Edward E. McCall, stood at the head of the honorary pallbearers. As the Big Feller's body was borne into the street from 207 Bowery, members of the Sullivan Association placed an enormous funeral pall comprised of 3,900 American Beauty roses and 200 chrysanthemums over the coffin.[93]

Sarsaparilla Reilly, who had loyally served Big Tim from his earliest days in politics, acted as coordinator and a kind of master of ceremonies. Five thousand people jammed the cathedral. Ten thousand had been turned away and made up part of the 75,000 mourners who crowded the streets around Old St. Patrick's.[94] Eight priests and a Fire Department chaplain celebrated a High Requiem Mass to speed Tim's soul to heaven, though he was never a practicing Catholic.[95] No eulogies were given. They would have been superfluous. At the end of the Mass a boy's choir sang "Rest, Rest for the Weary" and "O, Death Where is Thy Sting." As the coffin was carried from the church, the somber tones of "Dies Irae" sounded through the old building. A long train of carriages, including six hacks containing nothing but flowers, followed the hearse through the streets of the Lower East Side and across the Williamsburgh Bridge to Calvary Cemetery in Long Island City.

As the procession rolled through the old Bowery neighborhood, packed throngs of onlookers lined the streets, straining for a glimpse of the procession. Behind them shop windows were filled with signs reading "We Mourn Our Loss." Inside Bowery movie theaters, a black-bordered photograph of the Big Feller flashed at the conclusion of each film. When the cortege reached Calvary, Big Tim was buried near his "best loved kinsman and most loyal supporter," Timothy P. Sullivan, Little Tim.

The bizarre, and to many, mysterious death of Big Tim Sullivan, and the seeming inexplicable delay in identifying his body, led to a swirl of rumors and theories. Some supposed "friends" of Tim's told reporters that he was murdered by "footpads"— muggers. Speaking for the family, Patrick Sullivan denied his brother was the victim of a homicide. Police Commissioner Waldo chimed in, stating that there was no evidence that the Bowery leader had met his death through foul play.[96] Talk of suicide, which began while Tim was missing, rose anew. Ellison tried to squash such stories. He knew Tim as "well as any man on earth," he asserted to newspapermen, "and I know he wasn't one who would commit suicide. And besides, he wouldn't walk two and a half miles to commit suicide. He was accidentally killed."[97] Sullivan confidant, Alderman Johnny White, dismissed the suicide talk stating, "Tim was Irish and Catholic. That is the answer to that."[98] The theology was sound, but the psychology was flawed. Whether a man with a broken mind was capable of observing the strictures of dogma remains highly debatable. But the clan would not countenance any open-ended questions and stuck to their belief that Tim was trying to reach a railroad station. In defending this scenario, Patrick Sullivan claimed his brother had climbed over a bridge seeking a shortcut and fell to the tracks.[99] Whatever the details, the Sullivans and their retainers were adamant about one thing—Big Tim did not kill himself.

What happened to Big Tim Sullivan on the night of August 31 will probably never be satisfactorily answered. Despite denials, many people then and now believe Tim was the victim of foul play. That his death occurred in the wake of Rosenthal's murder and Becker's trial only strengthened that assumption. He knew too much, had ordered Rosenthal's death, or at least permitted it. Rumors spread that the Big Feller had been recovering his sanity and his memory and was ready to reveal everything he knew about the Rosenthal case when he mysteriously died.[100] Indeed,

16. Charles Francis Murphy at Big Tim Sullivan's funeral. *Munsey's Magazine,* **December 1913.**

after Becker's death house testament was released in 1915, newspapers felt the need to reassure the public that Sullivan's death was not due to foul play.[101] Perhaps the family and friends were correct. Tim had simply tried to make his way back to the neighborhood he had known and loved. In his diminished condition he became disoriented, blundered onto the tracks at the

17. Grave of Timothy Daniel Sullivan. Calvary Cemetery, Long Island. Author's Collection.

wrong time, and met his death. Or perhaps, as others have suggested, the clouds of unreason temporarily lifted, he saw his situation clearly, and realized that the future held only innumerable years of mental agony.[102] So with a last act of will he freed himself from the bondage that sprang from his own mind. Of the several scenarios, murder has the least evidence. Otherwise, Big Tim's death is a mystery he left his family, friends, followers, and chroniclers.

11

Legacies

Perhaps there was never a more perplexing admixture of good
and evil in one human character than in that of Timothy D.
Sullivan.

—Alvin F. Harlow, *Old Bowery Days*

BIG TIM LEFT HIS ESTATE TO HIS SURVIVING BROTHER PATRICK,
half-brother Larry Mulligan, half-sister Mrs. Margaret Hickey,
and the children of his deceased half-sister, Mary Ann Summers.
At the time of his death, estimates of Sullivan's worth ranged
from $2,000,000 to $5,000,000. But as his heirs and executors
began to examine his records, it quickly became apparent that
his finances were confused. By 1914, the Sullivan family's lawyer, William Ellison, stated that the estate might be insolvent.[1]
The Big Feller was a promiscuous investor, putting his money in
a wide variety of interests, not all of them fruitful. In the last
years of Tim's life there had been whispers that he had taken
some hard hits financially, but the disordered state of his financial affairs were revealed only after his death.[2]

According to Ellison, part of the problem lay in the fact that
Tim kept much of his business in his head—and surely there was
no paper trail for the money he made from his gambling interests. How that was divvied up and by whom can only be imag-
ined. Ellison also charged that "the cruelest advantage" was
taken of the "Big Feller's" diminished capabilities as he declined
mentally.[3] In May 1914, under pressure from William Fox, who
had filed claims against the estate, Patrick Sullivan and Larry
Mulligan drew up a list of Big Tim's assets, which were valued at
$975,000.[4] Tim's most important holdings were his shares in the
Sullivan-Considine Theatrical Circuit, which had recently been
sold to Marcus Loew for one million dollars. However, debts and
other obligations amounting to $236,000 reduced the income from

the sale.[5] Over the next few years Ellison worked to straighten out some of Sullivan's affairs, but legal maneuvering over the estate continued into the 1920s. On January 12, 1921, what was left of the Big Feller's estate, both real and personal, was sold for $97,000.[6]

The public may have been surprised to hear that Big Tim's estate was far below rumored levels, but another revelation likely led to nothing more than a shrug of the shoulders. In January 1916, Sarah G. Mohr sued Sullivan's estate for money she claimed Sullivan had promised her if she remained unmarried until their daughter reached the age of sixteen.[7] The daughter, named Mabel, was born September 23, 1892, and Tim immediately set up an allowance for her care. When she was nine, the Big Feller took out a life insurance policy for $50,000, naming her as the beneficiary. This had been paid when Tim died.[8] Sarah Mohr, however, claimed that Sullivan later agreed to pay her $10,000 if she did not marry until Mabel reached sixteen. Mohr fulfilled her part of the bargain and remained single until their daughter was seventeen. Tim gave Mohr, described as a childhood friend, $4,600 in 1910 and promised to pay the rest at 6 percent interest. In his last letter to Mohr, written in April 1912 as his mental problems increased, he stated he had recently been robbed of $350,000 and promised to pay the balance he owed as soon as it was possible.[9] Another daughter, Margaret Catherine, whose mother was Margaret A. Holland, was granted a bequest of $50,000 from Tim's estate on the order of Judge Daniel Cohalan.[10] While Mabel and Margaret Catherine were recognized as Tim's offspring, a chorus girl named Ada Sullivan, who professed to be another product of Tim's extramarital activities, was not accepted as such by either the family or the courts.[11]

During Tim's wake, Larry Mulligan vowed that the family would continue the most visible of all Big Tim's philanthropic activities—the traditional Bowery Christmas dinner. True to their word, the Sullivan Association served up Yule meals for 5,000 men who were fed in shifts 500 at a time.[12] Following the Big Feller's custom, tickets were distributed entitling the bearer to a new pair of shoes and socks. But with Tim in his grave only a little over three months, an atmosphere of melancholy hung over the festivities, and the conversations were dominated by reminiscences of the absent leader who had made such celebrations possible. At one point, an old man in ragged clothes and torn shoes rose at his seat and asked all to repeat in unison "God bless the soul of Big Tim Sullivan."[13] The response was unanimous and heartfelt. The dinner was also held the following year, though no shoes and socks were provided. In 1915, however, the Bowery's down-and-out found the doors to the clubhouse padlocked on Christmas day. In the disarray over Tim's finances, it had become too expensive for the remaining family and retainers to continue Tim's extravagant generosity. In May 1916, Big Tim's old clubhouse was sold.

When Big Tim's corpse was finally identified, the *New York Times* consoled itself that "there will never be another district leader of this type. . . . 'Graft' will not be exterminated quickly, but the audacious and domineering grafter of the Sullivan type has passed into history. . . ."[14] But even the *Times'* editorialist was forced to concede that the fallen Bowery chieftain possessed some virtues. "He lived according to his lights," the writer continued. "He derived his idea of politics from his teachers, and proved so apt a pupil that he bettered his instructors. Every man has his good points. Sullivan was true to his convictions and to his friends."[15] Tim would have smiled at the last sentence. It was his own credo throughout his life and career.

The *Times* was, of course, the mouthpiece of the uptown dwellers and the "respectable" classes. Those capable of seeing Tim in all his multivariegated guises—especially those not offended by the bare-knuckles character of New York politics and life—recognized the full import of the Big Feller's demise. Writing for *Munsey's Magazine,* Oliver Simmons declared, "[Big Tim's] death was the death of Sullivanism, the machine that held the East Side for Tammany Hall. His funeral was not only of Timothy Daniel Sullivan, king of district leaders, Congressman, State Senator, Assemblyman, millionaire, philanthropist, and gambler, but the funeral of the power that held together for the Democratic party the motley humanity of the East Side from Chatham Square to Fourteen Street."[16]

As far as the Sullivans were concerned, Simmons was prescient. Without Big Tim's personality and judgment, the surviving warriors of the clan faded into their political sunset. By 1914, a struggle for control of the Third Assembly District, the core of the Sullivan empire, had broken out with the family trying to hold on in the face of candidates backed by Charlie Murphy. In 1916, Patrick Sullivan was deposed as leader of the Third Assembly District. The following year, attempting to recoup his fortunes, Patrick attacked Murphy and the Hall as "a little coterie of greedy men . . . utterly out of touch with the progressive principles of democracy as expressed by President Wilson."[17] Patrick went so far as to support reformer John Purroy Mitchell for a second term as mayor, despite his being detested by virtually all Democrats. Big Tim would never have made such a blunder. Despite being publicly—and accurately—described as a man of "marvelous mental density," Murphy's candidate, "Red Mike" Hylan, won a smashing victory.[18] By 1920, Big Tim Sullivan's Bowery empire had passed into history—and legend. Tammany district leaders would remain important and locally powerful figures, but never again would Murphy be forced to tread cautiously around a leader who was virtually his equal—if not more.

Whether remembered with a smile, a shudder, or a shrug, the echoes of Big Tim's reign reverberated long after he was lowered into the ground at Calvary Cemetery. His legacies followed the pattern of his life, being rich, diverse, disturbing, and contradictory. Tim's involvement with gambling and connections with the underworld lived on in the career of Arnold Rothstein. Rothstein, boosted by the Big Feller early in his career—and who, some claimed, called Tim his "father"—became the nation's most influential gambler. It was he who realized that the days of illicit gambling houses were over, a development he surmounted by organizing the "floating" crap game. Probable Tammany bagman and conduit between the Wigwam and the underworld, he was instrumental in fixing the 1919 World Series and became the model, albeit distorted, for the master gambler Meyer Wolfsheim in F. Scott Fitzgerald's *The Great Gatsby*. Rothstein quickly realized the possibilities offered by Prohibition and employed the up-and-coming gangsters Charles "Lucky" Luciano, Meyer Lansky, and "Dutch" Schultz to run some of his bootlegging operations. Through his grooming and promotion of Rothstein, Sullivan became a distant benefactor of modern organized crime.

In terms of the Big Feller's favorite legitimate investment—entertainment—Tim was one of the many who nurtured the emerging popular entertainment called vaudeville. His financial—and political—support of amusement parks, boxing, and motion pictures certainly aided such enterprises, but his money, substantial though it may have been, was helpful but not crucial to the rise of such popular diversions. Nevertheless, in Albany and through his pocket, Big Tim helped expand existing stage entertainment while promoting the revolutionary new cinematic form. It seemed fitting that Sullivan posthumously made his way to the screen. On April 1, 1914, seven months after his death, a four-reel film titled *The Life of Big Tim Sullivan or, From Newsboy to Senator* was released by the Gotham Film Company. The picture presented Big Tim's life as a classic rags-to-riches story— which it was—and focused on his social charities, especially the Christmas dinners. The biopic concludes with Tim's constituents praying for his soul after his death. Big Tim remains the only Tammany leader ever given his own movie.

From the time he was eighteen until his death, politics stood at the center of Tim's life. It provided him with the money he put into investments as well as the incalculable amounts he dispensed through his charities, whether his Christmas dinners and chowders or the untold amounts he handed out to those who asked. His political power not only sustained him and his extended family, but it provided the pulpit and means to defend what he saw as his people—the poorly paid workers, or just plain poor—of the Lower East Side.

Big Tim's legendary philanthropy and concern for the residents of the Bowery and the other districts he directly or indirectly controlled were the natural responses of the man. In response to his aid, support, jobs, entertainments, and charities, the people of the Lower East Side were willing to overlook his flaws, gambling, and underworld ties. Tim would never allow a charge of dealing with prostitution to stand unanswered, but he never denied he knew many of the hitters on the Bowery, from the Whyos to Paul Vacarelli. In many ways he was a transitional figure, the last great—greatest—practitioner of nineteenth-century urban politics. Throughout the nineteenth century, city politicos often kept open relationships with the underworld, at least those who ostensibly practiced "victimless" illegalities. By the twentieth century, such relationships had become anachronistic. Partly this was the result of rising public expectations. The electorate would continue to shrug at minor infractions, but they increasingly balked at dirty cops and politicians who consorted with criminals. Charlie Murphy was ahead of Sullivan in seeing that "dirty graft" might cost more in political capital than it was worth in lucre. If nothing else, the Rosenthal murder, with its combination of police graft and conjecture about the Big Feller's role, underscored the dangers of such contacts to Tammany in the new century.

Murphy, possibly advised by Tom Foley, tried to insulate the Hall from charges of dirty graft by forbidding the machine's members from collecting tribute themselves. Henceforth, gangsters would do the sordid work of raking in the fees and protection money and acting as bagmen. The new system, however, a response to the Rosenthal scandal, left the Democracy increasingly reliant on its underworld allies. After Charlie Murphy's shrewd and steady hand was removed by his death in 1924, the Tammany politicians began to lose control over their criminal allies, and the balance of power began to shift from the politicians to the mobsters. By the 1930s, Tammany was more tainted by its underworld connections than it had been when Sullivan and Murphy ruled. The Great Depression not only set the stage for the kind of massive state support that undercut Tammany's hold on the urban working classes, it generated an intolerant attitude toward graft, corruption, and criminal involvement in politics. Mayor Jimmy Walker, who had much of Sullivan's charm but little of his judgment, was forced from office by a new set of investigations into municipal government. A reform government led by Mayor Fiorello LaGuardia took city hall and managed a feat no other such administration had achieved—re-election. Tammany bled votes and money throughout the New Deal and World War II. When it had a chance to return to office under Mayor William O'Dwyer, it was destroyed by revelations of Mafia connections. The Tiger lingered into the late 1950s, but the last of its nine lives was spent.

Yet, in many other ways, Tim, acting on gut instinct, was ahead of the calculating Murphy. The Big Feller was unfazed by the transition of the Lower East Side from German and Irish to a more polyglot, Italian, and Eastern European Jewish area. He readily adjusted his style and organization to accommodate and organize the newcomers, and seemed to enjoy the process. Though some predicted Tammany would lose the support of the

Lower East Side after Tim's death, such was not the case. Following Tim's example, Murphy slowly adopted the policies and interests of the mixed communities along the Bowery and Lower Broadway, and, despite some shaky moments, held the downtown areas for the Hall for another generation. In this he was greatly helped by his protégé, Al Smith, who in turn was the protégé of Big Tom Foley, Tim's old ally. Though essentially an Irish figure, Smith also had Italian and English strains in his background, and he was—as Tim had been—pure Lower East Side.

Smith had a lot of Sullivan's charm and verve. He also had little interest in gambling and kept his distance from the hoodlums of his day. Yet even Smith, as deeply concerned about the city's workers and poor as Tim, was behind the Bowery king in ensuring protections for the workers by means of state law. Smith was still following Murphy's orders to derail the 54-Hour Bill even as Tim rammed it home. Later, as governor, Smith would use the power of the state to improve the lives of New Yorkers. But in this he and Murphy, who was grooming him for the presidency, were simply following the path Big Tim had laid out in his own personal style. When it came to women's suffrage, Tim far outpaced Murphy, Smith, and most of the Tammany organization, publicly pushing the measure while Silent Charlie did all he could to impede it. Perhaps Murphy understood that state support and entitlements would pull the rug out from the machine itself, providing the services and defenses that Tammany and the "machine within a machine" had formerly offered in exchange for power. Big Tim may have known this too. If he did, he didn't care.

In 1938, Frances Perkins, who had become Franklin Roosevelt's secretary of labor and first woman cabinet member, went to the White House to ask Roosevelt to ease American immigration policy. During the 1920s, American immigration policy had become restrictive, and many fleeing Nazi Germany or the other fascist governments were often denied refuge in the United States. Perkins's plea put the president in mind of Big Tim, whom he had known and sometimes dueled with when he was a callow and self-important state senator in Albany. "Tim Sullivan," he recalled to Perkins, "used to say that the America of the future would be made out of the people who had come over in

steerage and who knew in their own hearts and lives the difference between being despised and being accepted and liked."[19]
The president paused for a few seconds, and then went on. "Poor
old Tim Sullivan never understood about modern politics, but he
was right about the human heart."[20]

Appendix

How Did Big Tim Really Speak?

THE NEW YORK ACCENT IS ONE OF THE MOST READILY IDENTIFI-able in America, and perhaps, via movies and television, the world. It has been imitated, mimicked, denounced, belittled and, occasionally, extolled as a badge of honorable plebeian virtues. When it began to take on its distinctive character is not known for certain. It was well established by the later nineteenth century, when its basic elements, the exceptionally broad A, microscopic final R's, and dental T's were all in evidence.

Though the speech of lower- and middle-class New Yorkers might have been evolving in its idiosyncratic fashion before the 1840s, it seems clear that the arrival of immigrants contributed to its style. Neither the Irish, the Germans, nor the later Italians and East European Jews have the TH sound that exists in Standard English. Even today, most people in Ireland pronounce the TH by placing the tongue directly behind the upper incisors instead of on the bottom, producing something like a Th as in "tough," as opposed to a TH as in "through." This is the reason why the common surname MacCarthy is often rendered as Mac-Carty, which is actually closer to the way it is pronounced in Ireland. It didn't take much for that to be reduced to a D. Even if it was a hard TH, newsmen might simply render it as a D, partly because it was close to the sound, and partly because it made the alleged speakers seem exotically low-life.

Of course, there have always been New York accents and New York accents, and class lines then and now have divided them. In the past, as today, almost all New Yorkers, excepting those sent to private schools, spoke New York style. Some neighborhoods, often characterized by both poverty and ethnic separation, had it in spades. In the post–Civil War period, the Lower East Side provided both the accent and the argot—the slang. This was the type of New York accent that Big Tim Sullivan and his compatriots grew up speaking. To the press, primarily made up of those at least one class level above them, this was often a source of amusement. Stories of Sullivan clan rallies often included quotes from the audience laced with references to "goils." Frances Perkins, who quoted Tim as saying "wid" for with, claimed Tim spoke with an Irish brogue, and his style of a turn-of-the-century New York accent probably was more heavily Irish-influenced than it is today. The author has known people who spoke an older version of New Yorkese who did say something like "earl" for oil, while turtle came out almost like "toitle." The plural of "you" was rendered "youse." The actual pronunciation was a bit more complex, but trying to write it in Standard English is difficult, which partly explains how the news reporters fell back on the conventions they did when printing Tim's talk.

While the upper classes might snicker or ridicule, for Tim and his "Wise Men," using Lower East Side speech was not only natural, but served as a badge of their authenticity and a link with their constituents. Indeed, news reports of Tim's first major address in the state assembly noted that his remarks were given in flawless Lower East Side style. Tim sometimes began a speech stating that he didn't talk "so good," which was often a way of connecting with his listeners, who were well aware they didn't talk "so good" either. It is likely that Tim ratcheted up the accent and the slang a notch or two when mood or need arose. Reporters covering Little Tim noted that he could speak "normal" New York style when he wanted, but addressing a gathering downtown, he was likely to adopt a more downtown style. There is no doubt the Big Feller did the same. So how did Big Tim speak? He spoke pretty much the way the newspapers recorded it. He spoke American English, Lower East Side New York, with the ability to juice it up or tone it down depending on circumstance.

Notes

CHAPTER 1. THE CITY AND MACHINE

Epigraphs were taken from William V. Shannon, *The American Irish: A Political and Social Portrait* (New York: Collier Books, 1974), 62 and "New York: Good Government in Danger," *McClure's Magazine* (November 1903), cited in Terrence J. McDonald, ed., *Plunkitt of Tammany Hall* (New York: Bedford-St. Martin's, 1994), 128.

1. Alvin F. Harlow, *Old Bowery Days* (New York: D. Appleton, 1931), 389.
2. Ibid., 400.
3. Christopher M. Finan, *Alfred E. Smith: The Happy Warrior* (New York: Hill & Wang, 2002), 20.
4. Ibid.
5. *Gotham,* (New York: Oxford University Press, 1999), 1112.
6. Luc Sante, *Low Life* (New York: Farrar, Straus & Giroux, 1991), 266. Tweed reputedly appropriated the tiger from the Americus Club, while others trace the tiger's origin to the game of faro, which was also identified with the great cat.
7. Ibid. By 1892, 61 percent of Tammany Society members were Irish. See Steven P. Erie, *Rainbow's End: Irish-Americans and the Dilemma of Urban Machine Politics* (Berkeley: 1988), 58.
8. Alfred Connable and Edward Silberfarb, *Tigers of Tammany: Nine Men Who Ruled New York* (New York: Holt, Rinehart & Winston, 1967), 175.
9. This account is largely based on Connable and Silberfarb, *Tigers of Tammany,* 176.
10. Ibid., 177.
11. Ibid.
12. Ibid., 187.
13. Erie, *Rainbow's End,* 53.
14. Hartley Davis, "Tammany Hall: The Most Perfect Political Machine in the World," *Munsey's Magazine* (1900): 65.
15. Connable and Silberfarb, *Tigers of Tammany,* 199–200.
16. Ibid., 201.
17. Ibid.
18. Ibid.
19. Another version has it that Croker himself had advised that Tammany have a "federative council" rather than a boss, but, "[b]y a common impulse . . .

all of the district leaders looked to him, and by formal agreement at last offered him the leadership." E. J. Edwards, "Richard Croker as 'Boss' of Tammany," *McClure's Magazine* (November 1895): 544.

20. David C. Hammack, *Power and Society: Greater New York at the Turn of the Century* (New York: Russell Sage Foundation, 1982), 162.

21. Erie, *Rainbow's End,* 111.

22. Edwards, "Richard Croker," 544.

23. Hammack, *Power and Society,* 138.

24. Richard Croker, "Tammany Hall and the Democracy," *North American Review,* 154, 423 (February 1892): 225–30, http://www.wadsworth.com/history-d/special-features/ext/ap/chapter 18/18.4 croker.html.

25. Connable and Silberfarb, *Tigers of Tammany,* 209–10.

Chapter 2. Upward Mobility

Epigraph was taken from Warren Sloat, *The Battle for the Soul of New York* (New York: Cooper Square Press, 2002), 109.

1. See the various dates in both the congressional and New York State memorial volumes issued after Sullivan's death. U.S. Congress, House, *Timothy D. Sullivan: Memorial Addresses Delivered in the House of Representatives of the United States (Sixty-third Congress* (Washington, D.C.: 1914), and *Proceedings of the Legislature of the State of New York on the Life, Character and Public Service of Timothy D. Sullivan* (Albany, NY: D. B. Lyon, 1914).

2. The New York State *Proceedings* cites both. There does, however, appear to be a church record bearing the 1862 date.

3. Daniel Czitrom, "Underworlds and Underdogs: Big Tim Sullivan and Metropolitan Politics in New York, 1889–1913," *Journal of American History* 78 (September 1991): 540.

4. If later memories were accurate, Catherine Sullivan took an active interest in the children of the neighborhood and was remembered fondly as "one of the noblest women" on the Lower East Side. In 1910, city aldermen named a new street providing access to the Williamsburgh Bridge in her honor, though pleasing her famous son was no doubt a consideration. Kenmare Street was named after Kenmare, County Kerry, where she was born. *New York Times,* March 3, 1910, 2.

5. Luc Sante, *Low Life* (New York: Farrar, Straus & Giroux, 1991), 214.

6. *New York Herald,* November 1, 1909, 4.

7. Ibid.

8. *New York Times,* October 16, 1902, 3.

9. Ibid.

10. Alvin F. Harlow, *Old Bowery Days* (New York: D. Appleton, 1931), 487.

11. Ibid.

12. *New York Times,* October 16, 1902, 3.

13. In 1902, Sullivan claimed he owned three saloons, the first on Leonard Street and two on Center Street—one directly across from the Tombs Police Court. Harlow lists four, including one on Chrystie Street.

14. *New York Herald,* May 19, 1907, section 2, 1.

15. "At the Court of 'Big Tim' Sullivan", *New York Herald,* May 19, 1907, Section 2 (magazine), 1.

16. Ibid.

17. Ibid.

18. Ibid.

19. Reminiscences of William S. Bennet, part 1, 102, (1951) in the Oral History Collection of Columbia University.

20. Alfred Connable and Edward Silberfarb, *Tigers of Tammany: Nine Men Who Ruled New York* (New York: Holt, Rinehart & Winston, 1967), 211.

21. Werner, M. R. *Tammany Hall,* (Garden City, Doubleday, Doran and Company, 1928), 438.

22. *New York Herald,* May 19, 1907, section 2 (magazine), 1.

Chapter 3. Running the Game

Epigraph is from the *New York Times,* December 23, 1909, 2.

1. Kate Holladay Claghorn, "The Foreign Immigrant in New York City," in *Reports of the Industrial Commission,* vol. 15 (Washington, DC: United States Government Printing Office, 1901), 465–92.

2. Alvin Harlow, *Old Bowery Days* (New York: D. Appleton, 1931), 403.

3. Oliver Simmons, "Passing of the Sullivan Dynasty," *Munsey's Magazine,* 1, no. 3 (December 1913): 412.

4. Henderson, *Tammany Hall and the New Immigrants* (New York: Arno Press, 1976),

5. *New York Times,* February 20, 1906, 6.

6. *New York World,* October 27, 1901, 10.

7. "At the Court of Big Tim Sullivan," *New York Herald,* May 19, 1907, section 2 (magazine), 2.

8. *New York Tribune,* December 7, 1902, 14.

9. *New York World,* June 14, 1903, n3.

10. *New York Tribune,* December 7, 1902, 14.

11. *New York World,* June 14, 1903, n3.

12. Ibid.

13. *New York Tribune,* December 7, 1902, 14.

14. Harlow, *Old Bowery Days,* 510.

15. Ibid., 494.

16. Ibid.

17. *New York Tribune,* January 13, 1913, 4. See also Harlow, *Old Bowery Days,* 513.

18. Henderson, *Tammany Hall,* 10.

19. Werner, M. R. *Tammany Hall* (Garden City: Doubleday, Doran & CO., 1928), 439.

20. Cited in Daniel L. Czitrom, "Underworlds and Underdogs: Big Tim Sullivan and Metropolitan Politics in New York, 1889–1913," *Journal of American History* 78 (December 1891): 538–58, 549.

21. *New York Times,* September 14, 1913, 2.

22. Cited in Czitrom, "Underworlds," 546.

23. Harlow, *Old Bowery Days,* 503.

24. Ibid., 505.

25. *New York Tribune,* September 19, 1901, 2.

26. Harlow, *Old Bowery Days,* 492.

27. David Hammack, *Power and Society: Greater New York at the Turn of the Century* (New York: Russell Sage Foundation, 1982), 141.

28. Timothy J. Guilfoyle, *City of Eros: New York City, Prostitution, and the Commercialization of Sex, 1790–1920* (New York: W. W. Norton, 1992), 188.

29. Hammack, *Power and Society,* 145.

30. Alfred Connable and Edward Silberfarb, *Tigers of Tammany: Nine Men Who Ruled New York* (New York: Holt, Rinehart & Winston, 1967), 213

31. Ibid.

32. Ibid., 214.

33. The police commission was an archaic, unwieldy, and inefficient institution in which four commissioners would oversee the police. One acted as president, effectively chairman of the commission. The commission was shortly replaced by a single commissioner with a chief of police directly beneath him.

34. Theodore Roosevelt, *An Autobiography,*. http://www.bartleby.com/55/6.html.

35. Ibid.

36. Ibid.

37. Connable and Silberfarb, *Tigers of Tammany,* 216.

38. Ibid., 216–17.

39. Van Wyck did better posthumously. The Van Wyck Expressway, running between LaGuardia and JFK airports is named for him. It is notoriously jammed.

40. Connable and Silberfarb, *Tigers of Tammany,* 217.

41. Hammack, *Power and Society,* 167.

42. Werner, M. R. *Tammany Hall,* (Garden City: Doubleday, Doran & Co., 1928), 463.

43. *New York Tribune,* September 19, 1901, 3.

44. Luc Sante, *Low Life* (New York: Farrar, Straus & Giroux, 1991), 172. Some have cast doubts on these numbers. They originated among anti-Tammany, anti-Sullivan Republicans which the pro-Republican *Times* was happy to print. Some authorities believe it was in the interests of the Republican-reformer faction to paint the darkest picture possible of Sullivan, and that no single group held such a monopoly on gambling in Gotham.

45. Harlow, *Old Bowery Days,* 501.

46. Ibid.

47. Reminiscences of J. T. Hettrick, part 4 (1949), 49, in the Oral History Collection of Columbia University.

48. Ibid.

Chapter 4. Taking His Opportunities

Epigraph was taken from the *New York Times,* November 4, 1907, 1.

1. Alfred Connable and Edward Silberfarb, *Tigers of Tammany: Nine Men Who Ruled New York* (New York: Holt, Rinehart & Winston, 1967), 222.

2. Daniel L. Czitrom, "Underworlds and Underdogs: Big Tim Sullivan and Metropolitan Politics in New York, 1889–1913," *Journal of American History* 78 (December 1991): 548.

3. Samuel P. Orth, *The Boss and the Machine: A Chronicle of Politicians and Party Organization.* (New Haven: Yale University Press, 1919), http://www. fullbooks.com/The-Boss-and-the-Machine1.html.

4. David Hammack, *Power and Society: Greater New York at the Turn of the Century* (New York: Russell Sage Foundation, 1982), 149.

5. Richard O'Connor, *Courtroom Warrior: The Combatitive Career of William Travers Jerome* (Boston: Little, Brown, 1963), 70–71.

6. *New York Herald,* April 19, 1901, 4.

7. Ibid.

8. Ibid., April 21, 1901, 4.

9. Ibid.

10. Czitrom, "Underworlds," 549.

11. Ibid.

12. O'Connor, *Courtroom Warrior,* 80.

13. *New York Tribune,* September 19, 1901, 1.

14. Connable and Silberfarb, *Tigers of Tammany,* 224.

15. Ibid.

16. *New York Tribune,* September 19, 1901, 1.

17. *New York Times,* February 9, 1901, 1.

18. Ibid.

19. *New York Tribune,* September 19, 1901, 1.

20. O'Connor, *Courtroom Warrior,* 76.

21. Timothy J. Guilfoyle, *City of Eros: New York, Prostitution, and the Commercialization of Sex, 1790–1920* (New York: W. W. Norton, 1992), 251.

22. O'Connor, *Courtroom Warrior,* 76.

23. Cited in Czitrom, "Underworlds," 550.

24. *New York Times,* September 9, 1913, 2.

25. Reporters of the time were divided about Tim's connection with prostitution. J. T. Hettrick pointed to a public smashing of a brothel by the Sullivans as proof that Big and Little Tim "would not tolerate a house of prostitution on the East Side." Time may have colored his recollections, as brothels were abundant on the East Side. Many othef reporters were certain Tim at least countenanced the sex trade. Reminiscences of J. T. Hettrick, part 4 (1949), 47, in the Oral History Collection of Columbia University.

26. Czitrom, "Underworlds," 550.

27. Harlow, *Old Bowery Days,* 503. Hochstim began as a bail bondsman working out of the Essex Street courthouse. He later became heavily involved in prostitution, allegedly importing whores into the city to satisfy demand and ultimately extending his prostitution ring to Newark and Philadelphia. See Warren Sloat, *The Battle for the Soul of New York* (New York: Cooper Square Press, 2002), 439. See also Guilfoyle, *City of Eros,* 261.

28. Guilfoyle, *City of Eros,* 261.

29. *New York Times,* September 14, 1913, 2.

30. Divver himself may not have been as pure as the driven snow. He was widely believed to have ties with criminals and was excoriated by the *Times* for these connections in 1890. On the other hand, the *Times* attacked virtually all

Tammany members. Charles M. Finan, *Alfred E. Smith: The Happy Warrior* (New York: Hill & Wang, 2002), 31.

31. Connable and Silberfarb, *Tigers of Tammany,* 225.

32. *New York Tribune,* September 19, 1901, 1.

33. Ibid., September 17, 1901, 9

34. Harlow, *Old Bowery Days,* 507.

35. Ibid.

36. Connable and Silberfarb, *Tigers of Tammany,* 227.

37. *New York Tribune,* September 19, 1901, 1.

38. *New York World,* November 6, 1901, 1.

39. Ibid. None of the other New York papers carried the story of Tim's decking Croker's critic. Probably no reporters from the other papers were allowed to accompany them into Ennis's Restaurant. This suggests that the reporter was Henry Bayard Swope, later editor of the *World,* who was on good terms with Tammany leaders, including Big Tim. On the other hand, Big Tim made good copy, and his activities were frequently exaggerated, and some possibly concocted, by reporters and editors.

40. Connable and Silberfarb, *Tigers of Tammany,* 232.

41. Ibid.

42. *New York Tribune,* September 14, 1913, 10.

43. Nancy Joan Weiss, *Charles Francis Murphy: Respectability and Responsibility in Tammany Politics,* (Northampton, MA: Smith College, 1968), 3.

44. George B. McClellan Jr. disputed this generalization claiming that he had seen Murphy the worse for wear from alcohol. McClellan's career was destroyed by his break with Murphy, and it is difficult to determine if his opinions and recollections of Tammany leaders were colored by his experience. George B. McClellan Jr., *The Gentleman and the Tiger: The Autobiography of George B. McClellan, Jr.* (New York: J. B. Lippincott, 1956), 231.

45. Weiss, *Charles Francis Murphy,* 19.

46. Ibid., 20.

47. Ibid., 21.

48. Ibid.

49. Ibid.

50. Ibid., 22.

51. McClellan, *Gentleman and the Tiger,* 212.

52. Ibid., 23.

53. Ibid.

54. Ibid., 27

55. Ibid., 28.

56. Connable and Silberfarb, *Tigers of Tammany,* 232.

57. David Von Drehle, *Triangle: The Fire that Changed America,* (New York: Atlantic Monthly Press, 2003), 227.

58. *New York Times,* October 9, 1902, 1.

59. Harlow, *Old Bowery Days,* 508.

60. *New York Times,* October 9, 1902, 1.

61. The practice of buying judgeships did not end with the fall of Tammany Hall in the 1930s. During the 1970s, the going rate for a supreme court seat was $75,000; lower court posts went for $35,000. Obituary of Matthew J. Troy Jr., *New York Times,* December 5, 2004, metro section, 51.

62. Ibid.
63. Harlow, *Old Bowery Days,* 493.
64. Ibid.
65. Ibid.
66. *New York Times,* October 4, 1902, 3.
67. Ibid., October 16, 1902, 3.
68. Ibid.
69. Ibid.
70. Ibid.
71. Ibid.
72. Ibid., November 2, 1902, 2.
73. Frances Perkins, *The Roosevelt I Knew* (New York: Viking, 1946), 12, and *New York Times,* November 2, 1902, 2.
74. *Times,* November 2, 1902, 2.
75. Ibid.
76. Ibid.
77. Ibid.
78. Ibid.
79. Ibid., November 3, 1902, 3.
80. Ibid.

Chapter 5. Extracurricular Activities

Epigraph is from reminiscences of J. T. Hettrick, part 4 (1949), 49, in the Oral History Collection of Columbia University.
1. *New York Times,* December 23, 1902, 2.
2. Ibid.
3. Ibid.
4. Harold Zink, *City Bosses in the United States: A Study of Twentieth-Century Municipal Bosses* (Durham, NC: Duke University Press, 1930), 90.
5. Ibid., 91.
6. William B. Ellison, "Mother's Influence Strongest in Big Tim's Life," *New York World,* February 16, 1913, n6.
7. *New York Times,* November 21, 1921, 14.
8. Ibid.
9. Alvin Harlow, *Old Bowery Days* (New York: D. Appleton, 1931), 511.
10. *New York Times,* December 26, 1910, 14.
11. Ibid.
12. Ibid., December 26, 1911, 16.
13. Daniel L. Czitrom, "Underworlds and Underdogs: Big Tim Sullivan and Metropolitan Politics in New York, 1889–1913," *Journal of American History* 78 (December 1991): 545.
14. Tim insisted on quality footwear for his beneficiaries. In 1911 he contracted for five thousand shoes from the Endicott-Johnson Shoe Company of Binghamton. They were to be the "best quality goods . . . waterproofed and made in the latest shapes with a view to durability. Such shoes sell at retail at $3.50 to $4.00." *New York Times,* January 23, 1911, 4.

15. *New York Times,* December 26, 1910, 14.
16. *New York Tribune,* September 14, 1913, 2.
17. Zink states they began in 1885.
18. *New York Tribune,* September 17, 1895, 1.
19. Ibid.
20. Ibid.
21. Ibid.
22. Ibid.
23. Ibid., September 15, 1903, 5.
24. Ibid.
25. *New York Times,* September 1, 1908, 5.
26. Ibid., September 1, 1908, 5 and August 31, 1909, 3.
27. Ibid., August 31, 1909, 3.
28. Ibid.
29. Ibid.
30. Ibid., August 30, 1910, 2.
31. Ibid., September 1, 1908, 3.
32. *New York Tribune,* September 17, 1903, 1.
33. Ibid.
34. *Tammany Times,* 2, no. 4 (December 2, 1893): 7.
35. Occasionally, Sullivan gave the "franchise" to hold a ball for a follower or friend, an important favor since they were moneymaking events.
36. Harlow, *Old Bowery Days,* 444.
37. *New York Tribune,* September 14, 1913, 2.
38. Ellison, *New York World,* February 16, 1913, n6.
39. Hartley Davis, "Tammany Hall: The Most Perfect Political Organization in the World," *Munsey's Magazine,* 1901, 66.
40. Steven Erie argues that Tammany Hall provided different benefits to the various ethnic groups. The Irish, their core voting bloc, received the bulk of political patronage and civil service jobs while the newer immigrants were given symbolic recognition, for example, Columbus Day, or business licenses and legal services. Erie argues that the latter were less valuable than the former. In the aggregate this seems possible, but the support for business and charity was not inconsiderable, and in the case of Sullivan it was extravagant. Steven Erie, *Rainbow's End: Irish-Americans and the Dilemma of Urban Machine Politics* (Berkeley: University of California Press, 1988), 14.
41. Czitrom, "Underworlds," 547.
42. Journalist J. T. Hettrick recollected that Tim could also call on some expert advice from the city's financial leaders. According to Hettrick, after Sullivan lost $250,000 in the stock market, Belmont gathered his investment accounts and transferred them to Belmont and Company. Supposedly he did the same for Little Tim, and guided their investments into the profit column. The Reminiscences of J. T. Hettrick, 1949, 48, in the Oral History Collection of Columbian University.
43. *New York Times,* May 6, 1914, 20.
44. Ibid., May 26, 1909, 9.
45. Czitrom, "Underworlds," 551.
46. *New York Times,* May 6, 1914, 20.
47. Czitrom, "Underworlds," 552.

48. Ibid.

49. Werner, *Tammany Hall,* 509.

50. Ibid.

51. Http://www.foe.com/history/pastgwp/sullivan.

52. *New York Times,* September 16, 1912, 1.

53. Ibid.

54. Ibid. September 18, 1912, 11.

55. Ibid., September 18, 1913, 6.

56. Ibid., July 23, 1908, 6.

57. Ibid., January 3, 1916, 9.

58. Ibid., February 8, 1909, 6.

59. Ibid., May 26, 1909, 9.

60. Supposedly, while Hearst and Sullivan avoided each other on the 1909 voyage, they had several talks or "conferences" when they found themselves traveling on the same liner the following year. *New York Times,* May 22, 1910, 3.

61. Ibid., June 6, 1909, secttion 3, 3.

62. Ibid.

63. *New York Herald,* May 19, 1907, magazine (section 2), 2.

64. Harlow, *Old Bowery Days,* 512. One of the few players Sullivan habitually bested was the future heavyweight champion "Kid" McCoy. Morris Strauss remembered "Kid could hit, but he couldn't play poker. He was duck soup for the gifted leader."

65. *New York Herald,* May 19, 1907, magazine (section 2), 2.

66. *New York Times,* June 20, 1910, 3.

67. Luc Sante, *Low Life,* (New Yor, Farrar, Straus & Giroux, 1991), 174.

68. Ibid.

69. Harlow, *Old Bowery Days,* 512–13.

70. Sante, *Low Life,* 270.

71. Ibid.

72. Harlow, *Old Bowery Days,* 511.

73. Ibid.

Chapter 6. No Final Victories

1. *New York World,* June 14, 1903, n3.

2. Ibid.

3. *New York Times,* October 1, 1903, 8.

4. *New York World,* June 14, 1903, 6.

5. David C. Hammack, *Power and Society: Greater New York at the Turn of the Century* (New York: Russell Sage Foundation, 1982), 157.

6. *New York Times,* October 1, 1903, 8.

7. Ibid., October 2, 1903, 1.

8. Mary Joan Weiss, *Charles Francis Murphy, 1858–1924: Respectability and Responsibility in Tammany Politics* (Northampton, MA: Smith College, 1968), 43–44.

9. *New York Herald,* November 2, 1903, section 2, 5.

10. *World of Work* magazine, December 1903, 4257.

11. *New York Herald,* November 1, 1903, 3.

12. *New York Times,* October 29, 1903, 2.

13. *New York Herald,* November 2, 1903, 6.

14. Ibid., November 1, 1903, 3.

15. Ibid., November 3, 1903, 3.

16. Ibid., November 4, 1903, 3.

17. Ibid.

18. Ibid.

19. Ibid., *New York Tribune,* November 2, 1905, 6.

20. *World of Work,* December 1903, 4256.

21. *New York Herald,* November 5, 1903, 9. On the other hand, the *Tribune* reported that Sullivan was part of a pool that made $100,000 on the election, with Tim taking $25,000 as his cut. *New York Tribune,* November 5, 1903, 5. Either way the "Big Feller" made a tidy sum from the Tammany victory. Even more if the reports were of two different wagers.

22. *New York Times,* December 23, 1909, 2.

23. Ibid., September 14, 1913, 2.

24. Obituary, Thomas J. McManus, *New York Times,* July 31, 1926, 11.

25. Harold Zink, who wrote the first academic study of political machines in the early twentieth century (*City Bosses in the United States: A Study of Twentieth-Century Municipal Bosses,* 1930), stated no one could hope to rule the city without his acquiescence.

26. Oliver Simmons, "Passing of the Sullivan Dynasty," *Munsey's Magazine* 1, no. 3, (December 1913): 413.

27. Ibid., 415.

28. Ibid.

29. *New York World,* February 16, 1913, N6.

30. Ibid. Tim was not invariably successful in winning judicial nominations for his friends. In October 1908 he threw his support behind Emmanuel Blumenstiel for supreme court Justice and got Murphy to back him. Blumenstiel had been a target of disbarment proceedings and was the subject of negative comments from other judges. Most of the other district leaders opposed him as a drag on the ticket. In the end, Murphy sided with the majority, and Blumenstiel was dropped. Probably personal loyalty induced Tim to stay with Blumenstiel. Murphy could claim he was forced to drop his support, which was a relief to him, and possibly Tim as well. *New York Tribune,* October 8, 1908, 3.

31. This account is based on Harlow, *Old Bowery Days,* 509–10.

32. *New York Times,* November 4, 1907, 1.

Chapter 7. George and Charlie

Epigraph is from the reminiscence of William S. Bennet, 19 , 102, in the Oral History Collection of Columbia University.

1. George B. McClellan Jr., *The Gentleman and the Tiger: The Autobiography of George B. McClellan, Jr.* (New York: J. B. Lipincott, 1956), 213.

2. Ibid., 221.

3. Steven P. Erie, *Rainbow's End: Irish-Americans and the Dilemma of Urban Machine Politics* (Berkeley: University of California Press, 1988), 91.

4. In the end, Tammany won 75 percent of the Irish vote. Erie, *Rainbow's End,* 91.

5. *New York Times,* October 6, 1905, 2.

6. Ibid.

7. Ibid.

8. Alfred Connable and Edward Silberfarb, *Tigers of Tammany: Nine Men who Ruled New York* (New York: Holt, Rinehart & Winston, 1967), 242–43.

9. *New York Times,* October 20, 1905, 12.

10. Ibid., October 26, 1905, 3

11. *New York Tribune,* October 24, 1905, 2.

12. *New York Times,* November 2, 1905, 1.

13. Ibid.

14. Ibid.

15. Ibid., *New York Times,* November 6, 1905, 1.

16. Ibid., November 8, 1905, 1.

17. *New York Tribune,* November 6, 1905, 2.

18. Ibid.

19. Ibid.

20. Ibid.

21. *New York Times,* November 8, 1905, 1.

22. *New York Tribune,* November 8, 1905, 1.

23. Ibid.

24. Ibid.

25. Ibid.

26. Ibid., 3.

27. For two years Hearst pursued litigation over the election. In the end 650,000 ballots were recounted, which awarded McClellan an additional 200 votes. McClellan, *Gentleman and the Tiger,* 229.

28. *New York Tribune,* November 9, 1905, 5.

29. McClellan, *Gentleman and the Tiger,* 231.

30. Ibid.

31. Ibid., 234.

32. *New York Herald,* September 26, 1906, 2. See also *Herald,* September 27, 1906, 6.

33. McClellan, *Gentleman and the Tiger,* 286.

34. *New York Times,* September 15, 1906, 1.

35. Ibid.

36. *New York Herald,* September 16, 1906, 5.

37. Ibid., 1.

38. Ibid.

39. *New York Times,* September 19, 1906, 1. Some reported that Sullivan had confided to a friend during the Labor Day chowder that he would stand with Murphy against McClellan in the primaries. The nature of the contests did not require him to openly oppose McClellan, but it provides evidence that when push came to shove, Sullivan stood with the Tammany Hall against city hall. See *New York Times,* September 12, 1906, 5.

40. Ibid., September 22, 1906, 3.

41. *New York Herald,* September 25, 1906, 4.

42. *New York Times,* September 21, 1906, 4.

43. McClellan, *Gentleman and the Tiger,* 286.

44. *New York Times,* September 25, 1906, 2.

45. Ibid.

46. *New York Herald,* September 25, 1906, 1.

47. Ibid.

48. Ibid., September 27, 1906, 8.

49. Ibid., 7.

50. Ibid.

51. Ibid., 6.

52. Ibid., 5.

53. *New York Times,* September 27, 1906, 1.

54. *New York Herald,* September 28, 1906, 5.

55. McClellan, *Gentleman and the Tiger,* 286.

56. Cited in McClellan, *Gentleman and the Tiger,* 288.

57. *New York Times,* September 30, 1906, 6.

58. *New York Herald,* October 5, 1906, 1, *New York Times,* October 8, 1906, 1 and October 11, 1906, 2.

59. In fact, the *New York Times* reported that Big Tim announced before the Buffalo convention that if Hearst were nominated, he would not run for the state senate. October 14, 1905, 3.

60. *New York Times,* October 5, 1906, 2.

61. Ibid.

62. Ibid., October 6, 1906, 2.

63. *New York Herald,* October 10, 1906, 4.

64. Ibid., November 2, 1906, 2.

65. *New York Times,* November 5, 1906, 2.

66. Ibid., October 6, 1906, 2.

67. Ibid., November 6, 1906, 1.

68. *New York Times,* September 26, 1906, 8.

69. Ibid.

70. *New York Herald,* September 27, 1906, 7.

71. Ibid., October 26, 1906, 1.

72. Connable and Silberfarb, *Tigers of Tammany,* 245.

73. Ibid., 245, and Nancy Joan Weiss, *Charles Francis Murphy, 1858–1924* (Northampton, MA: Smith College), 42.

74. Harold Zink, *City Bosses in the United States: A Study of Twenty Municipal Bosses* (Durham, NC: Duke University Press, 1930), 154.

75. *New York Times,* April 3, 1907, 1.

76. Ibid.

77. Ibid., May 2, 1907, 1.

78. Ibid.

79. Ibid.

80. *New York Times,* December 23, 1909, 2.

81. Thomas M. Henderson, *Tammany Hall and the New Immigrants* (New York: Arno Press, 1975), 7.

82. Alvin Harlow, *Old Bowery Days* (New York: D. Appleton, 1931), 517. McClellan argued that he fired Bingham, who "gave me more trouble than any

man who served me," because he refused a direct order. This seems accurate, but the timing certainly caused the removal to accrue to Sullivan's advantage. McClellan, *Gentleman and the Tiger,* 297.

83. *New York Herald,* May 19, 1907, section 2 (magazine), 2.

Chapter 8. The Progressive

1. Alvin F. Harlow, *Old Bowery Days* (New York: D. Appleton, 1931), 495.
2. *New York Tribune,* October 3, 1909, 4.
3. Steven P. Erie, *Rainbow's End: Irish-Americans and the Dilemma of Urban Machine Politics* (Berkeley: University of California Press, 1988), 103. By contrast the Irish made up only 5 percent of the area in the same year.
4. David von Drehle, *Triangle: The Fire that Changed America* (New York: Atlantic Monthly Press, 2003), 191.
5. Erie, *Rainbow's End,* 103.
6. Ibid., 36.
7. Von Drehle, *Triangle,* 255.
8. Ibid., 15
9. Ibid., 172.
10. Cited in Harlow, *Old Bowery Days,* 515.
11. *New York Herald,* November 1, 1909, 2.
12. Thomas M. Henderson, *Tammany Hall and the New Immigrants* (New York: Arno Press, 1976), 2.
13. *New York Herald,* November 1, 1909, 1.
14. Ibid.
15. Ibid.
16. Ibid.
17. Ibid.
18. Harlow, *Old Bowery Days,* 516–17.
19. *New York Herald,* November 1, 1909, 1.
20. Ibid.
21. Ibid.
22. Ibid.
23. *New York Times,* January 6, 1910, 3.
24. Alfred Connable and Edward Silberfarb, *Tigers of Tammany: Nine Men Who Ruled New York* (New York: Holt, Rinehart & Winston, 1967), 247.
25. Von Drehle, *Triangle,* 74–78.
26. Ibid., 80.
27. Connable and Silberfarb, *Tigers of Tammany,* 248.
28. *New York Times,* June 20, 1910, 3.
29. Harlow, *Old Bowery Days,* 517. See also *New York Times,* January 13, 1910, 3.
30. Ibid.
31. *New York Times,* December 24, 1909, 2.
32. Ibid. 28 January, 1909, 2.
33. Ibid., December 24, 1909, 2.
34. *New York Tribune,* January 13, 1913, 4.

35. *New York Times,* December 24, 1909, 2.

36. Ibid.; see also Harlow, *Old Bowery Days,* 518.

37. Ibid.

38. Von Drehle, *Triangle,* 201

39. Ibid., 191–92.

40. Connable and Silberfarb, *Tigers of Tammany,* 250.

41. *New York Times,* May 23, 1910.

42. Ibid.

43. Ibid.

44. Ibid., November 2, 1908 and February 14 and 17, 1910, 11.

45. *Proceedings of the Legislature of the State of New York on the Life, Character and Public Service of Timothy D. Sullivan* (Albany: D. B. Lyon, 1914), 31.

46. *New York Times,* April 26, 1911, 6.

47. Ibid.

48. Ibid., April 27, 1911, 8.

49. Ibid., May 11, 1911, 2.

50. Ibid.

51. Ibid.

52. Ibid.

53. Ibid.

54. For contemporary arguments of both sides of the Sullivan law, see the *New York Times,* February 25, 1912, 14 and March 3, 1912, 14.

Chapter 9. The Last Hurrah

Epigraph is from Frances Perkins, *The Roosevelt I Knew* (New York: Viking, 1946), 14.

1. Reminiscences of Francis Perkins, vol. 1, part 1 (1955) 225, in the Oral History Collection of Columbia University.

2. *New York Times,* January 22, 1912, 4.

3. Ibid., March 3, 1912, part 8.

4. *New York Times,* January 25, 1912, 5.

5. Ibid.

6. Daniel Czitrom, "Underworlds and Underdogs," Big Tim Sullivan and Metropolitan Politics in New York, 1889–1913," *Journal of American History,* (December 1994), 553.

7. *New York Times,* March 31, 1912, 6.

8. Harriot Stanton Blatch, and Anna Lutz, *Challenging Years* (New York: G. P. Putnam, 1940), 152.

9. Ibid.

10. Ibid.

11. Ibid., 166.

12. Ibid., 166–67.

13. Ibid., 167.

14. *New York Times,* March 31, 1912, 6.

15. Ibid.

16. Ibid.
17. Von Drehle, *Triangle,* 198.
18. Ibid., 199.
19. Perkins, *The Roosevelt I Knew,* 12.
20. Ibid.
21. Charles M. Finan, *Alfred E. Smith: The Happy Warrior* (New York: Hill & Wang, 2002), 237–38.
22. Perkins, *The Roosevelt I Knew,* 12.
23. Ibid., 13.
24. David C. Hammack, *Power and Society: Greater New York at the Turn of the Century* (New York: Russell Sage Foundation, 1982), 16.
25. Ibid.
26. Ibid.
27. Steven P. Erie, *Rainbow's End: Irish-Americans and the Dilemma of Urban Machine Politics* (Berkeley: University of California Press, 1988), 87.
28. Ibid.
29. *New York Times,* December 4, 1910, Sunday ??? 3.
30. Von Drehle, *Triangle,* 163–64.
31. Ibid., 209–10.
32. Ibid.
33. Ibid., 205.
34. George Martin, *Madam Secretary: Frances Perkins* (Boston: Houghton Mifflin, 1976), 92.
35. Ibid., 93.
36. Ibid.,
37. Daniel Czitrom, "Underworlds and Underdogs," 554.
38. Reminiscences of Frances Perkins, vol. 1, part 1, (1955), 108, in the Oral History Collection of Columbia University.
39. Martin, *Madam Secretary,* 94.
40. Ibid., 96.
41. Ibid.
42. Ibid.
43. Reminiscences of Frances Perkins, vol. 1, part 1 (1955), 111, in the Oral History Collection of Columbia University.
44. Martin, *Madam Secretary,* 97.
45. Ibid.
46. Ibid., 96.
47. Reminiscences of Frances Perkins, vol. 1, part 1 (1955), 111, in the Oral History Collection of Columbia University.
48. Perkins, *The Roosevelt I Knew,* 14.
49. Ibid.

Chapter 10. Decline and Fall

Epigraphs are from the *New York Times,* July 23, 1915 and Oliver Simmons, "Passing of the Sullivan Dynasty," *Munsey's Magazine* 1, no. 3, (December 1913): 416.

1. Jonathan Root, *One Night in July* (New York: Coward-McCann, 1961), 46.

2. Andy Logan, *Against the Evidence* (New York: McCall, 1970), 51.

3. David Pietrusza, *Rothstein: The Life, Times and Murder of the Criminal Genius Who Fixed the 1919 World Series* (New York: Carroll & Graf, 2003), 55.

4. Ibid., 60

5. Logan, *Against the Evidence,* 53.

6. Reminiscences of John T. Hettrick, part 4 (1949), 190, in the Oral History Collection of Columbia University.

7. *New York Herald,* July 25, 1912, 4.

8. Logan, *Against the Evidence,* 59.

9. Ibid.,

10. Pietrusza, 69.

11. Logan, 67. See also *New York World,* July 13, 1912, 1.

12. Logan. 67.

13. *New York World,* July 14, 1912, 1.

14. Ibid., July 15, 1912, 2.

15. Pietrusza, *Rothstein,* 74

16. Ibid., 75.

17. *New York World,* July 17, 1912, 1.

18. Von Drehle, *Triangle: The Fire that Changed America* (New York: Atlantic Monthly Press, 2003), 261.

19. *New York Herald,* July 19, 1912, 1.

20. *New York World,* July 17, 1912, 3.

21. *New York Herald,* July 17, 1912, 1.

22. Cited in Logan, *Against the Evidence,* 54.

23. Ibid.

24. *New York Herald,* July 17, 1912, 2.

25. Logan, *Against the Evidence,* 55.

26. Pietrusza, *Rothstein,* 79.

27. Ibid.

28. Ibid., 81.

29. *New York Times,* July 20, 1915, 6.

30. Ibid.

31. Ibid.

32. Ibid.

33. *New York Times,* July 21, 1915, 7.

34. Ibid.

35. Ibid.

36. Ibid.

37. Ibid.

38. Ibid.

39. Ibid.

40. Ibid., July 25, 1912, 1.

41. Ibid.

42. Ibid., July 22, 1915, 1.

43. Ibid.

44. Ibid.

45. Ibid.

46. Ibid., 6.
47. Ibid.
48. Logan, *Against the Evidence,* 307.
49. The best account of the Rosenthal murder is still Andy Logan's *Against the Evidence.* She presents a convincing argument that a consortium of gamblers killed Rosenthal and framed Becker with the aid of the ambitious Whitman. What Big Tim's role was she is not so sure.
50. *New York Tribune,* September 11, 1913, 1.
51. Ibid., 16 January 1913, 1.
52. Ibid., September 14, 1913, 2 and *New York Times,* 5August 5, 1914, 9.
53. Ibid.
54. *New York Times,* September 20, 1912, 1.
55. Ibid.
56. Ibid.
57. Ibid., January 3, 1913, 9.
58. Ibid., September 20, 1912, 1.
59. Ibid.
60. Ibid. November 6, 1912, 4.
61. Ibid., November 12, 1912, 1.
62. Ibid., November 21, 1912, 1.
63. *New York Herald,* January 11, 1913, 7.
64. *New York Tribune,* January 23, 1913, 6.
65. Ibid.
66. Ibid.
67. *New York Herald,* January 19, 1913, 1.
68. Ibid.
69. *New York Tribune,* January 23, 1913, 6.
70. Ibid.
71. Ibid.
72. Ibid.
73. Daniel Czitrom, "Underworlds and Underdogs: Big Tim Sullivan and Metropolitan Politics in New York, 1889–1913," *Journal of American History* 78 (December 1991): 557.
74. *New York Tribune,* February 1, 1913, 5.
75. *New York Herald,* January 12, 1913, section 1, 5.
76. *New York Times,* April 3, 1913, 1.
77. Ibid.
78. Ibid., April 7, 1913, 11.
79. *New York Times,* September 12, 1913, 11.
80. *New York Tribune,* September 10, 1913, 1.
81. Ibid.
82. Ibid., September 11, 1913, 1.
83. Ibid.
84. Ibid., September 12, 1913, 9.
85. *New York Times,* December 13, 1913, 1. The *Tribune* quoted Perfield, saying, "We have the body of Congressman Sullivan," which sounds a bit too official under the circumstances. *Tribune,* September 14, 1913, 1.
86. *Tribune,* September 14, 1913, 1.
87. Ibid.

88. *New York Times,* September 15, 1913, 9.

89. Ibid.

90. Ibid.

91. Ibid.

92. One result of Big Tim's death and belated identification was that the New York Police Department began photographing all unidentified dead and setting up a gallery where those searching for missing persons could check the pictures.

93. *New York Times,* September 15, 1913, 9.

94. *New York Tribune,* September 16, 1913, 1.

95. *New York World,* February 16, 1913, n6.

96. *New York Herald,* September18, 1913, 14.

97. *New York Tribune,* September 14, 1913, 2.

98. *New York Times,* September 14, 1913, 1.

99. *New York Herald,* September 18, 1913, 14.

100. Logan, *Against the Evidence,* 233.

101. *New York Times,* July 22, 1915, 2.

102. Kevin Baker, *Dreamland* (New York: HarperCollins, 1999).

Chapter 11. Legacies

Epigraph is from Alvin F. Harlow, *Old Bowery Days* (New York: D. Appleton, 1931), 488.

1. *New York Times,* August 5, 1914, 9.

2. Ibid., September 14, 1913, 2.

3. Ibid., August 5, 1914, 9.

4. Ibid., May 6, 1914, 1.

5. Ibid. Among Tim's other lucrative investments were Dreamland Amusement Park and the C. J. Sullivan [no relation] Advertising Company.

6. Ibid., January 21, 1921, 6.

7. Ibid., January 3, 1916, 9.

8. Ibid.

9. Ibid.

10. Harold Zink, *City Bosses in the United States: A Study of Twenty Municipal Bosses* (Durham, NC: Duke University Press, 1930), 93.

11. *New York Times,* September 18, 1913, 6.

12. Ibid., December 26, 1913, 2.

13. Ibid.

14. Ibid., September 14, 1913, 14.

15. Ibid.

16. Oliver Simmons, "Passing of the Sullivan Dynasty," *Munsey's Magazine* 1, no. 111 (December 1913): 408.

17. Cited in Nancy Joan Weiss, *Charles Francis Murphy, 1858–1924: Respectability and Responsibility in Tammany Politics* (Northampton, MA: Smith College, 1968), 67.

18. Alfred Connable and Edward Silberfarb, *Tigers of Tammany: Nine Men Who Ruled New York* (New York: Holt, Rinehart & Winston, 1967), 261.

19. Frances Perkins, *The Roosevelt I Knew* (New York: Viking, 1946), 13.

20. Ibid.

Bibliography

PRIMARY SOURCES

Bennet, William S. Reminiscences of William S. Bennet, part 1, 1951, 102, in the Oral History Collection of Columbia University.

Blatch, Harriot Stanton, and Alma Lutz. *Challenging Years.* New York: G. P. Putnam, 1940.

Claghorn, Kate Holladay. "The Foreign Immigrant in New York City." *Reports of the Industrial Commission.* Vol. 15. Washington, DC: United States Government Printing Office, 1901.

Davis, Hartley. "A Campaign for Decency." *Munsey's Magazine* (September 1901): 249–58.

———. "Tammany Hall: The Most Perfect Political Organization in the World," *Munsey's Magazine* (January 1900): 56–58.

Edwards, E. J. "Richard Croker as 'Boss' of Tammany Hall." *McClure's Magazine* (November 1895): 542–50.

Ellison, William B., "Mother's Influence Strongest in Big Tim's Life," *New York Herald,* February 16, 1913, n6.

"Glimpses of a Great Campaign." *World of Work,* December 1903, 4255–59.

Hettrick, John T. Reminiscences of J. T. Hettrick, part 4 (1949), 49, in the Oral History Collection of Columbia University.

McClellan, George B., Jr. *The Gentleman and the Tiger: The Autobiography of George B. McClellan, Jr.* New York: J. B. Lipincott, 1956.

Memorial Address delivered in the House of Representatives of the United States, Sixty-third Congress Proceedings in the House: June 12, 1914. Washington, D.C.: Government Printing Office, 1914.

New York Herald. Articles from 1901, 1912–13, 1907, and 1909.

New York Times. Articles from 1902, 1905–16, 1921, and 1926.

New York Tribune. Articles from 1895, 1901–5, and 1913.

New York World. Articles from 1901, 1903, 1912, and 1913.

Perkins, Frances. Reminiscences of Frances Perkins, part 2 (1955), in the Oral History Collection of Columbia University.

———. *The Roosevelt I Knew.* New York: Viking Press, 1946.

Proceedings of the Legislature of the State of New York on the Life, Character and Public Service of Timothy D. Sullivan. Albany, NY: D. B. Lyon, 1914.

Roosevelt, Theodore. *An Autobiography.* http://www.bartleby.com/55/6html.

Simmons, Oliver. "Passing of the Sullivan Dynasty." *Munsey's Magazine* 1, no. 3 (December 1913): 407–16.

Tammany Times, articles from 1893, 1894.

Wheeler, Everett P. "Tammany Hall." *Outlook,* September 13, 1913, 73–81.

Secondary Sources

Baker, Kevin. *Dreamland.* New York: HarperCollins, 1999.

Burrows, Edwin G. and Mike Wallace. *Gotham. A History of New York to 1898.* New York: Oxford University Press, 1999.

Connable, Alfred, and Edward Silberfarb. *Tigers of Tammany: Nine Men Who Ran New York.* New York: Holt, Rinehart & Winston, 1967.

Czitrom, Daniel L. "Underworlds and Underdogs: Big Tim Sullivan and Metropolitan Politics in New York, 1889–1913." *Journal of American History* 78 (December 1991): 538–58.

Erie, Steven P. *Rainbow's End: Irish-Americans and the Dilemma of Urban Machine Politics.* Berkeley: University of California Press, 1988.

Finan, Christopher M. *Alfred E. Smith: The Happy Warrior.* New York: Hill & Wang, 2002.

Guilfoyle, Timothy J. *City of Eros: New York City, Prostitution and the Commercialization of Sex, 1790–1920.* New York: W. W. Norton, 1992.

Hammack, David C. *Power and Society: Greater New York at the Turn of the Century.* New York: Russell Sage Foundation, 1982.

Harlow, Alvin F. *Old Bowery Days.* New York: D. Appleton, 1931.

Henderson, Thomas M. *Tammany Hall and the New Immigrants.* New York: Arno Press, 1976.

Logan, Andy. *Against the Evidence: The Becker-Rosenthal Affair.* New York: McCall, 1970.

Martin, George. *Madam Secretary: Frances Perkins.* Boston: Houghton Mifflin, 1976.

O'Connor, Richard. *Courtroom Warrior: The Combative Career of William Travers Jerome.* Boston: Little, Brown, 1963.

Orth, Samuel P. *The Boss and the Machine.* New Haven: Yale University Press, 1919.

Pietrusza, David. *Rothstein: The Life, Times and Murder of the Criminal Genius Who Fixed the 1919 World Series.* New York: Carroll & Graf, 2003.

Root, Jonathan. *One Night in July.* New York: Coward-McCann, 1961.

Sante, Luc. *Low Life.* New York: Farrar, Straus & Giroux, 1991

Sloat, Warren. *The Battle for the Soul of New York.* New York: Cooper Square Press, 2002.

Von Drehle, David. *Triangle: The Fire that Changed America.* New York: Atlantic Monthly Press, 2003.

Weiss, Nancy Joan. *Charles Francis Murphy, 1858–1924: Respectability and Responsibility in Tammany Politics.* Northampton, MA: Smith College, 1968.

Werner, M. R. *Tammany Hall.* Garden City: Doubleday, Doran and Company, 1928.

Zink, Harold. *City Bosses in the United States: A Study of Twenty Municipal Bosses.* Durham, NC: Duke University Press, 1930.

Index

220

INDEX

Gaynor William, 120; attempted assassination of, 140; as mayor, 138
George, Henry: and Independent Labor Party, 31–32, 154
Germans: and alcohol, 50; on Lower East Side, 41
Grace, William, 26
Graft: "dirty," 27; "honest," 27–28"
Grady, Thomas, 113–14
Grant, Hugh, 33, 52

Harlow, Alvin, 35, 188
Hearst, William Randolph, 80; mayoral bid, 111–16; challenges Tammany, 110
Hell's Kitchen, 105
Hesper Club, 165
Holland, Mary Catherine: TDS daughter, 189

International Ladies Garment Workers Union, 139
Irish, 22–23; and alcohol, 50; on Lower East Side, 41; political activism of 23; and Tammany Hall, 24, 131
Italians: employment, 48, 128; in Bowery, 41; political participation, 131
Ivins, William, 110

Jerome, William Travers, 48; anti-gambling measures, 61; character of TDS, on, 102; and Committee of Fifteen; on 1903 Tammany victory, 104; on prostitution, 65; attitude towards Sullivan, 83
Jews: attraction to socialism, 131; in garment trades, 133; on Lower East Side, 130–31

Kelly, John "Honest John": early career, 24–25; reorganizes Tammany, 25–29
Krause, George J., 134; partnership with TDS, 90

"Lawrence Mulligan Civic Ball," 133
Lexow Committee, 52

Life of Big Tim Sullivan or, From Newsboy to Senator (film), 192
Low, Seth, 56, defeated, 103–4, mayor, 68
Lower East Side, 13; accent, 196–97; character of, 41–42; demographic change, 130, 193; Sullivan's hold on, 43, 85, 104, 106, 192

Matamora Club, the: Sullivan Association headquarters, 86
Max Hochstim Association: connection with prostitution, 66, 202 n. 27
Mazet, Robert: and Mazet Commission, 59
McCall, Edward E., 75
McCarren, Hugh: anti-Hearst, 120, 125; allies with Tammany, 101
McClellan, George B., Jr: as mayor, 99; and Charles F. Murphy, 73, 99, 127; breaks with, 109–10, 116–17; 1903 mayoral campaign, 102; re-elected, 115
McClure's Magazine: attacks TDS, 133
McLaughlin, Hugh: Brooklyn Democratic leader, 100
McManus, Thomas J.: aids Frances Perkins, 152–53; 161; Sullivan ally, 105
Metroploe, the, 104, 164
Miner, Henry C.: partnership with Sullivan, 90
Miner's Bowery Theater, 62, 90, 102, 113
Mohr, Mabel: TDS daughter, 189
Mohr, Susan G., 189
Mulligan, Lawrence (stepbrother): 169; holds Christmas dinner, 189; and TDS decline, 177–81; and TDS death, 183–84
Mulligan, Lawrence: (stepfather) 34
Municipal Ownership League: and Hearst, 110; 1903 convention, 113
Murphy, Charles F.: background, 70–72; business support, 154–55; Dock Commissioner, 72–73; at TDS funeral, 184; graft (attitude